bamboo

A HAWAI'I WR...

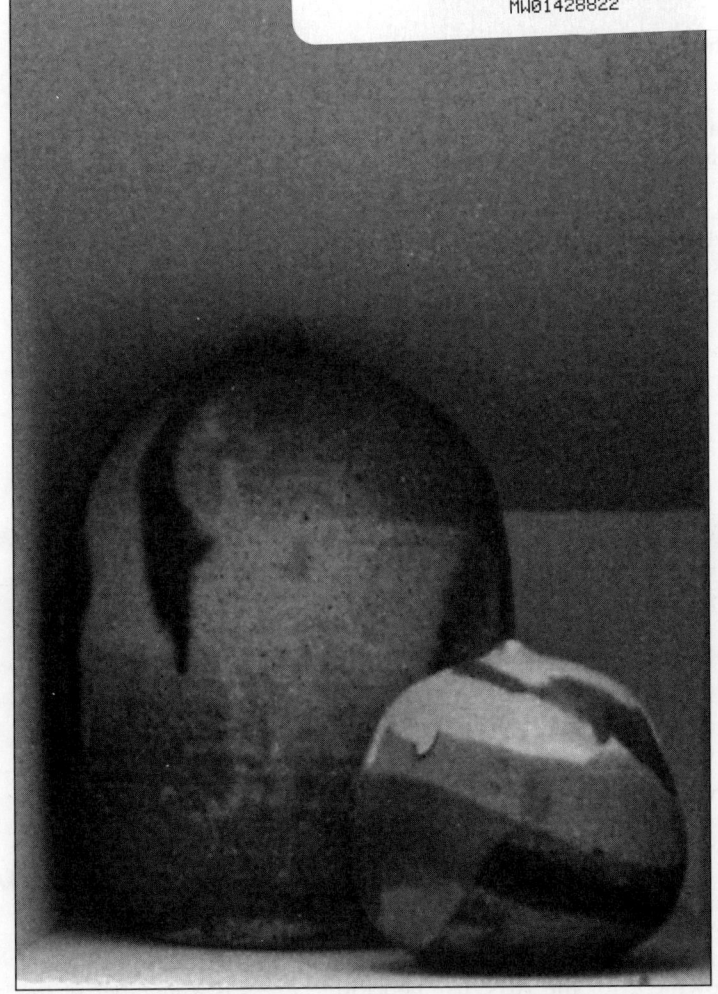

NUMBER SIXTY-NINE
SPRING 1996
NEW MOON ●

ISSN 0733-0308
ISBN 0-910043-48-5
Copyright 1996 Bamboo Ridge Press
Indexed in the American Humanities Index

All rights reserved by the individual authors. This book, or parts thereof, may not be reproduced in any form without permission of the authors. Printed in the United States.

"Filming Sausage" from *Her Wild American Self* by M. Evelina Galang, published by Coffee House Press. Copyright 1996 by M. Evelina Galang. All rights reserved.
"Prologue" and "Chapter 7" copyright 1996 by Shirley Geok-lin Lim. Reprinted by permission from *Among the White Moon Faces: An Asian-American Memoir of Homelands*, forthcoming from the Feminist Press at the City University of New York, by Shirley Geok-lin Lim. To order, please call (212) 360-5794.
"The Crossing" from *Wild Meat and the Bully Burgers* by Lois-Ann Yamanaka, published by Farrar, Straus & Giroux. Copyright 1996 by Lois-Ann Yamanaka. All rights reserved.

Published by Bamboo Ridge Press
Editors: Eric Chock and Darrell H.Y. Lum
Managing Editor: Joy Kobayashi-Cintrón
Copy editor: Gail Harada
Cover: *Shiro Momo* by Toshiko Takaezu, porcelain,
    21 1/8" high x 14 1/2" diameter, 1992.
    From the collection of the State Foundation on
    Culture and the Arts. Photo by Tibor Franyo.
Title page and portfolio photos: Shuzo Uemoto
Book design: Susanne Yuu
Typesetting & production: Wayne Kawamoto

Bamboo Ridge Press is a nonprofit, tax-exempt organization formed to foster the appreciation, understanding, and creation of literary, visual, audio-visual, and performing arts by and about Hawaii's people. Your tax-deductible contributions are welcomed.
Bamboo Ridge is supported in part by grants from the State Foundation on Culture and the Arts (SFCA), celebrating 30 years of culture and arts in Hawai'i. The SFCA is funded by appropriations from the Hawai'i State Legislature and by grants from the National Endowment for the Arts. Bamboo Ridge Press is a member of the Council of Literary Magazines and Presses (CLMP).
Bamboo Ridge is published twice a year. Subscriptions are $16/year. For direct mail orders or a catalog of our books, call or write:

BAMBOO RIDGE PRESS
P. O. BOX 61781
HONOLULU, HAWAI'I 96839-1781
(808) 599-4823

For Jen, Christmas 1996
love Dan

We gratefully acknowledge the charitable contributions made to Bamboo Ridge Press in 1995 by the following individuals and organizations:

Anonymous
Anonymous
Lori L. Ching
Susan Nunes Fadley
Blayne M. Higa
Bert & Mary Kimura
Terry Lau & Noe Tanigawa
Cynthia J.M. Lum
Jerry Martien
Adelin McMillin
Audrey L. Mueh
Amy Uyematsu
Lou Zitnik

Anonymous
Borders Books & Arts
Marjorie Edel
cate m. gable
Barbara Kagan
Jody Kobayashi
Peter C.T. Li
Wing Tek Lum
Noel Abubo Mateo
Grace J. Merritt
Tadashi Sato
Jean Yamanaka

this book belongs to
Jennifer Harris

CONTENTS

Eric Chock
11 THE NEOCOLONIALIZATION OF BAMBOO RIDGE: REPOSITIONING BAMBOO RIDGE AND LOCAL LITERATURE IN THE 1990s

Toshiko Takaezu
26 PORTFOLIO

Joy Kobayashi-Cintrón
31 TOSHIKO TAKAEZU

Margo Berdeshevsky
36 BLACK

Arlene Biala
40 PA'AUILO

Louie Bliemeister
42 SOME KINDA LOVE

Meredith Carson
52 FIREWORKS
54 MOTHER TONGUE

Sue Cowing
55 AT THE HONOLULU AQUARIUM, WITH CAMERA
57 NIGHT WATCHES
59 INK PAINTING BY LIU DAN, 1992

Brian Cronwall
60 THE ANT OF THE POEM

Kenneth Zamora Damacion
61 LAST NOTE BETWEEN HEAVEN AND HELL
64 THE ISLANDS

Diana J. Eicher
66 SETSUKO
68 VIOLET DARKNESS

M. Evelina Galang
70 FILMING SAUSAGE

Mavis Hara
94 REVERIE
98 BLUE WILLOW

Steve Heller
100 PRIVATE ISLAND

Laura Iwasaki
120 KAMIKAZE LOVE

Milton Kimura
129 CORONATION

Jeanne Kawelolani Kinney
136 REDRAWING THE BIG ISLAND

Peter C.T. Li
138 A FIRE IN THE FIELDS

Shirley Geok-lin Lim
156 Excerpt from AMONG THE WHITE MOON FACES: AN ASIAN-AMERICAN MEMOIR OF HOMELANDS

Mary Lombard
193 THE FINE ART OF COSMETOLOGY

Wing Tek Lum
205 POEMS AFTER WANG WEI

Noel Abubo Mateo
206　LAPU-LAPU IN NEW YORK, NEW YORK

Michael McPherson
208　THE LONG SWIM
210　THE MAYOR OF ALA MOANA
212　TAPES

Wendy Miyake
213　WONDER WOMAN AND MY JUNIOR PROM

William Starr Moake
217　MEMORIES OF A PLACE CALLED THE SEVEN

Kiyoshi Young Najita
242　I WOULD LIKE TO DANCE THE HULA WITH YOU

Carrie O'Connor
251　THE MAD PEOPLE IN THE ATTIC

Joan Perkins
255　CONVERSATION WITH MY EIGHT-YEAR-OLD SON

Ran Ying Porter
258　Excerpt from BLACK DRAGON RIVER

Albert Saijo
275　NIGHT LIFE WAKING STATE ZOMBIE
277　KARMA LOLLIPOP

Marjorie Sinclair
280　SENSEI

Lia Smith
282 SAFE

Indigo Som
297 MISSING
299 CORVINA

Joseph Stanton
301 SPRING TRAINING IN 'AIEA

Eileen Tabios
303 NEGROS

Kobai Scott Whitney
315 KONA GLITTER, 1964: A GHOST STORY

Lois-Ann Yamanaka
325 THE CROSSING

340 CONTRIBUTORS

ERIC CHOCK

This essay was presented as a talk at the University of Hawai'i–Mānoa English Department Colloquium Series, May 2, 1996.

THE NEOCOLONIALIZATION OF BAMBOO RIDGE: REPOSITIONING BAMBOO RIDGE AND LOCAL LITERATURE IN THE 1990s

There have been recent discussions about Local literature, and Bamboo Ridge Press publications in particular, which have been disturbing to me as co-editor of the press. We arose in controversy, and have been criticized since we started, so this in itself is not new. In our early days, with the many literary and political discussions of the times, there were ample opportunities for us to publicly discuss our purposes. Perhaps it is time that our goals are addressed again. This is a brief literary history to help reposition ourselves in the 90s. To some, this may be restating the obvious. But since I found out that most of my students here didn't know what I meant by the Hawaiian Renaissance, I guess this may be worth saying again.

Original Goals: An Alternative Literature

The original mission statement of Bamboo Ridge Press is derived from that of Talk Story, Inc., our original umbrella organization. It has appeared on the copyright page of most of our publications since our founding in 1978:

> Bamboo Ridge Press is a non-profit, tax-exempt organization formed to foster the appreciation, understanding, and creation of literary, visual, audio-visual and performing arts by and about Hawaii's people.

To project from this statement, I would add that our

expectations were that if we continued over a period of time to publish the best work that was sent to us, we would end up with a representative array of the best writing about Hawai'i by people of different ethnic backgrounds, a literary picture which was almost non-existent at the time. We set out to create this vision as an alternative to the mainstream, white literary canon. This resulted in highlighting the Local vs. mainland Haole cultural polarity of the times. This polarity was not only part of our social heritage, but was plainly evident in the university system as well, not only in the makeup of the faculty, but in the kinds of courses and texts available to students.

Part of establishing a sense of an alternative literature included publication of older, previously published works by Local writers in Hawai'i, creating some sense of the modern tradition of Local literature in English which we were hoping to nurture. These included work by Hawaiians about such things as Pele worship ("Pele's Own," Kong, 1979); fishing with sacred rocks ("The Mystery of the Ku'ula Rock," Chun Fat, 1979); early stories about Asian plantation workers ("The Forgotten Flea Powder," Ige, 1978), or on becoming "haolified" ("Letter to Hisae," Toshi, 1979). Building on these foundations, we hoped to develop a sense of a tradition of literature which was pluralistic or multicultural, but in a distinctly contemporary Local way. Although there have never been any stylistic guidelines, we hoped the writing would be representative of our regional, multicultural, modern, Local community.

The effect of this kind of general approach is that we did not have a specific political agenda beyond the idea that most of the work we expected would be written by people born and raised in the islands, or with very strong ties to life here, and that it would be largely about Hawai'i or Hawai'i-related themes. Generally, most of what we publish in our magazine is unsolicited. But, to demonstrate our expansive kind of definition and our openness to publishing a variety of writers from the Local community, our earliest issues included work we solicited from writers as diverse as Wayne Westlake and Frank Stewart, Michael

Among and Phyllis Thompson. We were from the beginning, from before the Talk Story Conference, trying to counter the attacks that our version of supporting Local writers was exclusionary. Of course, in the late 1970s, this meant that these charges were largely based on the Local vs. Haole polemics of the times. In retrospect, this was not a difficult charge to answer. Simply by looking at our Tables of Contents, it was apparent that simply by publishing what we liked best without regard to who the writer was led us to publishing a significant number of Haole writers. Perhaps because we were outspoken in our efforts to establish our sense of an alternate literary identity, we were perceived as putting down others. Or perhaps because we were beginning to tread on other people's already-established territory—in publishing, readings, teaching positions—we met with resistance.

Intellectual Space

What we have been doing is clearing an intellectual space in which Hawai'i writers can show their work. It is based on certain political realities happening in this geographical space, and there is interchange between the arenas, but there is a distinction between what happens in Hawai'i and what happens in the literary arena. In the intellectual space of the literary arena, we can project that more ideal sense of a multicultural world where many voices will be heard. In that arena, ethnicity will be an influential factor, perhaps a tool toward gaining visibility and the attention of people who can effect change in the real world. Ethnicity is a significant factor in describing Hawaii's peoples. But it is only one factor among many, one which we would hope would not preclude participation in the development and exchange of artistic ideas. We are attempting to encompass a variety of ethnic and other voices while moving toward some kind of ideal multicultural nation, of which Hawai'i itself is a kind of model.

Paradise Myth

What we have been doing can be aligned with a corrupted notion of multiculturalism which romanticizes the American dream (or the Aloha Spirit) while perpetuating the imbalance of power among ethnic groups in the United States. While it is easy to find overlap between working toward an ideal and having romantic visions, this is a necessary condition for all art. We would make the distinction that what happens in this intellectual space will reflect the real world but move toward an ideal. We should not be labeled or categorized as a static entity, though the perception of movement may be difficult in the short term. While it is true that the last five books we have published in between the regular literary magazines have been by writers of Asian ancestry, it can also be said that there was an earlier period where we had four books in a row on Hawaiian themes. Again, given the long view, it is a myth that we are ethnically biased in what we publish.

It is true that the 1978 Talk Story Conference focused mainly on Local and mainland Asian writers, though there was also significant representation by Hawaiian writers, kumu hula, and chanters. In as much as it was an ethnic writers conference in the 1970s, there was no representation of mainland born Haole writers. There were Local Haole and hapa Haole writers in the programs. Or, in the 1980 Writers of Hawai'i Conference (of which HLAC, Talk Story, and Bamboo Ridge were the main sponsors, and which I organized), the six days focused on the works of Ozzie Bushnell, Aldyth Morris, John Dominis Holt, Milton Murayama, and Maxine Hong Kingston. Although these were simply the best-known Local authors at the time, clearly, a vision of multicultural Hawai'i was being presented in which we tried to leave no one out.

Hawaiian Literary Appropriateness

But from the beginning, not many Hawaiians, or writers

with obviously Hawaiian names, have submitted work to us, although all those who have been asked have submitted work. But only when asked. Perhaps it is true that not many Hawaiians have had the time nor inclination to study creative writing and work at developing the level of their art. This is a particularly sensitive issue because we have always respected Hawaiian culture as the primary, base culture of this place, and now with the rise of the Hawaiian Sovereignty Movement, there is much more concern for that representation to be there. But from the time of the Hawaiian Renaissance in the 1960s, after John Holt's *On Being Hawaiian*, discussions have often settled on whether or not Hawaiians were more interested in oral forms (chants and lyrics) as opposed to written forms. Or whether or not English literary forms and academics were therefore not encouraged by the Hawaiian community.

Writing from the Inside

It was at this stage in the development of Local literature in general that Ozzie Bushnell became known for making his pronouncements regarding the initiative Local people must make. At the Writers of Hawai'i Conference, 1980, he restated his concerns:

> Nobody in this conference has sounded the alarm. I do this often enough; some of you may be tired of hearing this from me . . . . Whose gonna take our places when we're gone? Who's moving up in the ranks to get the mantles? Where are the young writers or the middle-aged writers of today? Alas, they don't seem to exist.
>
> At a recent conference I prodded George Kanahele. He was talking about Hawaiian Renaissance. I said, "Where are the novelists?" And after a while he got tired of me pushing him and he turned, and with a withering look and a scornful expression he said, "Why should anybody bother to write a novel?" Well, maybe

that's the answer. If it is, then maybe somebody should tell me, prick the balloon in which I live! . . . And when there aren't anymore novels being produced by novelists in Hawai'i, we goin' be sad and sorry. Because all those outsiders coming in then, to tell us about ourselves. Instead of ourselves, from inside, telling us about ourselves.

Writers of Hawai'i, Bamboo Ridge Press, 1981

Bushnell was restating several concerns here. First, the concern that outsiders will be getting our stories wrong, or worse, will be appropriating them for their own purposes. That they will care more for commercial value than for authenticity. He was also alluding to the colonial, or provincial attitude as it was then called, which had us believing that everything good came from the mainland; that what we read is written by others, for others, and we need to learn how to become like those others to appreciate things of real value. He was alluding to the fact that his books were hard to get published, here or in New York, and that even when published there was not a well-developed reading audience here for literary books about the islands. He also articulated the belief by some that literature in an American style may not be interesting or appropriate for people from an oral tradition. But his statements in effect were advancing the idea that language and literature, even though taken from the dominant culture, were essential tools in constructing a narrative of truth against those outsiders. The Local literature movement of the 70s and 80s was based on ideas like these. All of these concerns are still with us today.

The Paradigm Shift: Literary Entropy

One of the ironies of the beginnings of Talk Story, Bamboo Ridge, and other ethnically-related movements of the 1970s is that they have led to a greater focus and understanding of our differences. The irony is that after Talk Story brought a statewide focus on our literature, efforts were made by *Bamboo Ridge, Seaweeds and Constructions, Hapa* and others to promote Local writers. And part of the success of that movement is that writers or groups of writers have become more categorized by ethnicity, and that has led to a separateness by racial categories which at times seems to fall into the divide-and-conquer strategies used by the old plantation system to keep the working classes weak. Or, it is as if the UH representatives of the mainstream literary canon were weakened in their colonial role, and, like decolonization movements everywhere, the remaining Locals started to form alliances and fight over the new political territory. Instead of the original Local vs. Haole dichotomy being the focus, it has led to the splintering of what was called the Local into various factions, with native Hawaiian writers gaining focus as the sovereignty movement continues its momentum. In effect, some are calling the Local vs. Haole paradigm a mask behind which all non-white Locals can hide behind if sides are to be taken; that if Caucasians are neocolonial in this scheme, then so is everyone else who is not Hawaiian, working class origins or not. In literary terms, this political argument is translated into phrases such as "usurping the space" which belongs to Hawaiians, when referring to the non-Hawaiians published in the pages of Local literary journals and books like Bamboo Ridge. Hence the irony that a literary venture started with the logo of contract plantation laborers is now called, by some, neocolonial.

Exploring the Paradigm: Minority Movement Comparison

Like the rise of the Black Civil Rights Movement, which provided much of the impetus for all the minority American movements of the last thirty years, there was the need to develop a sense of ethnic pride. Only after that has been sufficiently established within not only the mainstream society, but within the ethnic community itself, can institutions be created which nurture the members of that specific culture. It might be notable that the most visible sense of a Hawaiian movement in recent years started with the Hawaiian Renaissance of the 1960s and 70s, which in actuality existed more on a cultural front with the emphasis on rejuvenating the hula kahiko, as well as the popularity of contemporary Hawaiian music. The Merrie Monarch Festival, Kanikapila, Prince Lot Hula Festival, and the television popularity of the Kamehameha Schools Song Contest, among others, became Local cultural icons; not to mention Gabby Pahinui, Olomana, Country Comfort, the Brothers Cazimeros, and others.

The more political Protect Kaho'olawe Ohana was by contrast not as well received at first, and was treated as other political movements of the time were treated by a skeptical, hesitant Local community. There was a separation of cultural issues from the hard politics of reclaiming land, and this has been part of the many differences within the Native Hawaiian community.

Pacific Island Nation Comparison

This is one way to interpret political movements in Hawai'i, as part of minority American movements like the Black American or Native American movements. But these movements in the 1970s were also tied to the term Third World. And many in Hawai'i would place Hawaii's political struggles in the context of Pacific Island national struggles. In this context, indigenous Hawaiian culture is on its home grounds and must fight not just for recognition and status among the many ethnicities in America; it must also fight for its very survival, since the struggle is taking place in this presently American context, or not at all. This Pacific Island context of struggle has not been fully embraced, and it is a large question as to whether it will or not because not only have most other Locals become assimilated Americans, most Hawaiians have too. Using the one drop rule of blood quantum, most Hawaiians are Christians, dress Local, know more American TV heroes than

Hawaiian legends, and would rather eat Big Macs than the Wai'anae diet.

So, in effect, a unified political movement is fairly new, and the development of institutions to nurture people of Hawaiian ancestry is also in a kind of nascent stage. Regarding contemporary literature, in the last two decades there have been a few books of poetry or fiction published by Native Hawaiians, and there is not yet a well-established Hawaiian literary magazine. While it has been described as an emergent literature, contemporary literary production has been established and it can be expected that literary production in English will continue to blossom.

New Definitions and Realignment

With the changing political context and the Hawaiian Sovereignty Movement of the 90s replacing the Hawaiian Renaissance, there has been a realignment of power and redefinition of terms. Instead of the old, colonial Local/Haole paradigm, present day Hawai'i politics also forms around other groupings. Perhaps the main political perception is the Hawaiian/Other paradigm, in which Other includes all others. Or, restated in light of historical change, the Hawaiian/Local/Haole paradigm may be the more common culturally-recognized definition by some. Or, some may find focus mainly with a Hawaiian/Local Asian/Haole breakdown. This is problematic because the change from the old to the new definitions complicates the meaning of Hawaiian vis a vis Local. The overlap that exists is sometimes overlooked in simplified versions of who we all are. Translated into what this means for Local publishing, there is a shift of emphasis toward Native Hawaiian cultural production as opposed to a general, all-inclusive Local cultural production.

This complicates the role of Bamboo Ridge. There is a shift of emphasis of the literary polemics toward this new front, replacing Local vs. Haole issues. For example, instead of Local

Literature being used as a term when referring to UH English Department curriculum, you may hear that Hawaiian Literature or Literatures of Hawai'i are the more correct terms, and literature by Local Asians will be separated under the Asian American Literature category. What was for many years seen as a common Local culture based on the predominant ethnic mixtures of the post-plantation period is now being dismantled, or perhaps re-labeled and reassigned, and there will of course be a time of transition. The distinctions are being expanded in terms of how people distinguish themselves within what used to be acknowledged as Local culture, singular, and therefore, the switch from Local Literature to Literatures of Hawai'i, with priority placed on the indigenous Hawaiian literature.

Because these issues are not clearly defined, I think that Bamboo Ridge is still trying to focus on one encompassing Local, and the role this concept must play as the intellectual space in which to work through Hawaiian/Local/Haole issues.

Defining the Intellectual Space

Looking back from my particular perspective, I would take Talk Story as an arbitrary marker because it made such a big impression not only on the overall Local literary community, but, for the first time, on the Local community at large. Not only were writers interested in its events, but Local educators at all levels as well as ordinary readers attended the panels and followed the coverage in the papers. It was the first time that we had a large visible display of Hawaii's ethnic writers. Because of the obvious model it provided for Local writers who had not yet made the leap into ethnic literature, and because conditions here were so ripe for exactly that kind of change, the effect was noticeable. It crystallized an attitude already extant on the mainland regarding the role of ethnicity in culture.

The mainland ethnic writers criticized the Local writers for not being political enough, and although Local writers protested that the political levels were implicit in our writing, there were obvious differences in both the writing and the presentation and management of the writing after the conference. Instead of debating the programming of literary events as we had done for several years, a Local contingent organized and took over the Hawai'i Literary Arts Council in 1979, changing its focus away from a heavily mainstream canonical approach. More ethnic literary conferences, panels, readings, and events which focused on Hawaii's literature were staged in the next few years. Little magazines rode this wave into the 1980s. Local magazines and books began to be assigned reading in university level classes. Parallel to this literary movement of course, the Hawaiian movement was moving beyond its Hawaiian Renaissance stage into a much stronger political phase, and Hawaiian writers underwent a significant change.

Although some Hawaiian writers began to involve themselves in the political aspects of the Hawaiian movement, it should be noted that for most of them through the mid-1970s, this was not their primary concern. Westlake and Among were known for their interest in Chinese poetry; a young Joe Balaz was vanity-publishing romantic lyrics; Naone was influenced by the Merwin-Bly-TM group of poets; and it was not clear that McPherson was interested in being defined as a Hawaiian writer. Leialoha Perkins was mostly self-published and not well-known until some time after Talk Story. And till recently, Carolyn Lei Lanilau was still Carolyn Lau, her book of poems carrying a Chinese title and having no Hawaiian focus to it. There were few other identifiably Hawaiian creative writers who had published more than a small handful of poems or short fiction in English.

Talk Story Writer Models Expanded

But the Talk Story Conference provided several models for Hawaiian writers as well as Asian American writers. First, the conference featured kumu hulas and chanters, and these represented Hawaiian language literature. Second, Talk Story also published and/or had readings by young Hawaiian writers, like those mentioned above, who I would say were attempting to gain entry into mainstream American models of contemporary literature. They were attempting to be accepted on an assimilationist model like most of the Local Asian American writers here. The third possible avenue was the model brought by the mainland ethnic writers who showed that you could actually break away from mainstream models and form your own styles, focus on ethnic themes, create your own publishing and performing venues, create your own university courses, and take over or create your own literary organizations. It is not a large coincidence that the ethnic literary movement in Hawai'i blossomed after the Talk Story Conference, that more pidgin, Local themes, characters, or imagery began to pour out of Hawaii's writers. And, while these three models were being debated and worked over by Local writers, there was a fourth model that was being developed along with the Hawaiian Sovereignty Movement. Writers aligning themselves with a Pacific Island emerging nations model realized that there was a distinction between being a militant minority American writer or a writer of an indigenous people fighting for independence.

These four models apply to most Local writers: 1) writing in a language other than English which therefore focuses on a non-American culture; 2) writing in English to participate in a mainstream context, in a predominantly universalist or assimilationist style; 3) writing in English in an acculturated or ethnic style, or to participate to some degree in an ethnic context; 4) writing in English, or in Hawaiian and translating into English, as a statement of indigenous Hawaiian, or non-American status.

There is of course much debate as to the overlapping and differences between these categories, and this is part of the evolution of our contemporary literature. In Local literature, publishing debates have evolved around these differences, or related ways of defining them. There is obvious cultural/linguistic overlap between styles which use a common language.

There is confusion over writing as an ethnic American writer versus an indigenous writer. All people raised in the United States are assimilated to some extent, and many so-called indigenous writers are from multiethnic backgrounds of which more than half is often non-Hawaiian. The overlap between Local and Hawaiian becomes confusing. Lines of distinction are hard to draw, yet there is enough reason to keep these definitions in mind as we explore the changes in Local literature. Many writers define their work with two or more categories. Again, Bamboo Ridge is trying to maintain an intellectual space in which all these issues may be explored and none excluded.

But because of the confusion and overlap, it can be convenient to label us as neocolonialist. It can be easy to lump all the non-Hawaiian writers in opposition to Hawaiian writers, and call the first group neocolonial. And while it may be important for someone to establish a primarily Hawaiian-focused literary journal, there will be a need for a Local community journal like Bamboo Ridge for a long time to come. But if no Hawaiian writers develop and send us their writing, this would defeat the purpose of Bamboo Ridge, and it would change to something other than what we started out to be.

Given the American background of Hawaii's residents, our literary publications do reflect contemporary American tastes. But rather than thinking of this as colonial or limiting, we choose to see the ethnic American cultural developments of recent decades as models which allow us to express radically different ideas from mainstream ones, while still using the language and literary background of English. This view comprises a vision of America as a leader in the development of World Culture. While remaining grounded in our separate histories, we all seek ways to create a better composite future. For us, it is a kind of "Think Global, but act Local."

Summary: The New Warning

Perhaps with all the Local literary activity these days, Ozzie Bushnell would feel satisfied that his warnings have been heeded, that Hawaii's writers are indeed creating narratives of truth from the inside, that now, it is more a matter of sorting through them. And perhaps the new warning is that with all the multiplicity of literature being created, we need to nurture and support the writers we now have; that instead of concentrating on the differences among these narratives, we should also remember the commonalities of the literature of this place. And not forget the original overriding political situation which gave us impetus to start our alternative literary ventures in the first place.

There is a time for politics and a time for art. To quote Michael Among in a toast to Wayne Westlake:

> my friend said never get involved in politics
> you'll never write any poems
> *Seaweeds and Constructions*, 1976

Over the years I have often wanted to stop the press because it's too much work for too little reward. In nurturing other people's writing, it keeps us from doing our own. People seem to think that we are some kind of powerful, strong organization. We don't have an office or university support. We work out of our homes. We are always struggling to survive. But writers keep developing and sending us stuff. We are kept alive not just by our own considerable efforts, but because there seems to be a community need we are filling; we exist only because others want us to. That's the nature of our game. If you are a dedicated Local writer looking for a home for your writing, we want it to be here. We will not publish everything you send us, but if you are a serious writer and continue to develop your craft, Bamboo Ridge will probably want to publish some of your work eventually. But it may take some time.

We're just trying to produce the stuff which is the truth of this place in all its variety. As literary artists and publishers, we just want to keep developing the literature, and scholars will categorize the work however they do, and that's not our main concern. So don't stop sending us your stuff, even if you do get rejections now and then. There are writers who have sent us dozens of submissions before we published one; and there are those we've published before who we haven't published again. It is the job of the writer to read the magazines out there, to choose which poems to send to which magazines, and to keep at the process even though relatively few pieces will get published. It is the job of the editors to select what they see fit; we want to be open to diversity, but we'd like to publish only the best of that diversity. We also want to be open to suggestions. Perhaps we need your essays to educate us on our aesthetics, because, ultimately, the aesthetics of the editors define a magazine.

Perhaps the natural outgrowth of Talk Story and the national ethnic movements is that we further define the various ethnic groups of Hawai'i in literature; that we attempt to publish more Hawaiian, Filipino, Portuguese, and those other underrepresented local writers. But to do this, we need for many more of those writers to send us material to choose from. And we need for everyone, over time, to trust our choices. Perhaps we should pull back from publishing any more of those mainland ethnic writers who helped us by providing the models for how we could revolutionize our literary scene. Perhaps we should stop publishing those stray poems or stories which we just happened to like but which have nothing to do with Hawai'i and are by writers from New York or Kansas. Those especially may be too much of a dilution of our purposes. These are issues which we are now working through, and if you have any suggestions I would welcome them.

TOSHIKO TAKAEZU

PORTFOLIO

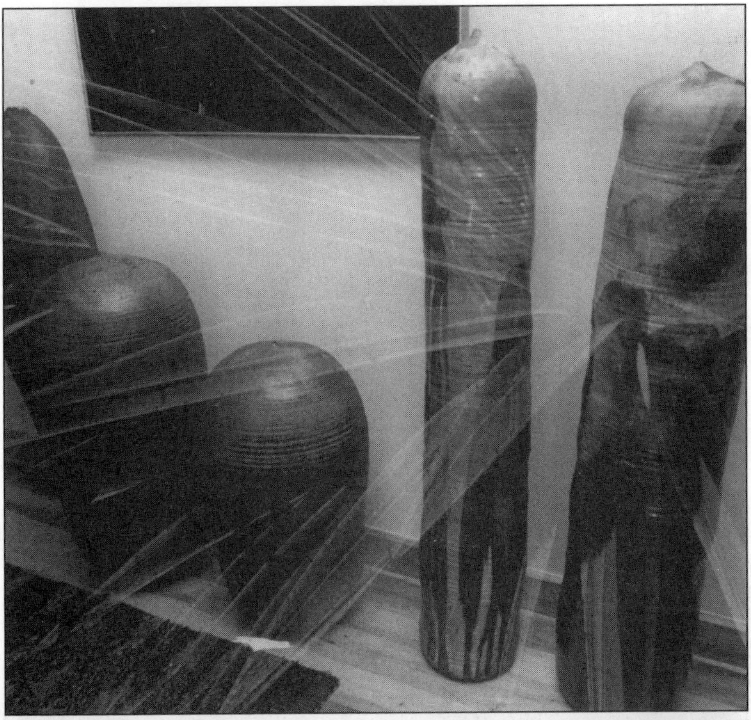

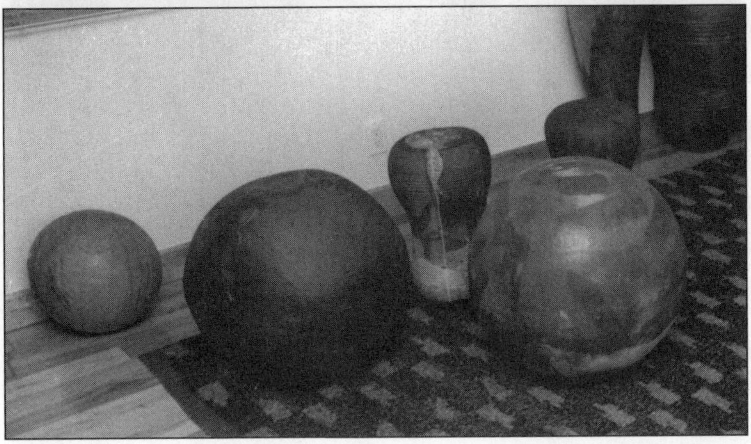

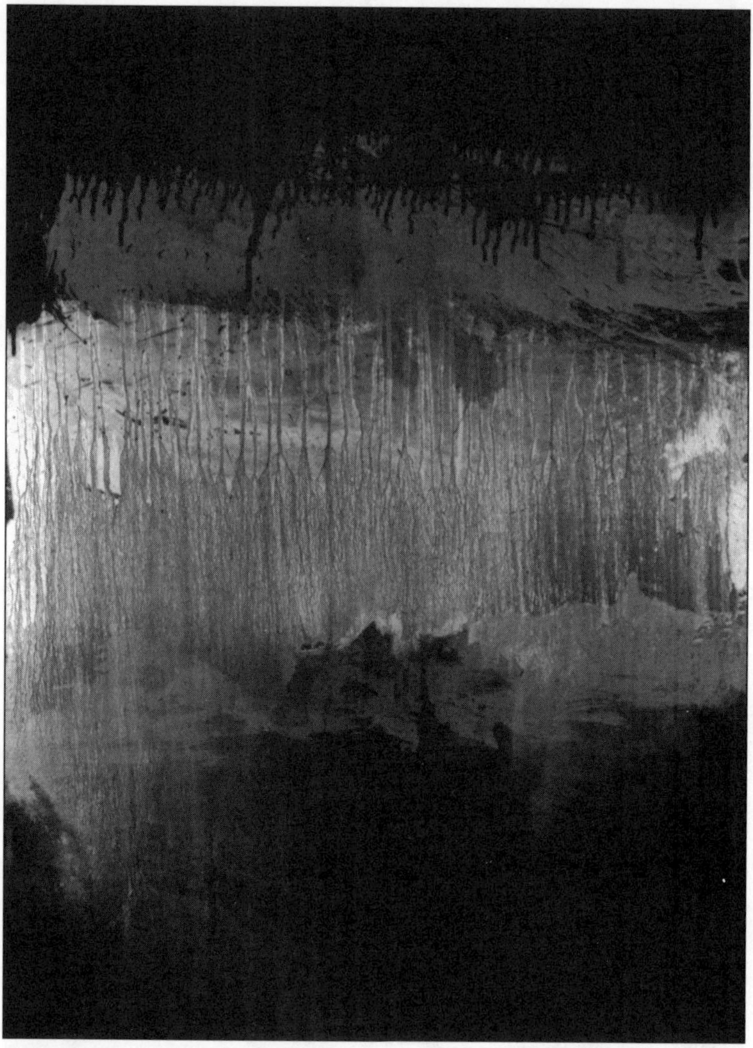

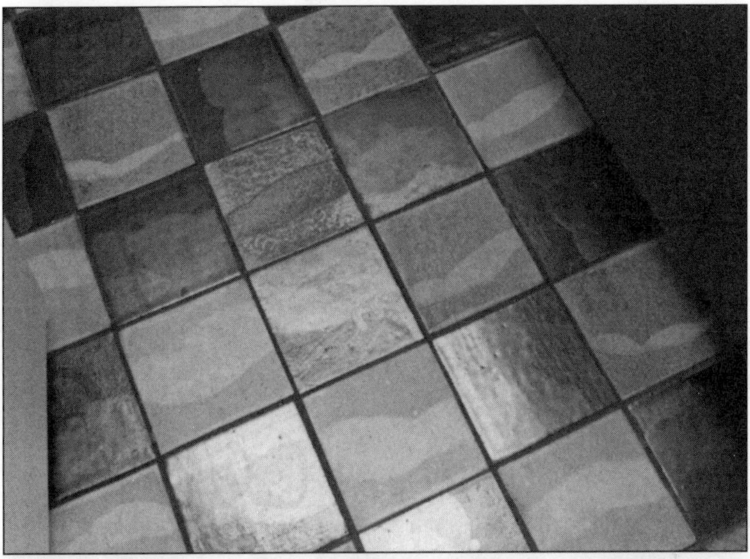

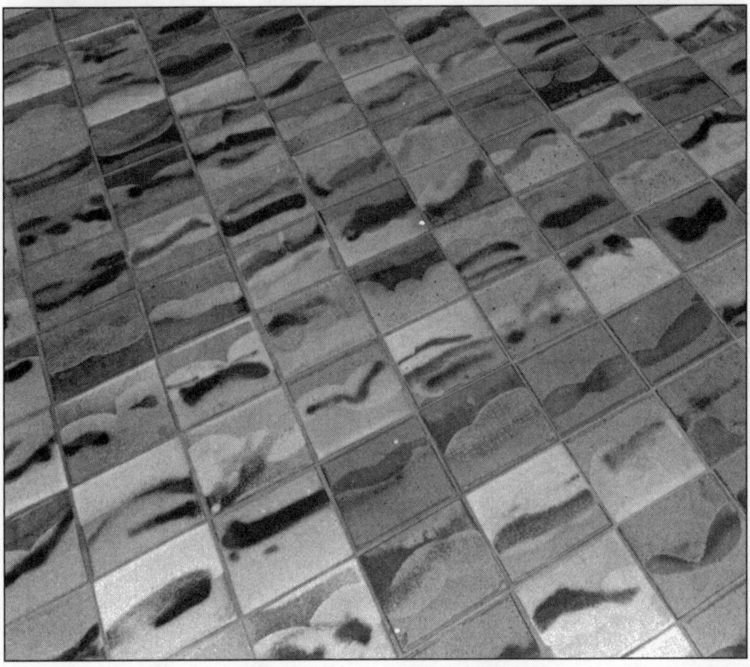

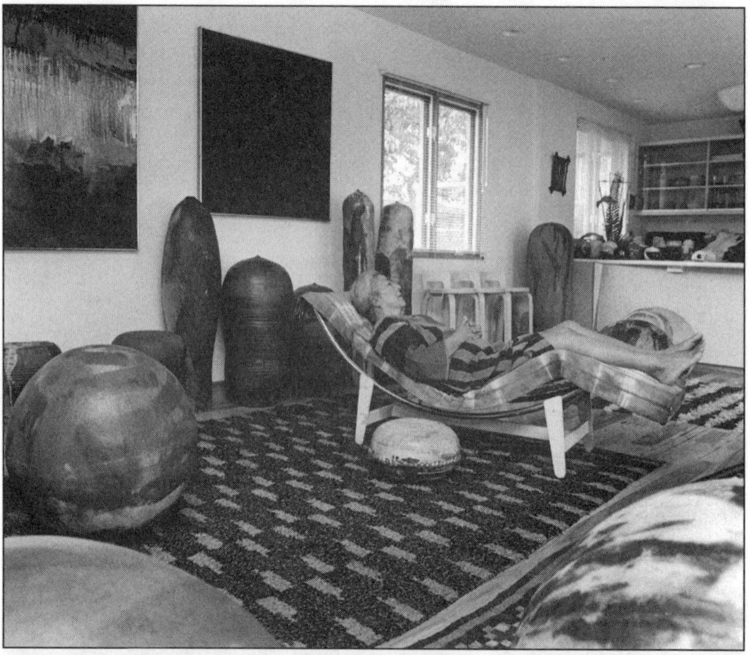

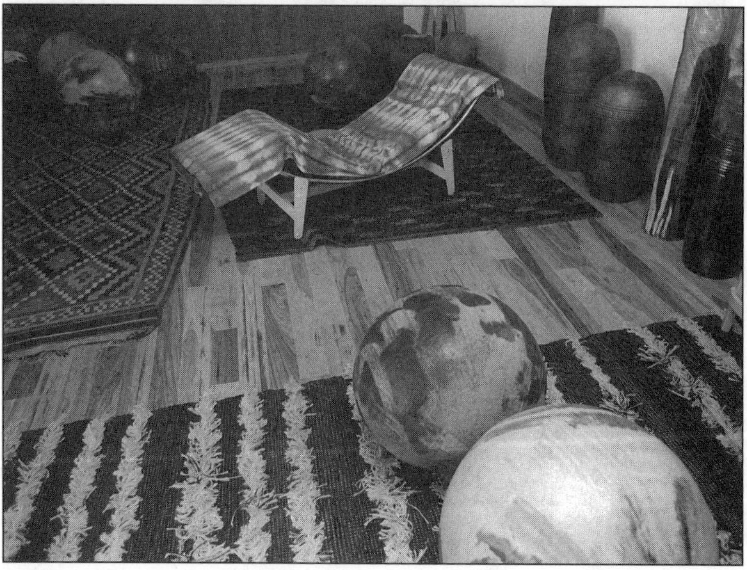

JOY KOBAYASHI-CINTRÓN

TOSHIKO TAKAEZU

In the fall of 1955, when she was thirty-three years old, Toshiko Takaezu journeyed to Japan. During her eight-month stay, she traveled around the country her parents emigrated from, lived in a temple, visited some of Japan's best-known potters, and experienced the tea ceremony. There she realized that she wasn't ready to make tea bowls.

"It was easy to make bowls, but to make *tea bowls* I first had to be an individual. I had to wait until making tea bowls came naturally to me. It wasn't a question of technique; it was the question of being ready as a person."

Forty years later, Takaezu sat at the potter's wheel in the ceramics studio named in her honor at the Honolulu YWCA where she had taught her first ceramics classes. She was spending her Hawai'i vacation throwing a hundred tea bowls for a fund-raiser to benefit the YWCA and its ceramics program. It was an opportunity to see a master artist at work, to watch what she calls her interplay with clay. In her life, Toshiko Takaezu has not differentiated between her artistic pursuits and her spiritual development. By waiting until she was "ready" to make tea ceremony bowls, she exemplified the Zen principles of harmony, respect, purity and tranquility. On the occasion of the 1995 opening of her retrospective at the National Museum of Modern Art in Kyoto, Japan, she wrote that her journey of many years was coming full circle. "Now," she declared, " I can begin anew."

Takaezu is a nisei born in the plantation village of Pepeʻekeo, near Hilo on the Big Island of Hawaiʻi, the sixth child in a family of eight girls and three boys. By the time she was ten, her family relocated to Maui and after graduation from high school, she moved to Honolulu to live with her sisters. She worked at the Hawaiian Potters Guild, took Saturday classes at the Honolulu Academy of Arts and studied with ceramist Claude Horan at the University of Hawaiʻi.

While still a student, Takaezu began teaching ceramics at Mānoa Elementary School a couple of days a week and evenings at the YWCA. She taught her students how to make pinch pots and how to handbuild with coils and slabs. Sometimes she had them work on a group project with the clay form extending around the work table " . . . like a rope, almost like a lei. And everybody touches the clay. Just have fun doing it. And, after a certain time, we move them. Like musical chairs. So you'll have another person's work to go on from. Or, say, you could take it apart . . . or continue, or add on. I said, no one should have any ego because it doesn't belong to anyone. And then we let them go around and around and select the place that they thought they could enhance, do something with. Enhance it, or take it down completely and start over again. And I tell them not to break the chain, the feeling around it. And then I said, 'The ceiling is the limit and the floor is the limit.' People started making things to touch the ceiling . . . and then go down, onto the floor, all kinds of things."

Although she had already started teaching, Takaezu felt the need to continue studying the medium, so in 1951, decided to attend the Cranbrook Academy of Art in Bloomfield, Michigan, where Finnish potter Maija Grotell taught. Takaezu wrote of her mentor, "She was an unusual and rare human being who felt it was important for students to become individuals, and it was through her criticism that I began to discover who I was."

Encouraged to nurture her individuality, Takaezu experimented with ceramic glazes and forms while also studying weaving and sculpture. She sought to create in clay "a natural pure form" that she could use as a three-dimensional canvas on which to paint. She faced the challenge of developing glazes which would maintain their colors through the high temperatures of stoneware firing.

Takaezu's earliest pieces were utilitarian—bowls, pots, teapots—but these became less functional bottle-like shapes with narrow necks and smaller and smaller openings. Continued exploration resulted in double- then multi-spouted and multi-chambered pieces. Her hallmark "closed form" evolved from these shapes with the spouts becoming mere nubs and then disappearing altogether.

"I started with a bird shape for a teapot; tail end, the handle, and the head, the spout. And that got to be two-spouted bottles and it didn't look like a bird anymore, it became abstract. After that, I decided to make multiple spouts and connect the two forms, put together and create all kinds of things. I made two-spouted bottles. From one particular view, it was like a mask. You could see a mask, which I didn't plan. So I decided, well, why not make a mask? So I put a nose and two eyes or a mouth and two eyes. The mask got smaller and smaller and gradually got to be a closed form. So see, I didn't say I'm going to do closed forms, it just happened—gradual, natural growth."

"The other thing is, I have beads in my pieces. That came

as an accident. I was trimming the top and clay fell in, I was making a closed form. I fired it and it started to ring and I thought, 'Oh, what a wonderful idea!' So I started adding it to every piece but sometimes it gets stuck. In time some beads loosen and it rings. But every piece has it, I make sure they're there."

Recognized as being the first ceramist to create a totally rounded and closed form, Takaezu's ongoing exploration of less functional forms made her instrumental in the movement of the 50s and 60s to elevate ceramics from a craft to a sculptural art. Her closed forms grew to massive proportions as she produced spheres, ellipsoids and a series of "Moons" and flat-topped garden seats. In the 70s, she began elongating her pieces into tall cylindrical "tree forms" inspired by the burned trunks remaining in the stark volcanic landscape of Hawaii's Devastation Forest and, in the 80s, the large organic shapes evolved into "Hearts" and "Torsos." Another recent sculptural development is the *momo* (peach) series of ovoid forms with stem-like protuberances at the top. These forms have slits cut from side to side across their tops and are significant because she has deliberately created an opening in one of her closed forms.

As her sculptural forms evolved, Takaezu's ongoing experimentation with glaze formulas resulted in the extensive palette of colors which she applies uninhibitedly to the three-dimensional canvas of her ceramics. Her early work was often in tans and shades of brown, pale yellows and blacks, but more recent pieces range from subtle pastels to vivid hues of blue, green, pink, orange and red. She can achieve iridescence, metallics and gold. Glaze application ranges from calligraphic brushstrokes to dipping, dripping, pouring and even splashing or flinging the colors onto the forms.

Takaezu's teaching career on the mainland began in 1954 with summer sessions at Cranbrook and a year in the Art Department at the University of Wisconsin in Madison. After her trip to Japan, she joined the faculty at the Cleveland Institute of Art, where she headed the Ceramics Department. She left Cleveland after establishing a studio in Clinton, New Jersey, in 1964. From 1967 to her retirement in 1992, she taught at Princeton University.

Like her teacher Grotell, Takaezu encouraged individual expression while requiring a certain discipline from her students—orderliness in the studio and no idle chatter during workshops. She used to begin by teaching her workshop students the process of making tofu. Pointing out the inefficiency of feeding fifteen to twenty pounds of soybeans and grains to cattle for each pound of meat produced, she would talk about combining the complementary proteins of grains and legumes to get complete protein in the diet without eating meat.

"When I'd do a workshop, I'd carry with me soybeans and Epsom salt and a linen pillow slip. I'd say, 'This workshop is important but not really. I think making tofu is more important than making ceramics.' So I taught them how to make tofu. Of course, I did demonstrate and talked about clay and how I feel about the clay."

When Takaezu left Hawai'i in 1951 to study at Cranbrook, she expected to be gone for only a year. Instead, she stayed on the mainland to teach and in the early 70s, bought acreage in Quakertown, New Jersey, where she has her home, studio and extensive vegetable and flower gardens. When she does come back to the Islands, she lives in a recently completed two-story addition to her sister's house which features handmade tiles in the bathrooms and shelf-lined walls for the display of decades-worth of ceramic creations. The bright and airy living room has a few carefully selected pieces of designer furniture and lots of open space to accommodate numerous large sculptural Takaezu forms grouped on rugs woven by the artist, in front of walls hung with her paintings. The portfolio here provides a glimpse of Toshiko Takaezu's Hawai'i home.

MARGO BERDESHEVSKY

BLACK

Friede lives across the street from the City Marble Cemetery, where only squirrels are frenetic in the placid heat of August. Her tricky black cat watches them, and the monument stones that never move, through the grill of her street-level apartment. Thefts and more thefts in her neighborhood. August licks, with its thirsty tongue. The cat does not like to see strangers.

Friede drags her left foot like a recalcitrant dog. She's an older woman, this Friede. "I have nothing essential to say, don't listen to me," Friede, the city's black-polyester-clad-interesting-older-woman-playwright says. "I only write." She wears black clothes, only black clothes, and black shined fingernails. She speaks like a hand pistol, on one breath. Pop-blast. Hush. Silence. Blast. Pop. She has a visitor: Alice.

"So?"

The visitor's heart is unquiet. "What kind of a week have you had?" Alice sweats with her airy effort to impress. She would like to get published. She needs a recommendation. She needs a lifeline. Friede is worth this demure visit. She would like to be cooler.

"It was a week, what else?" Blast. Hush.

The girl watches the cat, wears a mentor-attentive face, for the older writer. The cat watches her too, black, with eyes in the back of its head.

I have eyes in the back of my head, Alice's Mommy used to say when she was so little, in the coop of a white slatted crib, and did not want to nap. *I'm sleeping,* she would plead. *No, I can tell,* her Mommy would say, *I have eyes* . . . . Eventually there was no need for Mommy to finish her sentence. Or find a word. Alice was always seen.

Friede studies her visitor—eager, semi-talented, an intrusion to be rid of. "So, what brings you to New York?" She is sharpening a number one pencil painstakingly, with a half-inch pen knife, shavings curling minisculy and ignored around her black synthetic-lizard shoes.

"Watering my root system," Alice tries a metaphor. "And I have . . . my parents are buried up the Hudson River somewhere. I think I want to visit their graves. I never have." She perspires at the roots of her pale hair. *I want to be wanted,* uttered, barely loud enough.

"I would not. Personally, I think root systems strangle. I cut them, myself. But don't listen to me. But don't go." She applies the pen knife to one pencil after another. There is a twenty-count box on the unsteady table before her.

The interview is over.

Alice wants more. Urgent: What color is mission? What color is surrender, or the sudden waking *is it good enough? I'll die not knowing.* Stamp your willful feet, worried girl. What color is the will to make words into suns that warm, don't burn, clarify, leave room for shadows? What color is a word that you can't, must find? Black.

Alice, heart like a red fist, thanks the woman for her audience. "If there is ever anything I can do for you . . . " she holds out the branch, hoping the black bird might, just might, might hop on and become her elderly friend.

"I can't think what that might be. Adieu."

Alice swallows rejection like a prune, deposits one precisely black-typed page, an example of her best, on the table with its jittery leg. Maybe the old woman will read it. Call her back. Announce her genius.

The door is shut. Tall, cool marble stones.

Bring red roses. Six. To the graves. Go. It's goddam more important than a page. Go. Never been. Always afraid.—to catch death—like a bad wind. Never stood at their stone. Never, grown child. I rode there in a limousine, in the blind snow. Couldn't find it now, not even if I was lined up in front of—It was snowing, both black winters. I'll find it. Find it. Go to the city, take a train up the river, get off at a town and find it. Reach in a trunk. Cockroach-chewed wills. Unearth a cemetery, in a town. Numbers, for a piece of the ground, in a town up a river, off a train and I'll go where death has an address. Should. Want. Go. Get roses. No friend. No recommendation. No Adieu.

No right lane no left, death had no color, no marker, white inside white, maybe, all Alice remembers is a thruway, a limo, a smell of old upholstery and damp, snow, white, dirty white, and don't look death in the eye, it will bite, while she waited, numb as a pulled tooth, both times. So she let the others walk to the graves. Pink and blue bunting . . . like a baby blanket covered . . . urn . . . and a man in a herringbone coat bows low, says *this is your mother,* and Alice in an overheated winter-waiting-room dressed in a tight-bodiced black velvet jumper like Alice in Wonderland. Eyes bite. Won't weep. Fragments of tears, all over her hands.

Alice is a graveyard, dreaming of herself. A forest of ironwoods like spider-woven women, dropping their browned needles, whistling for the fear, in the dark. Her dress is too tight.

. . . The trunk has rotted hinges. The wills have, sure enough, chewed borders stained brown. The site is up a river, take a train. Her hands shake like Juliet playing with her encaved imagination. . . . *if I should wake, and go mad, playing with their bones* . . .

Bear six roses, five to offer, one to keep, defying the black advice. *Don't go.*

Plot number 465. George Gershwin in a crypt at the bottom of the hill . . . it's *a helluva town . . . the people ride in a hole in the ground . . .* Billy Rose in a mausoleum, half way up. Two tall stones. A heavy man is leaning his swollen-tired head against one. Rows. Rows. A bell-sound of an ice cream truck over a fence beyond trees that sound of insects sawing the Sunday air. And rows. And Plot 465. A half-circle stone. Grey glints, knives of light off marble.

No names. This stone has no names.

No names. Here is 465. Here are no names. Here is empty marble.

One by one she severs petals from her roses, forgetting to save even one, they love me, they love me not, one by one, scattering red ovals. She abruptly sits, legs thrust straight out, like a dropped doll. No names on this stone. No root, and no one knows.

Dinner was burnt. *It's been an honor to be your father.* He never said that. Buzz-rattle-tremors in the trees. A chorus of little buzz saws, a rattle of buried hands and feet, crescendo, silent. Again. Crickets? Katydids? Speakers of the Hudson River Valley, daughter listening. She was carrying six flowers, now emptied stems. *Where is my mother? Where is my father?* She wishes she had paper, to write their names, one perfect, genius page, and leave it on the ground, and put a shaved, pointed stem on top.

Black polyester Friede, limping closer. No cat.

ARLENE BIALA

PA'AUILO

Uncle Rudy fans flies
off chicken long rice
pinakbet chiccaron macaroni salad
barbeque fish oysters

come
you eat now
bumby i eat don't worry
eh, you like the new house
my daughter like one
construction worker
i show her one time
then she do it
she fix everything
i tell her okay
you hook
electricity
to the new room
she do it

he fills a box
papayas hard green
what you mean
no can carry
take it

drinking tall beers
repeating
you come to the house
next tuesday

he says
the fifth time
bumby i call you
next tuesday
i cook for you
you eat here
sixth   seventh time
come on   get more rice
yes
uncle tuesday
okay

LOUIE BLIEMEISTER

SOME KINDA LOVE

She stretched through the setting sun in a dancer's arch, graceful and defiant. I could only watch from the shore, the sense of desperate awkwardness stealing into me again. Any sense of rhythm I might have felt on the water was gone, the dull ache in my arms and the backs of my shoulders my only reminder of a day's paddle to the Mokes. Wishing again for some subtlety, for a style less martial and direct, I watched this last gesture of a last moment, as usual, in silence.

There was nothing I could say, I knew, as she finished the dive. Even if I should summon the courage to speak, something in my tone would betray, sound forced and unnatural. As I turned to help load the kayaks on the car, I could feel the holes in my life, each one individual and glaring.

The cold from the beach shower helped me to feel alive again, the water sweet after the accustomed taste of salt. I opened my eyes in the stream, the water pushing back my hair, streaming down my neck. She was standing across from me, also rinsing, all cold in wet curves. At that moment I might have told her how beautiful she looked, but her eyes flashed towards mine once in the failing light and I could say nothing. I turned back to the car, dripping, the sand growing cold beneath my feet.

I think of her now as I ride home with my father, neither of us speaking for a while. By now, it seems, I can only remember her in outlines and gestures, or perhaps this was the only way I saw her to begin with.

"She was beautiful," my father says. Sometimes I swear he reads my thoughts, or perhaps I, too, hide less behind my eyes than I believe. I am more like him than I swore would be possible. "Why didn't you say anything to her?," he asks, echoing the question I have been asking myself since leaving the beach.

"She probably had a boyfriend," I reply. "And knowing my luck, at the exact moment I spoke, he would be standing right behind me. And then I would have felt bad for having to beat up her boyfriend." As I say this, I tense with glee at the thought of punishing someone for having something I could never know.

"A couple of lonely hearts, that's us," is his only answer, and I know the distance that lies in his eyes, have measured it myself. I also know that there is nothing I can say that will change the way his nights look, the way the empty house sounds, so we drive on in silence for a while.

We are on this route so frequently, he and I, this stretch between 'Aikahi and Lanikai. Here he worked me through the backwards controls on a motorcycle (clutch - left hand, gear shift - left foot, throttle and front brake - right hand, rear brake - right foot) over and over, from fumbling to fluency. Here, just past the bridge and Buzz's is the wall where, following him one night, my headlight caught him, leaning into the curve ahead of me. His shadow leapt out like a child into the road, snapping my heart into my throat in an instant. After Kalapawai Store, the road seems endless, a stretch of 30 mph speed limits and stops.

It is some time before my father speaks again, so I watch his hands on the wheel for a while, noting how they move surely, only releasing to shift. I remember how, as a child, I watched him carve a clipper ship in teak, four feet by three, every curve in every sail correct. (To this day, when I dream of ships, that is the one sailing towards me, and the hands that guide it are my father's, powerful and sure.) I swore he created the world with his hands, but then I think of how his left crashed into my fourteen-year-old nose, his eyes blazing with fury over something neither one of us really understood. The drops that fell in the sink in stark contrast, blood on porcelain, destroyed a world of mine. I remember again how his hands, almost gently, pinched the neck of a slowly dying kitten. I could never understand that type of mercy, even though I was the one who found the mangled wreck in the attic, torn apart by a too-young mother.

Looking now at my own hands, I trace the bones and scars, and recall the blood which has spilt across them, the gentleness with which they can trace the curve of a face. I realize now that this dual capacity for love and violence runs deep and long between us two, and despite the love, we can never forget the blood on our hands.

"I've never come that close to a turtle before," he says. "I could see into its eyes, right before it dove."

"Yeah," is all I can reply, remembering. Its old man's face was serene, the Zen master who could never teach his wisdom, and I remembered being twelve, a different turtle the only thing in sight on that flat and empty horizon that stretched towards Cabo San Lucas, Mexico. We altered course, any change welcome after ten days at sea, just to watch it dive down in its crystal world. It did not disappear, the clarity of the water betraying its presence if not its safety. Later, back on course, we caught a dorado. Not knowing then to call it *mahimahi*, we watched its colors fade with the light in its great, gentle eyes.

"I could see him underwater forever," I say. "It was almost like being back in the Tuamotos, wasn't it?" The look in his eyes says more than anything either of us could in reply, not sad or regretful, but distant. He and I are there more and more these days, remembering diving the atolls or climbing to waterfalls amid Marquesan hieroglyphs.

We continue in silence for a while, not knowing what to say, or how to say it, past the sewer ponds without the usual jokes, under the freeway, and left into Yacht Club Knolls. A home, of sorts, I think as we walk down the stairs, feeling the usual tensions of home replaced by something more tangible which only time will repair.

"I'll cook dinner. Go sit down," I say, glancing over the food with a practiced cook's eye, searching for the beginnings of something which I have never made before. The refrigerator looks bare now, its contents having been lessened in stages over the years: first my sister, then me, and now this final transition towards emptiness. I can sense the changes here perhaps more than anywhere else. Food, I had thought, held the family together, mealtimes and cookies expressing what often became hard to show in any other way. I see now also how the kitchen was where the first sign of my parents' disagreements appeared, how my father mixes ingredients in ways that no one would ever think of, how my mother refuses to change the slightest recipe that her mother had taught her.

I have always been in between, here as well as most other places, though the kitchen is where I have always felt most at home, moving with grace and precision. I concoct something with chicken and lots of vegetables, adding spices almost at random from the shelf, balancing flavors in my head, experimenting. I see some old pictures on the counter as I dish up, and one falls out a little past the others. It is from my first and last taekwondo tournament, and my leg is extended in a line with my body. It seems so strange how this moment can be frozen for so long: me forever kicking but never hitting, my opponent leaning back into eternity, his face locked in bracing for a kick that will never arrive. Thinking back, I regard this, like so many of my other losses, as a moral victory, overcoming fear and insecurity. At the end of the fight, I could barely hold my hands up, and kicking required every thought and muscle. I wanted so much to win, I think, and wonder if the referee felt my hand try to rise when he announced the winner. I shove this thought aside as I walk to the living room with dinner.

"How's work been?" I say, unsure of how to talk gently here. My mother's absence seems to loom within these walls, and I do not want to amplify that.

"Pretty well," he replies. "I've written a new program that simplifies stack testing to the point where emissions can be monitored hourly by a single person at each power plant. I wrote it using Visual Basic and Excel, so it's pretty simple, but it does the job."

"You do realize that for the most part I don't have a clue what you're talking about," I say. "Not a clue." I want to tell him, This is not life for us; this is too narrow, too stable. You have ridden manta rays — I have body surfed with sea lions. This life is not cut out for us. All these things that we don't need, we have. As usual, I say nothing, though my father's eyes are distant, almost sad. I never could quite understand this look, as though he found some regret, some wishing for another place, but then I realize that this, too, is a heritage of mine.

"Did you find a boat yet?" I ask, hoping that he has, that he realizes this house is not for him.

"I still have to put the house on the market," he says. "And then, since most of the down payment was from your mother's inheritance, I don't know what I'll have left. Forty-eight years old, and all I have is an Isuzu Trooper with 110,000 miles on it and a couple of scuba tanks." His eyes are dull with the fears of a middle-aged man, fears of being alone and worth nothing.

"Don't sell yourself short," I tell him. "You have me." The cat runs through the cat door, and between the double slaps of the door settling back, I feel the incredible stillness in the house. I stare out the screen door, trying to pick out a constellation in the darkness, thinking that the light we see is from stars which died millions of years ago. Looking back, I see my father's eyes well with tears that he can never shed. Even in the silence of the room, I can barely hear his response.

"Thanks."

I get up, gathering plates and carrying them into the kitchen. "I'll do dishes before I go," I tell him as he settles back into his recliner.

"You cooked," he says. "I'll clean up." I know somehow how the sound of dishes must echo in this quiet, how it must almost mock, so I only argue a little.

"I don't mind."

"Leave the dishes; I'll wash them later."

"You sure?"

"Leave them."

I cannot stay the night, though my bed is made downstairs. Too many things echo back at me, the downstairs always damp and full of memories I have yet to discard. There is something else, though; somehow I don't want my father to become dependent on me, knowing that his strength depends only on his getting through this, alone.

Shrugging into jacket, boots, gloves, reflective vest, helmet, and night riding glasses, I feel encased and removed from the air. I hug my father, giving him the usual soft left hook to the ribs—my trademark.

"Thanks for spending the day with your old man," he says, almost knowing why I must leave, not wanting me to.

"Anything for free food," I reply, and run up the stairs to my bike. I climb on and rock it twice to free the clutch disks, which stick after a day of not being run. I start up and short shift to keep the rpms low and the bike as quiet as possible. I inch out of the complex at fifteen miles an hour in third gear, then downshift out onto the road.

I take the first turn onto H3 at about 50, scraping my right footpeg as I lean into the curve. As I shift to fifth, my hand opens wide to grab the clutch, and I feel a dull pain in my first two knuckles, reminders of taekwondo, my last belt test. My forms were the best I have ever done them, forceful and smooth, and I survived sparring through my usual tactic of misleading. The breaking was the last, and I, as senior belt, was the last to break. The two inches of pine finally gave way on the fourth punch, and both the boards and my hand were spotted with blood. I felt the whole room stop with my hand when my full force failed to penetrate. That was also the last time I saw my parents sitting side by side, almost comfortable, still looking as though they belonged together.

Everything is physics, I muse to myself, trying to calculate wheel rpms, thinking about rotational inertia and centrifugal force. I remember once, when I was around ten, after helping me to patch a tire on my bicycle, my father told me to hold the axle between my hands. He started spinning the tire faster and faster.

"Now turn the tire," he told me. I tried, only to feel some force countering mine.

"It fights it," I said. "Why?"

"It's called rotational inertia," he replied. "It's the force that keeps your bike upright."

"And what if it goes faster," I asked. "Does it become more stable?"

"Sometimes."

"And what if it stops? Will it fall over?"

"Sometimes."

I don't see any cars coming, so I blast through the red light at the intersection, turning left onto Kam Highway. I know that I should slow down, but am somehow unable. I know where slowing down leads, for in different days when 150 miles in a day was traveling fast , every wavetop was different, and each star was distinct, almost marked against the night sky. For some reason I can't let that happen now, so I try to twist the thoughts out of my mind with the throttle. I'm doing 65 as I turn onto the Pali and start heading over the mountain, trying to place the changes within me, trying to understand where I am going so rapidly. I have marked these changes in their passing, but their placement in my world is still to be figured out, and no matter what the speed with which they occur, I still feel no sense of motion.

I take the big right on the Pali at 70, as fast as I have ever taken it, leaning inward on nothing for 180 degrees. I pray not to slip, but almost wonder what the guard rail would feel like at this speed. A benediction perhaps, and I can see myself sailing end over end, but never landing. I think about the physics involved, how my father showed me how angular momentum is conserved.

"Take a weight on a string," he told me. "Spin the weight

in a circle, around and around, then pull in on the string, so that the diameter is half of what it was. Does the weight change in speed?"

"No," I said. "It keeps going the same speed, but since it has less distance to travel, it would make more revolutions per minute."

"And how would the force on the string behave?"

"It would increase." I thought a moment.

"Why?"

"Because, even though the speed stays the same, it is accelerating. The direction of its travel changes, which means that the more sudden the change, the greater the acceleration, and the greater the force."

I think about the effects of this as I lean into the turn. The faster and sharper the corner, the harder the lean, the more force acting at once. Perhaps our lives are like that as well, once they are set in motion. The greater the change that occurs, the more speed at which our lives change direction, the more we react against it. It's simple inertia, I tell myself.

I feel a surge of adrenaline as I weave towards the tunnels, not wanting to look at the thousand foot drop on my right, and yet strangely attracted at the same time. I wonder what freefall would feel like, what I would think on the way down, how much time I would have. If an object falls at 9.8 meters per second squared, and the fall is approximately 300 meters, I think, it would mean that the square root of 9.8 times 300 would be the time to fall. I can't do the math in my head, and by now I am at the tunnels.

My bike drones like an old turboprop plane through the tunnels, and I think of my father's explanation of my engine, almost hearing each cylinder fire, at least as fast as I can think. "On your engine, for instance, do the cylinders travel in unison or in opposition?" Most of my father's explanations have always been questions. I thought for a while, using what I knew.

"On a four stroke engine, two cylinders, each piston firing once on every other revolution, one firing, the other recovering . . . That would mean the pistons must travel in unison." I have always marveled at the way in which my father can teach without tainting the sense of discovery, how he hides lessons inside lessons. I can see now how this relates to my parents, in a way: both caring, both striving, but in such opposite ways. Their timing has been off forever, and I remember a remark from my father, walking back to work after baguettes and ham in the park: "If they don't get the timing right at the factory it'll never be right, no matter how you adjust it."

They did make it work, held it together for twenty-two years, but it was never quite right. I can only allow myself to begin to understand the relief of, after a lifetime of almost working, finally admitting that it didn't, and that they couldn't make it.

I think about stability now as the needle creeps up to 100 and then past, but suddenly the thought occurs of sliding and spinning out of control, leaving my life in bits and pieces on this stretch of road. At this speed, you're just a streak on the road, I think, and wonder how long I would slide. Still, I don't back off the throttle, realizing that my life runs on a similar principle of inertia. Only in speed does my life have stability, or at least the sense of it, but I wonder how fast before something breaks, before the variables catch up with me and my reflexes cannot overcome them. But the miles and days slide by like melting ice, too fast to focus, and I think that suits me as I blast down the front side of the Pali, cold and damp, heading towards the city lights.

Somewhere in this mad rush must lie an answer, something beyond inertia, more than centrifugal force. I try to remember the Southern Cross, and the pull of the boat on night watches when the moment was beyond the scope of experience: the hiss-slap of waves on the hull and the driving sense of every moment in motion. I see some stars through a break in the trees, and think about their light and how it gets here. In some ways, the travel does not sound so bad, an unattainable speed with a precisely fixed rhythm, the only changes occurring from the outside, and no time for reflection until arrival.

I am pulled from my thoughts at the first light on the down side. An oncoming car, both of us going too fast, turns left in front of me, perhaps not seeing me, maybe not caring. I jerk on both brakes, feeling the back tire skid, but I can control this, so I look for an opening, but all I see is headlights and the driver's eyes locked on mine. The front tire goes into a skid, and the bike starts to slide out from under me. All I hear is squealing and my heart beating once, blood rushing cold and preordained, when something in the back of my mind stops. I let go of both brakes and lean hard to the left, to the right, that fast, missing his bumper by a heartbeat. I taste the fear, almost like blood in my mouth, but everything else appears in stark relief.

Every pinpoint of light is distinct as I pull over, slowing down and looking at the stars. Their light has traveled so far to get here, and all we do is keep moving away from its source. It's all a cosmic dance of attraction and motion, I think to myself, and I'm already a part of it. I put my foot down as, for the first time since I began, the wheels stop.

MEREDITH CARSON

FIREWORKS

After their galaxies
thumped out our patriotism
upon the city sky, and the
sizzle of rockets reaching up
plastered their brilliant star spit
in circles and slow cascades of
blue, green, red and diamond,
I slept.

Close to dawn I awoke and
saw from my hill the city silent
under the hung moon, with
beacon blinking from the radio station,
the lighted windows of some highrises
still glowing softly where
people lay restless,
still sighing for a tomorrow
which might have hopes for greater visions.

Yet I read of one who said,
"Look at those clouds!"
and held a party.
Some know the earth shows off continuously.

Cold sparks lie in the hand as
glow worms and fireflies.
Ripples along comb jellyfish
are incandescent.
The sea can shiver with phosphorescence.

There is an explosion of wings in the
lifting of shorebirds.

Those we love shine wonderfully.

In a finale the volcano's fire
sums up and promises
more of earth's celebration.

MEREDITH CARSON

MOTHER TONGUE

I have been practicing within myself
the voice of my mother
who has been dead now for fifty years.
I have been afraid to lose it.

The doves in the early morning
call from their throats:
"We do yes, oh we do yes,"
but their tongues have not spoken.

This wild wolf howling in me
is the world crying. Too great a sound
is meaningless.

But when I listen to my mother's voice
I hear my name spoken with
all inflections perfect
as in a mother language
whose subtleties are understood
and solace if repeated softly.

SUE COWING

AT THE HONOLULU AQUARIUM, WITH CAMERA

I frame the outdoor tide-pool exhibit
in my finder. Who would know
this rush and backwater over reef rock
is simulated? Instead, I shoot the sign
over the Hawaiian monk seals' pool, warning me
to keep my body parts behind the rail.

Inside, it's dark, except for the displays.
The Day Octopus is always flattening himself,
falling again for the illusions of glass,
propelling backwards with all eight arms behind
like a long banner, smack into one wall
of this four-by-one-by-two-foot tank.
His sack-like body looks instead
like a scrotum or a large, soft, comic nose.
At the end of each arm, a permanent tendril curl.
These arms are never still.
He pulls his silk sleeves in
and out of themselves, shakes out his scarves
as though in a light wind.

Today, instead of taking refuge at the back,
the octopus dances in the window of his tank.
His audience, a shirtless surfer with windburnt hair,
has kicked his slippers off and kneels
at soft attention close to the glass.
Each time the octopus unfurls an arm and flourishes it,
the surfer chuckles, whispering *"tako, tako"*,
traces the movement gently along the glass.

If you could say what goes on in anyone
of his three hearts, the octopus delights in this.
The movements of the pair
grow slower and more intricate.
No lovers' stroking could be more tender.
I hesitate, then slip on a close-up lens
and steal this shot.
                What won't come out on film
is that second after the click, when first the surfer,
then the octopus, turn stone red.

SUE COWING

NIGHT WATCHES

Wheezing again. Your cobweb dream.
Lung-fibers closing in like driftnet
on what's left of availing air.
You want to be out, you want me
humming or singing, repeating things. Clear nights

we lie on a reed mat out in the yard.
Somehow you are always reassured
by this vigil for meteors. Or else the car's
continual motion. I like that too.
Windshield wipers at 4 AM.
As long as we don't stop, you may even sleep
and the sudden solitude nourishes me.

At dawn I drive to Hanauma Bay
where the ocean keeps pouring into the side
of a blown volcano, carry you down
to the sand. Only somebody out that early
could find what we find: a single glass
fishing-net float washed in from Japan,
blue lava, glinty, imperfectly round.

I turn into our carport, pull up the brake,
but you cry, so I back out again.
Blue lights. Policeman behind me wants to know
where do I live and why at this hour . . .
I explain that he hasn't caught anyone.

I wish I could tell you how long this will go on.
The little that can be done, we have already done.

But the stars keep their appointments to fall down
or shine, and the man in the squad car
stays awake all night like us, his motor running.

SUE COWING

INK PAINTING BY LIU DAN, 1992

I want to see this
as the landscape it remembers.
It is not landscape.
Whatever the matter is here
it is breathing.
Is it rock? Wet?
Isn't this water? frozen? calcified?
No, it is quivering.

The longer I stare the more I desire
      one small form I can transfix and say:
at least I know this.
          Liu Dan has seen and meticulously brushed in
no such thing, but the very field
      energy flows through continuously
from spirit to matter through form
         and back again. Wherever I look,
              this happens and I'm drawn in
    to the shifting plane where he shuddered and stood
        to ask for his life.
This painting has no name.

BRIAN CRONWALL

THE ANT OF THE POEM

So when the ant, delicate
as rust filagree, crawls
onto the second page
of Matsuo Takahashi's poem
while I am reading it
at Kalapaki Beach this morning,
clouds move from eggplant to eggs;
when this ant crosses
from page two to page three,
stopping on one line then another,
it dots an "i" or fills an "o"
with a living thought;
when the ant crawls past "you"
without a stop and heads
toward the edge of the page,
I simply watch, calm, rapt;
and when the ant reaches
the end of the page and hesitates
before the gulf
between book and blanket,
poem and sand, a clear
intent bids me lower the page
so the ant can cross
the shadow effortlessly:
the sky opens into a single blue eye,
winking, calling attention
to the pores, certain
in the heat of the beckoning
and compassionate sun.

KENNETH ZAMORA DAMACION

LAST NOTE BETWEEN HEAVEN AND HELL
for A.W.

The artist has to find something within himself that's universal and which he can put into terms that are communicable to other people. The magic of it is that art can communicate this to a person without his realizing it. Enrichment, that's the function of music.
—Bill Evans

How could Bill Evans' sax player not notice
the last album of his mentor?
      The playing was agile and eloquent,
his hands climbed the ladder of the night sky to the stars.
          On the balcony, I feel
we are alone and we are not.

What if the joy we desire is to lie beside an angel,
         her wings trembling like a frightened bird,
and startled by our humanness and vulnerability,
      the large wings spread open, unlocking our grasp
          and despair.

Over the phone you complain
    you cannot see the stars as you could
in your West Virginia. I spin a record on the turntable.
      Connected like two lonely stars
flirting in the night sky,
    I try to listen to your breathing.

      Evans shot heroin
between his fingers because the veins on his arms

were bruised and mottled, you could have drawn a line
from one to another to show constellations of despair.
And what sadness is conveyed by the bassist
or the drummer stroking the snare gently with his brushes,
as they coaxed their friend to live
                    or eased him towards his dying?
What a way to go the sax player muffled through
his morning coffee and scones.

Suicide is Painless, We Will Meet Again,
            and *You Must Believe In Spring.*
Liver bad. His habit of bowing his head
        close to the keyboard, listening introspectively as he played.
wanting to talk to his dead
                brother Harry again,
his feet modulating sound, space, and thought on the foot pedals.
        I think of you and how someday you'll return
to West Virginia.
                    We are alone and we're not.
I'll think of you and how your mouth turned sourly
then sadly when you said the world was too cruel for artists.
            Their frailty becomes our music
                                and despair.

I know how I'll exit out:
                    the music of Monk, and Coltrane,
maybe Armstrong's *St. James Infirmary*
playing as a mirror and a reminder
that the moon bears down upon us,
that we want to lie beside angels,
that we want to be fixed among the stars.
        But the coda
is a shimmering cymbal stricken by the brushes
of the drummer,
        and a bassist plucking his instrument
as if it were his own heart, and a pianist

>   playing chords and melody
>   one last time between Heaven and Hell,
> the last note lingering for us still
>   around the empty piano bench.

KENNETH ZAMORA DAMACION

THE ISLANDS

Lying in bed in the dark,
    I listen to the muted trumpet,
the circular wash of brushes against the snare's skin,
someone is swirling
    circles in the sand, pensive.
The saxophone strikes in,
quarreling, moody, accusatory.
Another saxophone answers, cajoles.
    Why is it that I designated
the first sax a man's voice,
    the answering one a woman's?

*

    I can't swim.
I'm ambivalent about being thousands of miles
    from real land.
      But, I'm not certain why,
I wanted to keep treading further,
      sadness perhaps.
I turned and watched her reading beneath the palm tree.

*

We were talking about the sacrifices
of a divorce,
      the small and the grand,
her money which I did not want, the few items of furniture
I was proud of, my joy in awakening
    to find my young daughters sleeping beside me.

Maybe it was being on the island,
maybe it was our years together,
    our words came so naturally.
It must hurt you not to be intimate
with someone, she said.
    It must hurt you too, I answered.

*

I think of those last months before I left,
    lying on the couch, listening
to her footsteps overhead,
wondering could I ever love her again,
and knowing without looking
    that the hall light had flicked off,
knowing the darkness
    had closed in upon us.

DIANA J. EICHER

SETSUKO

My lover tells me the story
about her mother,
who summoned
ancestors
as her five-foot frame blocked
the doorway
to her house on
Kauhakō Street.
Erasing sounds from her daughter's
lips,
she demanded silence in
the labor room.
Arms folded like a scissors,
she whispered,
"Remember, you're Japanese and we don't scream."

Like a child, you had
courage
to trust her.
A woman with a husband you drove away.

Your silence
echoed to Kolekole Pass.
Hala trees
heard
your
pelvis
gripped with pain.
Pele's
tears showered

red flowers in place of your own.
Your mother heard nothing.
Pleased
her favorite daughter
obeyed her.
Any sound,
mistaken
for a haole daughter.

*Setsuko means faithful daughter in Japanese.

DIANA J. EICHER

VIOLET DARKNESS

I step into the water, evelyn
and
crabtree
surrounds me.
Rivers and veins
line pink marble walls,
a Glow-in-the-dark
crucifix,
shell surrounded,
traces a forgotten owner.

The bath water ignites
my torso,
ivory and raw,
stretched tight like a bolt of silk.
My breasts,
half-in, half-out,
become sugary pears,
warmed by
solitary
diamonds of water.
Silver coated
with ribbons of metal,
my fingers leave behind
confused
lines
across my stomach.
Soaked with skin,
I wring
a blue and white washcloth

over my head.
The heavy liquid
falls
like bronze,
the water
melts
my body.

Slice of golden
light, slides
under the
door,
carries notes of a
bedtime
song.
The teakettle,
whistling on the stove,
forgotten.

M. EVELINA GALANG

FILMING SAUSAGE

Day One of Nine
The assistant director, Bud, welcomes you with a huge hug. You have never met him before. He gives you the materials you need to keep the continuity on this job: a script, the storyboards, a shooting schedule. You're to make sure that each camera shot is legal—that clothes are exactly the same for each take, sleeves rolled three-quarters up each time, hair parted on the camera right side, every time. You will see to it that the plates have three Danny Boy sausages, one with a bite, the other two pointing camera left, every time. You watch the details in the spot. You keep the director honest.

"Why don't you get settled—grab something to eat," Bud tells you, "then I'll introduce you to Dick, he's the director."

The craft service table is in the backyard, under the shade of a hundred-year-old maple tree. To get there you must weave your body around the cables and giant lights which sit cold on the lawn of this house. Wave to some of the guys hauling lights from the truck. "Hey Tom! Solly! How ya doin', Mike?" They look up and call your name, grunt hello while you crawl beneath the scaffolding.

Your friend Katy drags two different kinds of rocking chairs around the corner of the house. "Elena!" she calls, "How are you?"

Standing at craft service where there is always something to graze on—bagels and cheese, chocolate donuts and ham sandwiches on white, you coddle a hot cup of coffee. Jump out of the way of a toddler as he runs about your legs, chasing a man in a jean jacket and baseball cap. The man dodges the boy, pretends to be scared of him, then turns about to capture the child and nibble at his belly. The boy laughs and mutters,

"Daddy, daddy, oh daddy!" You smile at them. It's nice, you think, to see a father and son in love like this. Imagine your boyfriend, Aaron, imagine a son and think you'd like this someday too. A small woman peeks around the tree and approaches the two. "Okay, Samuel," she says. "That's enough. Daddy has to work now." She takes the boy from the man and balances the child on her narrow hip.

After your coffee, Bud ushers you into the house, holding his palm to the small of your back. Wriggle ahead of him. He doesn't seem to notice this and places his hand on your shoulder, leading you to a room that's cramped with lights and sound blankets, teeming with grips, prop people, account execs from Harbor, Conahan and Lunt. Already the air is hot and stale inside the house; already it smells of sweat and burning rubber and it's only seven thirty in the morning.

"Dick," Bud calls, "This is your script and continuity, Elena." Bud holds his arm out to Dick Reinhonker. Reinhonker stands tall and skinny liked a newly sharpened pencil. He has salt and pepper hair which recedes from his forehead, slipping quietly underneath a baseball cap turned backward. His sparse beard runs along the edge of his face, linking his sideburns to one another. He has brown eyes that are wide and laugh lines that crease nicely as he welcomes you. He puts his hand out and draws you to him. "Nice to meet you," he says.

Say, "That's quite a little boy you have."

"Samuel—he's a little monster all right. I'm Dick." He offers you his hand. "Ellen?"

"Elena," you tell him. "Elena Romero."

He wants to know where you are from, so you tell him Ann Arbor.

A production assistant approaches the two of you, she carries a cup of coffee and a donut. She holds it out to Dick, says, "I have some more hidden in the back."

He takes the offering from her, kisses her thanks and you gather this was his special request—grape jelly donuts. He turns back to you and asks again, "Where are you from?"

You're used to people asking you this question and never being satisfied when you answer, Ann Arbor, but this really is where you're from. You know he wants to know the history of your black hair, the brown in your skin, the almond of your eyes, but you will not give in. You like to make people work for this answer. You enjoy seeing them squirm, but Dick doesn't squirm. Instead he laughs and says, "And where are your people from, Elena?"

"My people? You mean my ethnicity?"

"You're quick," he laughs as he brushes the hair off your forehead. "You'll keep me honest, won't you? " He winks at you then and you laugh.

The two of you find a corner in the house and begin to review the spots. You will be shooting three commercials in nine days, he tells you. Long days.

"I know this sounds a bit sick," Dick says as you page through the script, "but what the agency wants us to do is to send out the message that America is sausage in the morning, sunrise at the farm, spicy pork links, grandma and love." He looks at you, smiling, his eyes friendly as a puppy dog. "What do you think, Ellen, sick?"

Smile back at him, say, "Elena."

Dick tells you that he is going to rely on you. "I need to know what comes before the shot, and then what comes after it. Continuity is important on this one."

You think that you will like working with him okay, he seems nice enough, if only he'd get your name right. You imagine that in his youth, he was probably attractive.

The first shot is of an elderly woman named Bel Moss who's dressed in a gingham checkered apron. She has blond-white hair and light blue eyes. She stands at a kitchen stove, one that Katy rented from Period Prop Rentals, and stirs a pan of Danny Boy sausages.

The camera is set upon a dolly, a giant tripod on wheels which holds not only the camera, but the director and you. Underneath the actual camera, Dick wraps his hands about two metal wheels—one at the back of the camera's neck, and one to the left of the camera. He guides which way the camera floats, spinning the metal wheel much like a sailor would at sea. You sit at the back of the dolly, notebook on your lap, pens in your hands. Label your notes "Day One of Nine." Around your neck, wear two digital stopwatches that glow in the dark. Use these to count the seconds, the tenths of seconds.

The house is slowly quieting as everyone finds a place to sit. The grips walk out into the yard to smoke a cigarette or have another cup of coffee. They've lit the kitchen, made it warm and cozy, created that loving feeling. Katy tiptoes about the set, carrying a cloth diaper in her hand and occasionally wiping a smudge off the counter, the refrigerator, the toaster oven. The only voice that can be heard now is Dick's. He tells Bel to stir the sausages counterclockwise—"It's more appealing," he says. Bel follows directions well when she can hear them. Her hearing isn't so good. He is tilting the camera from the frying pan to her face and it is important that she smile on cue. You will count three seconds out and she will smile on three and sigh, "Danny Boy," on four. Bud struts circles about the camera dolly, heaving his jeans up to his swollen belly as Dick squints into the camera's eye piece. Dick mutters, "Yes, yes, yes, in a minute. Hold on."

"Let's shoot this baby," Bud tells him. "We gotta go." He tap dances in place and then asks, "Ready?" Dick nods. Bud turns to face the rest of the crew and calls out "That's it! Close it up and keep it down!"

Call out, "Scene One-oh-One take one is up!" and a series of voices—the assistant camera, video, and sound—acknowledge you as each one repeats, "One-oh-one, take one."

Bud rattles off a chain of commands, "Roll sound, roll camera, speed!" Dick looks over his shoulder, smiles at you, winks and says, "Let's ride this baby." When he's not looking, roll your eyes. Finally Dick calls out to Bel, "Action!"

Bel misses her cue. "Damn," Dick whispers after the twenty-seventh take. Though she can't hear him, Bel senses his hostility and she drops the frying pan on the floor, splattering grease on her one-of-a-kind apron. "It's okay sweetie, it's okay," he tells Bel, as he climbs down from the camera dolly. To you he says, "Let's look at what we've got."

Jump off the dolly, carting your pens and pad. The stopwatches swing across your breasts as you chase after Dick. Walk past his wife, who is standing behind the clients. Smile and say hello. She's looking right at you, but doesn't bother answering. Dick's strides are long and he is hard to keep up with. You hop over boxes and cables, trying not to trip, trying desperately to hear what he is saying. He is fast and unaware of how closely you trail him.

"The first nineteen were no good," you tell him. "You said they 'sucked egg.' You liked take twenty and twenty-two. You said take twenty-five was 'Awesome for action, shaky on camera.'"

He says, "You write down everything I say?"

"Verbatim," you tell him. "I figure writing down what you say will jog your memory—help you look for certain things."

"What if I don't mean it?" he asks.

"Mean what?"

"The stuff I say, what if it's all bullshit and you write it down?"

"Then you'll have to keep track of what you mean and what you don't mean. I just write what I hear."

He smiles at you and nudges your arm. "You're good. Not only beautiful, but smart too."

Stand with your back straight, not lilting to his touch, not recoiling either. Stand perfectly still. Turn your attention to your work. Your notes are detailed color coded messages. You know you are good at this, that editors love to get your notes because they are clear and to the point. Write down that the first shot was shot at eight-ten. Circle the takes that Dick liked. Put a triangle around the ones the client liked.

A dozen agency people huddle around Dick. Remain just outside their circle. The men wear baggy pants with teal blue and burgundy shirts, loud ties and tennis shoes. The women have on heavy eye make-up and blush. Their lips are lined with red pencil—they wear expensive sweaters and pant suits, red leather mini-skirts and white blouses with leather ties to match. They sit in front of the monitor with their yellow note pads and wind-up toys. "She's perfect, she's beautiful," they're saying. "We love when she smiles like she's going to cry."

"Yeah, yeah, like the thought of her grandson coming home moves her to tears."

"Yeah," Dick says. "You know, I work with a lot of old people and she's one of the best. She's right on."

"There's one take that we just loved," says a man. "Which was it, Kerrie?"

Kerrie, one of the women in red leather, snaps her fingers, says, "Oh yeah, it was, it was . . . which one was it?"

"You liked take twenty-one," you remind her. Look up at Dick, he's smiling at you, nodding.

"You can hear from all the way over there?" he asks.

Say, "Of course."

You all watch take twenty-one in playback, a take that Dick had labeled, "Fucked up" and the agency people say—"See how her lips tremble like that? Beautiful."

"Circle that take," Dick tells you. "It's a beauty, a true keeper."

He turns to run back to the camera and you follow him. He smiles and reaches out to you, wraps your shoulders with his arm and says, "Well, Ellen, looks like we fooled them."

When Bel comes back on set, she has on different glasses. "Are those the ones you normally wear?" you ask.

"Oh dear, I forgot my prop glasses," she sighs. Dick taps your shoulders, says, "Good call, Ellen, good call." Remind him that your name is not Ellen, it's Elena and he grins at you and says, "Whatever."

Katy walks up to the camera, carrying two footstools—one is hand-carved with little hearts at the legs and the other is plain and painted white. She holds them up to Dick and says, "Which one, Dick?" She winks at you.

"That's for the porch?" he asks.

"Uh-huh." She holds the white one up and says, "This one doesn't match the rocking chairs, but it looks good on the porch. The other one is grandma-like and matches the chair."

"That one," Dick says as he points to the white stool.

Katy turns to leave, but he calls her back. "Come here," he says. He puts his arms around Katy's waist and she returns his hug. "You're doing a wonderful job, Katy."

"For you, Dick," she says laughing, "anything."

When Katy walks away, Dick turns to you. Look past him to the set up in the kitchen. He says, "So, you and Katy friends?"

Tell him you are. He watches you out of the corner of his eye and whispers, "Really?" Look at him, confused, almost ask "What do you mean by that?" but don't.

At lunch, Bud tells you that Dick's impressed. "He likes you," Bud says, "He never likes script supervisors."

Letty, the wardrobe lady from L.A. who reads peoples' palms in between the filming, whispers, "Oh honey, that's because he has a thing for Asian women."

Say, "I'm not Asian, I'm American."

She laughs and lifting your hand up to the light, she runs her fingers along the creases of your palm. Smile at her. Say, "Well, Filipina-American, really." You are glib because you have heard this joke too many times for you to react—that you are all alike, that you are all exotic, that there are men in this world who are into "Asian" women. You used to get worked up over this. You used to despise men like that. Now you are too old to care. The Mata Haris of this world are in the movies, not making them as you are. And that is the woman those men seek, not you.

"Yes," Letty hums. "Your lines are strong. You are stubborn. Know what you want. You will live a very very long life, honey. I mean it honey, you will."

Just then the woman from this morning walks into the room, carrying the toddler. Everybody stands to greet her.

"What's her name?" you ask.

"Keiko," Letty says. Keiko's hair is not exactly black—actually it looks a little like it's supposed to be, but some dye job contaminated the color and now it's more like black and red. Her skin is olive and her eyes are brown. "She's not Asian either," Letty laughs. "Right." Samuel's screaming, "Daddy!" He reaches out his arms to Dick and dives right out of Keiko's arms.

"Hey Samuel, what's up, dude?" Dick says. He rubs his beard across the child's face, tickles him, kisses.

"They travel with him on all his jobs. Before Chicago, they were with us in Seattle," Letty informs you. "Before that, Toronto."

Say, "That's nice. I mean, that she can take off like that to be with her husband."

"Yeah," Letty says, blowing smoke out from her nostrils. "Suppose it's a way of keeping an eye on him."

Keiko wraps herself around Dick's long torso, whispers in his ear. Her hair falls back and exposes the white line of her neck. "She's pretty," you say. Letty laughs cynically.

That night, Dick asks you to come out with him and Bud and a few of the clients—to discuss the next day's shooting schedule, he says. To make sure you're all working like a team. Because you are not really being asked, but being told, you accompany them to dinner. Dick tells you to have anything you want, "It's on the company," he says. Order a plate of grilled calamari and a rich salmon linguini. Have two glasses of wine. Enjoy your meal, but not the company. This is part of your job, to sit with these people and talk about ways to shoot sexy sausages and eggs. You think it's strange that other than Bud and Katy, you are the only one from the crew, but the meeting's at an Italian restaurant, and you love eating Italian.

Finish work at midnight. When you arrive at home, sit at the foot of the bed and watch your boyfriend Aaron sleep. It's dark and all you really see is his shadow—but you imagine the look on his face, a slight smile, dark lashes, the angle of his chin. He's curled up like an infant which makes you want to crawl alongside him, rest next to him. He reaches, pulling you to him and whispers, "Long day, huh?"

Mold your body into his and sigh. Lots of the guys are on the job, tell him, Solly, Jeff, Andy, even Katy. Tell him that the director insisted you attend the pre-pro meeting. Say it wasn't bad. "The food was good," you tell him. "And I was on double time."

Aaron wants to know what the director's like. Say, "He has a thing for Asian women."

"Not that," he sighs, "I hate that."

Close your eyes and try to stop thinking. For a while, the day flutters past your lids, rolling out like a series of unfinished scenes, until your mind, like the rest of you, slips under the covers and sleeps.

Day Two of Nine

Tell Bud that Dick has rearranged the shooting schedule. Show which shots have been canceled. Dick crossed them off the storyboards himself. "He doesn't think we need them," you say. "He's trying to buy time for that one shot, at sunrise, the one in the field with the cows."

When Dick arrives he kisses everyone hello. Someone brings him a cup of coffee and a grape jelly donut. Dick reaches out for you and tells you that you look great today. He uses the word, hot. Smile at him uncomfortably. When you back away, he moves in even closer, brushes your shoulder with his. "Are those really your legs?"

You're standing against the house, wearing black leggings with a baggy sweater. You're wearing boots that climb your legs, hit past the tops of your knees. Your notebook rests on your hip as you finger the buttons on your stopwatch. Not sure if he's joking or what, ignore him.

He reaches out to graze the top of your thigh with the tip

of his finger. Back away. Don't let him touch you. Decide he's joking. Say, "No, Dick, these are not my legs. I borrowed them from props."

He smirks out loud. You feel his laughter rolling into your ear like morning fog off a summer lake. "Kidder," he whispers. Dick tosses this empty, awkward moment at you like an NBA basketball and somehow, you miss the toss, let the ball hit your hands and dribble down the side of you. He smiles as if to say, "Two points." Then he calls out to Katy, "Come here, Katy my dear and tell me how things are going."

Katy puts her arms around Dick's waist, tells him that things are going just swell. Look at them and sigh, think maybe it's time for more coffee and walk away. Dick calls to you, and so you turn to see him kissing Katy on the cheek. "Could you bring back a cup for me?" he asks. Shudder.

The first shot for today is of a man driving a black Saab. He races up a dirt road at dawn, drives past a flurry of chickens, a corral full of dairy cows. He's coming home. The prodigal son. The country boy gone city. The assistant camera person rattles off a list of filters—colors that will enhance the homecoming—corals and pinks, reds and ambers. The crew works together to achieve this sincere moment. Dick approaches from behind, kisses your cheek and laughing, asks, "Are you teaching her camera techniques, Joe?"

"Elena's the one keeping me on my toes—did you want a Coral-grad-one or was it a Coral-grad-two?"

"I wanted two," Dick says. "I want it to be rich."

"See?" You wink at Joe. "Told you."

"This girl knows what she's doing, Joe," Dick says as his palm rubs the back of your neck. Though his hand is warm, you shiver coldly, feel goose bumps rise in your arms. "She scares me."

"I'm not supposed to scare you, Dick," you say as you step away from him. "I'm supposed to make you feel better."

"Oh?" His eyes widen and you can feel a flush of red color your face like a filter out of Joe's kit.

"I mean, with me around you're not supposed to worry about these details."

He leans into you—brushes your forehead with a kiss. Laugh nervously. Say nothing. This will pass. Think of your mother—she would frown if she knew that people were so casual about touching her daughter at work. She'd frown at men and women behaving this way in public. It means nothing, you whisper to your mom as if she were next to you, it's just the way they are in this business. Everyone does it and you know that for the most part, so do you. You have to.

The camera dolly has been placed at the edge of a farmer's driveway. As you wait for the sun to create that homecoming moment, sit on the dolly and count out the length of the shot. Hit the button on the stopwatch and read: "Working in the city made breakfast a thing of the past. I never had time for anything more than coffee . . ." Sit with your legs crossed at the edge of the dolly, mumbling the copy to yourself, timing and re-timing the words that run about ten seconds. Every now and then, you look up to see what the rest of the crew is doing. Mostly they run about, scattered across the field between the camera and the house, hauling large pieces of scaffolding. Dick sits in a high-backed director's chair, drinking coffee with a little kick as Bud circles him, talks at him. Twice you look up and Dick is staring at you. Ignore him. Don't blow your top. You need to get along. Go back to the script, but he is getting on your nerves and you begin to shake your leg, swing it off the dolly. "What?" you finally ask him, "What?"

He grins and says, "Nothing, Elena, just looking."

Slam your notebook shut and walk away. Maybe it's you. You're being too sensitive. Think about your niece Amanda who knows an imaginary person named Roy. According to Amanda, Roy makes mud cookies and feeds them to her dolls—dirties them, undresses them, and pulls out their hair. Of course you know it's Amanda baking mud pies—not Roy. No one believes the child when she blames Roy. You want to think of a way to bring up this uncomfortable feeling, you want to tell on

Dick, the way she tells on Roy, but who would you tell? What would you say?

An hour passes. The light filters over the horizon and the man in the car drives into the camera's point of view. Just as he begins to pass the chicken coop, the animal wrangler who is stooped underneath the hen house wiggles an invisible prod and the chickens dance into the camera's frame on cue. The city boy pulls up to the farm house just as Bel's supposed to come onto the porch with her plate of sausages. Bud yells into a walkie talkie "Action." This is Bel's cue, but no one comes through the door. "Action," he calls again and still there is no movement.

"God damn it!" yells Dick. "What the hell's happening in there?"

Shoot this scene fifty-five times. The sun rises fast into the sky and that magic moment's lost. The clients from Harbor, Conahan and Lunt sit behind the camera dolly, whispering to themselves words so small you can barely make them out. Write down, "Clients brood over shot. Look a bit worried." The crickets have stopped chirping, and Dick and Bud are pacing the fields, arguing one hundred yards away.

Remind both Bud and Dick of the shots Dick has eliminated, assure them that they're not behind when they consider this, but Dick explodes, "Who said we're not shooting those shots? We have to! Who says we can buy time? Impossible."

Step away from Dick, toss a look at Bud who runs his palm up and down the stretch of his face. Show Dick your notes, show him where he's crossed shots off the list himself. He looks at you and says —"Why do you write everything down? Everything I say? Stop that. You have to stop that." He turns away from you, storms across the open field, screams at you, "Write this down, Dick is always right, he's the director!"

Keiko brings their son, Samuel, to location during lunch. She sits at a table conversing with Letty, smoking a cigarette while she pokes at a salad. She drinks seltzer water from a bottle and watches Dick and Samuel strut around the set with

Bud. Samuel rides on his father's shoulders, laughing as he tugs at Dick's gray wisps. They are singing the song, "I've Been Working on the Railroad."

At a table with Katy and some of the grips, finish the last of an apple cobbler doused in a melting mound of vanilla ice cream.

"I don't know how you all put up with him," Solly says.

"Well," Katy says, "it's just not worth getting worked up over." Katy drapes her arms across two folding chairs making her look like a scarecrow dressed in some man's hand-me-down clothes. Her blond hair is piled high upon her head like an empty hornet's nest. She winks at you, says, "Right, Elena? Not worth it."

Look across at Keiko who is watching her husband and child. She is waving at them when she catches you looking at her. You nod your head at Keiko and smile. In return, she looks away, tosses her head back at your table and blows a heavy dose of smoke from her red lips.

That night, Aaron cooks *pansit*, stir-fry vegetables and chicken with noodles.

"Where'd you learn to cook *pansit*?" you ask him.

"Your *lola*," he answers as he heaps the noodles onto your plates.

"What, you called my grandmother? Aaron, this is my favorite." Lean over and kiss him, rub his back. "I can't believe you did this."

"This job's a rough one," he tells you. "I wanted to make something that would help you get through it. Then I remembered how your family always makes *pansit* on birthdays," he says. "So, I called your *lola* and asked her for the recipe for —"

"Long life noodles!" you say laughing. Look into Aaron's face and carve the lines of his smile with the edge of your finger. "You're such a modern guy," tell him. Feel the tears rising up inside you, you are so tired. "What did *Lola* say?"

"She said next time she'd teach me how to make fresh egg

rolls and she wanted to know why don't you just tell that guy off."

"You know why." Tell Aaron that half the time you don't know what Dick means—is he joking, is he serious? Is he coming on to you? What? Sometimes he's nice. Sometimes he's charming.

"Charming?" Aaron asks.

"Well, with his son, he's charming, other times he's just sleazy."

Day Three of Nine

Today you are shooting more interiors of the kitchen. Walk around the set snapping Polaroid pictures for continuity. Walk around with your notebook and mark the little things—the sugar bowl's position, the time on the kitchen clock, the angle of the table to the lens. Dick follows you says, "I feel like you don't like me, Ellen. Do you?"

When he looks at you, you feel like the gaffer has turned the lights on you—your face gets hot and you can feel the perspiration seeping from the pores of your skin. He grabs onto your arm and turns you to him. He is waiting for an answer. "Elena, do you like me?"

Ignore him. Turn away. Walk over to the camera dolly and look at the markings on the camera—a ten to one zoom lens, no filters, roll number ten.

He sneaks up behind you, whispers, "You know, Ellen, you're not being honest with me. I like my script girls to be honest." Walk to the back of the dolly. Though your instinct is to lash out, say you are not a script girl, you're a script supervisor and you are not HIS script supervisor, you are not his anything, you say nothing. Feel him standing next to you, his shadow creeping over you. Scribble into your notebook, hear him tell you to add to your notes some obscenity—the obscenity for day three. Walk up to Bud say, "I'm stepping off set for a minute."

As you walk away Dick yells after you, "Something the matter?"

Later, your face is buried in your notes, but you feel another's presence. You feel someone almost touching you, seeing right into you and you feel naked. Continue to look down at your notes. Flip the pages of the script, run your fingers along the storyboard. Dive into the pages of your notes, scribbling things you will remind Dick later on.

Finally look up, as you continue to write. Dick is staring at you and his eyes, the ones that were warm like that puppy dog's have grown dark and sullen. Possessed, you think. "Always writing little notes. Got the world on a note pad. Here," he whispers as he leans into you, breathing words onto the nape of your neck. "Write this down," he says, "suck director's dick after wrap."

Squirm forward, dropping several pens and markers from your pouch. Reaching down, you pick them up, move away from Dick. Your notes go flying—the script, the storyboard. Katy runs over to help you pick up the papers before they blow about.

"My God, you're still a klutz," she says laughing. "Ever since I've known you, Elena, you've been a hazard on the set."

She hands you your papers and as you take them, she squeezes your hand and smiles.

There are six days left, after today. You think you can put up with Dick just long enough to do the job and take your pay check. Scribble down his words. Write them big and dark. They appear heavy on the page. Note the time.

Day Four of Nine

At five in the morning, the production company closes down LaSalle, a boulevard that leads right to Chicago's Board of Trade. The sky reflects blue/black against a moon that still shines white light, a light which contrasts with bright copper street lamps along the avenue. The street is wide and empty and lined on either side with tall granite buildings. The shot will be of the man in the Saab sitting in the middle of morning rush hour traffic. His black Saab is stuck between a city bus and a chauffeur-driven limo. A yellow cab cuts him off. A bike messenger swerves into his lane. None of this helps his attitude—he's grumpy, which makes him remember he's hungry, which leads him to fantasize about going home for a good breakfast, home to Grandma O'Connor and Danny Boy Sausages.

The police have blocked off the streets while Bud directs prop-car drivers into appropriate lanes to create a controlled rush hour environment. Several production assistants line the sidewalks, guiding extras to walk past the camera on cue. The crew is setting up to shoot at sunrise.

Wrapped in a down coat, you stand along side of the camera, next to Dick, jumping up on your toes to keep warm. He tells you, "Remind me that I want to get an extreme close-up of his hands hitting the horn, and remind me not to forget to get both a hand-held shot and a steady camera shot from in the car looking out. Oh—and I want to get close-ups of other drivers too for cut-aways."

Still jogging in place, you keep your hands deep in your pockets, nod your head up and down. He looks at you and smiles. "So Asia," he says. Asia, like the continent, like the band.

"Elena."

"I'm the director, Asia, I can call you anything I want. Anyhow, are you going to remember all those reminders or are you going to put them into that pad of yours?"

Jot down, "Remind Dick." At five a.m. it's cold and though it's only October, you're wearing knit gloves. You've cut the fingers off like a pauper kid, so your fingers can move freely between the buttons of your stopwatch, the pen and the pages.

"How many rolls of film have we shot so far?" he asks. You tell him seventeen rolls at four thousand feet a roll. He nods his head then turns away from you. Follow him into the trailer where the actor is getting dressed.

The motor home is crowded with clients. They are looking at ties—paisley, polka dots, stripes and flowers. Wide ties, bow ties, narrow leather ties. They look at navy, reds, teals and burgundy and bright yellows with purple accents.

"What do you think, Dick?" Kerrie asks. "We want our country boy to look powerful and yet not snobbish, rich but still down home."

"We want him to read 'America' and 'Danny Boy Sausage' at once," says a man in a Hawaiian shirt, baseball cap and trench coat.

"What do you think, Asia?" Dick asks you. Glance about the motor home, see people picking at their clothing, scribbling into note pads, trying not to catch your eye. "Navy and red striped, don't you think?" No one is speaking. There is only the hum of the motor home engine. You know that they are waiting for you, waiting to see what you will do.

Say nothing. Pretend you haven't heard him. Open your notes to yesterday and say, "Yesterday, you all thought that navy/red stripes would be too obvious. You narrowed it down to the teal and burgundy paisley and the navy with white pinpoint polka dots." Say this to the group of clients, completely aware that Dick is looking at you with his brows ruffled together like the feathers of an angry bird.

When you leave the trailer walk ahead of Dick. March back to the camera which stands at the end of the block. Dick calls out to you, "Hey, Asia!"

Keep walking. "Asia, come back here!" he yells. "I'm talking to you! Answer me when I speak to you!"

When you get to the camera, look at Bud who is hunched over with his hands in his down vest, blowing smoke from his mouth into the air. Next to him stands Keiko in an oversized parka, smoking another cigarette. When Bud sees you his eyebrows rise, ready to greet you, but you beat him to it and say, "Hi Bud, Dick wants you to check with weather one more time."

"Okee," he says, leaving you two alone. Turn to Keiko. "We haven't been introduced," tell her, "but my name is Elena."

She looks at you and says, "I know." Tell her that you admire her for being such a dedicated wife, dedicated mother. Tell her you couldn't do what she's doing.

"Oh well," Keiko says. Her voice is thick with a Japanese accent. "He's my husband and Sammy's father. We go where he goes." Look at the roots of her hair, they're dark and miscolored, awkward as snow on the beaches of Hawaii. You want to advise her, "Don't follow him, leave him." Instead say, "You must love him very much."

As the two of you stand there, watch Dick at the end of the block. See him shifting on his feet, staring. She looks towards Dick too and after a while Keiko turns to you and says, "It's not so hard." Her eyes are wet and you aren't sure if it's from the chill in the air or if she's crying. "Just have to be patient."

"Still," you say, "I'm not sure I'd have the strength to do what you do."

After work, sit in a tub full of bubbles. Stretch your neck forward, resting your forehead on the tops of your knees. Aaron washes the tension from your back, pushing suds along the lines of your torso, the curve of your waist. He tells you this isn't worth it—coming home so upset. Coming home with pains in all your bones. Not worth it.

"He's an idiot," you tell him. "I've never dealt with a director like him."

"He's frustrated. You ignore him and he lashes out. How do you feel when he calls you Asia?"

"Do I look like the continent of Asia?" you snap and seeing the worried look on Aaron's face, soften, say, "I'm too annoyed to feel anything." Tell him it won't be much longer. "We need the money."

Day Five of Nine

Today you sleep in a little. Your call time is a little later than usual, eight o'clock a.m. This is because the production is moving onto the stage. On the one hand, this is good, you start a little later. On the other hand it also means you could stay and work there till six a.m. tomorrow.

Drive along the lake in silence. Still sleepy, you barely notice the rush hour traffic around you. The sky is gray and you can hear the wind dash along the beach. You think you hear the waves crashing onto rocks, but you're travelling much too fast to actually hear the water. You've stopped dressing up for work—not that you ever were dressed up. You've taken to wearing old t-shirts and faded jeans. Instead of boots, wear tennis shoes that are weathered with dirt and mud. You shower but no longer blow-dry your hair or curl it. You've given up on make-up.

Driving, you wonder how long the day will be. What insults you will be subjected to today. For the past few mornings, Bud has thanked you for coming back to work, has told you how much the company appreciates your patience. Patience, my ass, you think, I can't afford not to come in. Last night your *lola* told you to sue the man. "Where we come from young ladies don't let men act this way."

"*Lola*, it's not like I'm encouraging this," you cried to her.

"Then you should speak up, *hija*, you should speak up."

Imagine telling Dick off, or walking off set for the day—or burning all your notes and quitting the job for good. That would screw him big time. No one would be able to pick up where you left off. He'd be lost. Think about turning him in, filing a suit, writing the *Chicago Tribune* or *Variety*. Imagine you and Keiko, friends, sisters, pow-wowing, letting him have a taste of his own recipe, coming up with other ways to cook sausages. You could fry them, roast them, bake them, skewer them on metal sticks, cut them up into little round pieces. You could—A taxi cuts you off and you slam on the breaks, honk the horn, you scream, "Asshole!" You hope the day is short.

Dick stands in front of a kitchen facade and stares at you as you sit on an applebox, reviewing your notes. The page before you is sparse. You've stopped writing down the things you hear. Wonder if you're even hearing conversations at all any more. You can feel him watching you, sense him out of the corner of your eye. Finally, look up and ask, "Do you want something?"

"Nothing," Dick says, "Well, actually, tell me something, Elena."

Begin poring through your notes, looking for the answer to the question he will ask. "What were you and my wife talking about?" he asks.

"Didn't she tell you?" you say as you continue to search your notes. You see that yesterday you forgot to write down what time the camera rolled first shot. You've stopped writing down complete sentences too. Sometimes you wrote, "Good" or "Okay," sometimes "Not good."

"I guess I forgot to ask."

"Well then, I suppose you'll have to remember, won't you?" Smile at him. Challenge him.

"You know, Asia," he says, "you don't need to be so meticulous." He leans over you, casting a shadow onto the pages of your notes. He whispers into your ear, says, "I mean, it seems that you haven't caught me being untrue—not to the script."

You decide not to answer him at all. He is talking to someone in the room named Asia or Ellen and you are neither of these persons.

Because you do not answer him, he stands and strutting far from you calls out, "You know Asia, your notes are looking pretty bare—I sure hope you haven't missed anything. Could cost us a lot of money, you know. Could cost you your job."

He gets up and walks over to the clients. Unclench your hand from the pencil. You haven't even noticed how hard you've been holding on. Glancing at your notes, see the words you've written down etched deep into the page.

Watch Katy scrubbing at the O'Connor's kitchen sink. Her hair bobs frantically as she scours the sink with a shower of cleanser. "Elena," she says, "do you remember if we had the shade drawn in the wide shot last Friday, or was it up?"

Stare at the O'Connor window. Examine the light yellow drapes that hang above the sink, the little green ruffles that tie the drapery back. Imagine the wide shot in the O'Connor kitchen. You remember you shot that on day three—or was it four? Bel, alias Mrs. O'Connor stood in front of the window and talked to Dick's twenty-five millimeter lens. Bel had a tendency to tilt her head to the right or camera left—you can see that—and the light which hit her from the back of the facade—but you can't imagine how the window looked exactly. Did you see glass or was it that white shade? You look through the Polaroids you'd taken—there aren't many. Which is unusual for you—you always take so many pictures when you're covering continuity on set.

Rifle through the Polaroids, never looking up. "I can't remember, Katy," you tell her. "I was a bit distracted."

"You're too soft skinned, Elena. You shouldn't fight it. Play along—you'll die in this business if you don't."

"That's not true," you tell her. Continue to flip through the pictures, say, "I work with all kinds of directors—nobody in Chicago has been this rude. Makes me want to file a complaint—or write a letter to someone—I don't know. God, I could quit. Screw 'em all."

"You wouldn't do that, would you? Think of all the people you'd piss off—you'd be a wave maker. No one would hire you."

Look up from the stack you've been shuffling. Stare at Katy. Pause and then say, "Thanks, Katy, thanks for the support."

"Plus," she calls to you, "you wouldn't get paid."

When Bud calls lunch at one o'clock, everyone leaves the room except you. You run your hands along the pages of your notes searching for the words you've written—or thought you'd written. It's weird that the pages are as empty as they are, because you seem to have been writing all this down—yet none of it exists except for cursory words like "Good" and "Best" and "No Good." Standing up, you place your notes on a chair against the wall. When you turn to leave you are caught off guard by Dick who stands in front of you. He presses up against you. Pinches you between him and the studio wall. He laughs. "Do you like lunch?" he asks. "Keiko likes lunch, that's why she comes to set, for lunch."

"Let me go."

"Elena, you're not coming onto me, are you?" He smiles at you and you can see the yellow of his teeth. "I'm flattered, Elena, but I'm a happily married man, you know."

"You bastard, you wouldn't." He leans down and the breath of his words land in little moist clumps on your nose and the brim of your lip. You can smell stale bits of nicotine and coffee. A wave of nausea rises from the knots inside you. "That's sick," you say. "You're the one." His eyes widen and you can see tiny red veins cracked in the white of his eye. Push him away.

"Name calling? Lies? Promiscuity? Careful Asia," he whispers. The weight of him against your breasts, sends sharp pains through your chest. Hold still, try not to breathe his smarmy scent. His eyes penetrate your skin. "You could be fired over something like this," he says, "lose lots of work, you know?" He rubs his face against yours the way he rubbed his beard against his son's small belly that first day. He pricks you with the bristles, and you can't believe you thought he was a good father. "This," he says, "is not the kind of behavior I tolerate on sets."

The door squeaks open and Samuel comes running through. Bud follows next, chasing the child and screaming in a high falsetto voice, "I'm gonna get you!"

When Bud sees you standing with Dick flat against your chest he laughs and says, "Excuse me—I didn't mean to interrupt."

Samuel runs to his dad and Dick tells them, "That's okay. We're just coming to lunch anyway."

Keiko, trailing after Bud and Samuel, enters the room and gives you a long cold look. You push your hair, out of your face, out of the corners of your mouth. She grabs onto Dick's arm and kisses him hello. They leave you standing at the wall while you wipe the sweat from your lips, your brow and forehead. You hold your hands out in front of you and watch them shake. Quickly gather your notes which have fallen from the chair you placed them on. The lines you've drawn on them are blurred. You blink tears from your eyes. The papers seem to stare at you blank as white walls. How can she put up with this, you think? How can she say nothing? Toss the papers, kick them out of your way. Leave.

Day Six of Nine

Sleep until noon. Speak to no one, not even Aaron. Walk around the house. Start to do things. Chores. Eat. Watch T.V. or read a book then stop. Accomplish nothing. You're not sure what has happened, only this: You feel weird.

Day Seven of Nine

More of day six.

Day Eight of Nine

Come out of hiding. Put your arms around Aaron and hold him for almost an hour. Tell him how much you want to cry. "Go ahead," he whispers. But you shake your head and say, "Can't." Tell him it's like being in shock. Tell him you are numb—your chest, your limbs, your heart.

Go for a walk. Answer the fifteen messages on the machine. Book yourself on two jobs. One starts next week. The other starts in three weeks. Ask who's directing.

Day Nine of Nine

Sit by the window of Millie's Matzo Madness, drinking bowls of soup. Your stomach's sore. You are alone and mumbling into matzo ball broth, reading matzo dough like a gypsy reads tea leaves. Rub the palms of your hands, trace the lines that Letty said spell out your life. You're confused and don't know which lines meant long life, stubbornness or strength.

Cup your hands in order to define the creases—the lines are gone. The palms are blank as white paper.

Dream about life-size erasers and gallon tanks of white-out. Wish you had some. On the napkin before you, scribble notes to yourself. You will write a letter, call a senator—maybe the one from Pennsylvania, make up a song or poem, a cautionary jingle. Warn everyone. Tomorrow you'll get tickets to Oprah's show—you'll offer to be a guest on her program, "The Choices Women Make."

You should have gone with your gut. Quit the moment you saw it coming. Did you see it coming? Left the day Danny Boy's sausages were no longer Danny's. When filming sausage was no longer the point. Now, even though you're the one who left, it seems that he has won.

Look down the center of your body. What do you see? A pair of legs. Legs that begin just beneath your chin, stretching long and narrow like a strip of highway somewhere in the middle of desolate Nebraska. Turn your head and look out Millie's picture window. Stare at your reflection, the contours of your face, the way your cheekbones sit wide and high, cocked at angles—the way your chin draws to a point and your hair feathers and frames your face like the Pacific Ocean borders Asia. You are Asia. The continent of Asia. Asia with long highway legs and blue-black hair. You are a slender hand. A delicate foot. The curve of a woman's hip. A teacup breast. You are an entire race of women. Chinese, Japanese, Filipina, Vietnamese. Fragmented and seemingly free, you have lost your edge. Your name. The soul that you once recognized. You've lost the continuity of self.

MAVIS HARA

REVERIE
She gives me a knowing look...
                            Wing Tek Lum

I walk from my hotel
to the orphanage to see you.
Mt. Unzen's plume of steam
motionless behind me.
In front of me
green morning glory vines climb
up and down wire fences
I've been thinking
of infants on baby food jars,
innocent smiles on soap boxes,
and I am unprepared
when I see you
for the first time.

Your hair is black,
your face, wrinkled,
uncontrolled muscles grimace.
Your mouth is open and dribbles,
 tiny old woman.
Your eyes open,
shine, volcanic stones,
they would glow in moonlight.

I remember Aunty Tanaka
in her dark hospital room,
the priest giving us each
a small blue sponge.
We crowd around her bed.

The green lines of the heart monitors
glowing above us, almost flat.
"They always crave water
before death," the priest tells each of us.
"You will give her an offering,
a last gift of water."
We dip our sponges
in the priest's wooden bowl.
We move toward her pillow,
he's chanting the sutra.
It settles on us heavily
slowing down all our movements.
I don't want to go.
She doesn't move,
she's barely breathing.
Her eyes are dark,
all pupil,
they don't connect with ours.
I'm afraid to touch her,
I hear my heart
and my breathing.
My husband is pushing me
toward her pillow.
I am afraid
as I edge toward the pillow,
she doesn't even know me.
I put my sponge to her open mouth,
smooth water across her wrinkled lips.
She moves her mouth slightly,
relaxes and sighs.
My terror turns to silence,
 the priest is chanting,
"Namu amida butsu"
drawing all suffering toward him,
wrapping it in monotones,
draining it away.

I watch you in your wooden crib,
white sheet wrapped,
around your bent, curled body.
They lift you out
and put you into my arms.
They hand me a bottle,
tuck a soft cloth under your chin
and wait
as I stare into your open mouth.
Your gums are wrinkled,
no teeth are showing.
But your lips are the color
of morning glories.
Only fourteen days old,
you know this position,
open wide for the nipple.
I bring it nearer,
touch your lips with white liquid.
You open your mouth wider,
bite hard, furrow your brow
and suckle,
to start the fluid flowing.

"I'm your mother,
I'll take care of you,"
I promise into your opaque eyes,
trying to convince you.
You bring your eyebrows together
to frown at me.
You are still suspicious.
Your eyes glitter like obsidian.
You give me a knowing look.
Life is short and uncertain,
you seem to be saying.
Raising your eyebrows like a teacher,

telling me I should remember,
 you swallow and sigh.
I watch your throat moving.
You nestle into my body,
forgiving me my ignorance.
The woman may be talking to me.
I can hear only silence.
It condenses into wonder.
I feel the rhythm of your suckling.
We breathe together slowly.
We sing a sutra with these rhythms.
It wraps itself around us,
and drains quietly away.

MAVIS HARA

BLUE WILLOW

You would be surprised, Mother,
I go to Tokyo shrine sales in the dark, at 5 a.m.
Old Japanese men dressed in patchwork scraps
of indigo dyed cloth stand over their grass mats
herding the hoard of cast away things.
Ohayo gozaimasu, Oku-san
"You are early today, Mrs . . . ,"
they murmur at me while I duck my head.
I avoid their eyes in imitation
of a proper Japanese housewife
so I do not have to speak.
It is the porcelain called "Blue Willow" that I hunt for,
not a Japanese pattern:
pine needles, bamboo leaves, and plum blossoms,
Sho-chiku-bai.
"Blue willow, a Japanese copy of Minton's china,"
the vendors say. Minton, the Englishman
copying the Dutch trade porcelains invented the scene
of winged pagodas, of fences and geometric borders
and in the center, a weeping willow tree over a bridge.
"Foreigners collect them," the old men whisper to me.
The Japanese believe that ghosts live under the weeping
    willow's branches.
"These dishes were made only for export."
Of course no Japanese would serve guests food
off such an unlucky plate.

But I remember us
in Hawaii, nearly forty years ago,
in Baba-san's basement kitchen.

I am seven and I am careful
as I dry each blue and white plate,
with the bleached ricebags
we use as dish towels.
You work over the sink and will not show me your face.
"Baba-san was always coughing and scolding you," I say
as I open the screened dish safe.
Auntie comes down the stairs bringing trays
of dirty dishes from the wake.
I stack the dry plates gently,
"You were always grumbling about her."
You run from the kitchen, hands covering your face.
I can still feel
the warm droplets of water
roll across the blue and white bridge
on the smooth porcelain plate.

STEVE HELLER

PRIVATE ISLAND

As he eased himself up the short steps to the entrance of the Hotel Lāna'i, Shigeo Masuda whispered a private vow: "One beer, den home."

Inside the narrow sunlit lobby, he discovered Vincente Espelita had started without him.

"Ey, ey! Mistah Big Greenskeepah! Ovah here . . . save you one seat." Vincente patted the green and yellow flowered cushion on the wicker chair across the table from his own.

"Thanks, eh. " Shigeo felt his belly fold a couple of inches over his belt as he settled himself in the chair.

"So," Vincente said. "What you been do all day, Mistah Big Greenskeepah?"

Shigeo rolled his shoulders to loosen up a kink in the middle of his back. "Da kine drive-around job. Check out da greens and fairways, you know? Make sure da grass all short for hit da ball straight."

Shigeo waited for Vincente to make a joke. Vincente had come straight here from the pineapple fields: streaks of reddish brown, the color of the old dirt roads that still crisscrossed the vast abandoned fields of Pālāwai Basin, marked every wrinkle of his gray long sleeve khaki shirt and tan leathery face. Shigeo could smell the sweet and sour tang of the pineapple clinging to Vincente's skin. The tang mingled with the musky aroma of dirt and sweat, and the bitter stinging odor of chemical poisons. Vincente and a few other old part-timers were the last of a dying breed. At one time the plantation had employed over a thousand workers, but all that was *pau* long time now. Only a couple of small fields next to the new airport remained in production, providing the "King of Fruit" fresh each day for the guests at the two new elite resorts at Kō'ele and Mānele Bay.

Dole Food Corporation owned Castle & Cooke, which owned the Lāna'i Company, which owned the two new luxury resorts as well as the tiny Hotel Lāna'i—and 95% of the island overall. Shigeo was lucky. In his youth, he'd been a field hand, then a boom spray operator. Now, at the age of forty, he was Assistant Head Greenskeeper for "The Experience at Kō'ele," which the Company had carved into the cool green leeward slopes of Mount Lāna'ihale behind the Lodge.

"What, dey don't make you look for da lost balls, too?" Vincente asked with a wink, and took a pull from his bottle of San Miguel.

Shigeo smiled back at him. "I got men for do dat for me."

"Well, look who da cat finally wen' drag in."

Shigeo turned and saw Suzie Castillo leaning against one of the French doors, her order pad in the front pocket of her blue jean shorts.

"Ey, ey! Show 'lil mo' respeck!" Vincente tilted his bottle in Shigeo's direction. "Dis da one an' only Shigeo Masuda, personal frien' of Mistah Bill Gates!"

Shigeo felt heat rise up his neck and flood his cheeks as Suzie lifted an eyebrow. At the registration desk, Albert looked up from his cash register.

"Dat mean you a big tippah now?" Suzie asked.

Shigeo shook his head. "Just big drinkah."

Vincente reached across the table and poked Shigeo in the belly with his index finger. "Biggah dan you use' to be, dat for sure!"

Suzie laughed. "So what you gone have, mistah big drinkah?"

"One Bud Light."

Vincente shook his head as Suzie retreated to the bar. "Budweizer . . . Da King of Piss."

Shigeo frowned at him. "How many dose you drink already?"

"Too many!" Suzie called from the bar.

"Bring me annudah one!" Vincente yelled back.

Shigeo noticed a slim, deeply tan young man talking to Albert at the reception counter. It was Ernie Galang's boy, Johnny. Shigeo couldn't see his face, but recognized the stringy black hair that hung all the way down to his buttocks. A couple of years ago Johnny had driven a van for the Lodge, but the Company had fired him for being unreliable. Everyone expected Johnny to leave the island after that—but he'd stayed on, collecting unemployment, then welfare.

"Ey, Johnny!" Vincente yelled across the room. "Barbah strike, o' what?"

Johnny turned away from the counter and faced them. "Boddah you?"

The two men fell silent. Displayed on the front of Johnny's T-shirt were the words "Lāna'i Growers." Beneath the words was a picture of a tall leafy green marijuana plant.

Johnny smiled expectantly for a few moments, but received no response. Finally, he shrugged and resumed talking to Albert.

Vincente shook his head and muttered, "No respeck."

Shigeo sighed as Suzie returned with the beers. He laid a five dollar bill on table, then said, "So, we gone toast o' what?"

Vincente pulled himself up straight again and raised his San Miguel. "To Antomino."

They clinked bottles. "To Antomino," Shigeo said.

They both took a sip. "Too bad you can't go Maui for da service," Vincente said.

Shigeo gazed through the picture window at a stand of Norfolk pine trees trembling in the midday breeze. "No can get off work. Got to shape up da course. Big tournament next weekend, you know. Mānele an' da Lodge all jam up . . . Uncle Toshio gone be dere."

Vincente nodded. "Anyway, I goin' miss dat guy. I used to stack da pineapple boxes on da back his truck, you know, back when he drove dat truck Lāna'i."

"I remembah." Shigeo stared at the brown bottle in front of him.

"Antomino," Vincente said, "he like a faddah to you when you was growing up, yeah?"

In his mind's eye Shigeo pictured a slim Filipino man about the same age as Vincente was now, sitting in the same chair, wearing a bright aloha shirt covered with orchids. In the breast pocket rested three fat black cigars. "Yeah."

"You need a faddah when you ain't got one . . . I remembah when Antomino teach you how to shoot da rifle, hunt da goats an' deer."

Shigeo stared through the window at the pine trees and said nothing.

Stay calm when you see him. Nevah jerk. Jus' squeeze sloooow li' dis . . .

"He teach me too, you know."

Shigeo turned away from the window. "I nevah know dat. I nevah know you even know how for shoot. When he teach you?"

"Small kid time. Just shoot, though. No hunt. My faddah, he nevah let me have da guns, you know. Pilipino pacifist. Only one *dis* island, dat fo' sure. I tell Antomino 'bout my faddah no let me have one rifle, and Antomino, he ask me: 'Yo' faddah say you no can shoot da gun at all?' I think about it an' tell, 'No, just no can hunt—and no can have rifle in da house.' So Antomino say, 'Den I teach you shoot da rifle.' Den he take me way down Polihua, past Garden of da Gods. Not all da way to da beach, just to da green. Know where I'm talking 'bout?"

Shigeo's mind stretched out across the high central plain of the island, over the rusty brown grid of the abandoned fields, beyond the desolate Garden of the Gods to a spot where the raw red, rock-strewn earth gave way to a lush lemon-lime carpet of pili grass. He nodded.

"Down dere," Vincente continued, "no one around for get shot by accident, you know. Antomino park da truck just before da green, den set out three tin cans on dis big square rock. Den he walk off twenty step and make a mark on the ground."

Shigeo pictured the precise spot where the twin ruts of Polihua Road sliced their way out of the red earth into the luminous green relief of the pili. About twenty yards to the west sat a reddish brown rock about the size of a large overstuffed chair, its flat surface pitted and scarred by multiple impacts. "I nevah knew was you shot up dat rock!"

Vincente nodded. "Antomino, he was a good teacha, you know? Bumbye, I pick off dose cans *bing, bing, bing,* ja' like shooting gallery. I figure aftah Antomino finish teach me, I go buy one Remington breach loadah. Figure I keep it ovah Lorenzo's house where faddah no can see. Figure I go find somebody else for teach me hunt. Ol' Pete Agliam, maybe. But after learn shoot, I nevah go buy one rifle. All dis time. Crazy, eh? Maybe I think: Now I know how for shoot, no need for hunt and disappoint faddah. Maybe was enough just know I *could* do it . . . " Vincente's eyes grew distant. "'Course, now I nevah know what it feel like for hunt da goat an' sheep an' deer . . . like you an' Daniel."

Shigeo felt a twinge in his chest as Vincente's eyes refocused and looked him up and down.

"Daniel, he beddah shot dan you yet?"

Shigeo smiled. "Way beddah. 'Course he got more time for hunt now."

"No more school for him, yeah?"

Shigeo shook his head. "He hate it worse dan me."

"So what he gone do now? Work for da Lodge? Or down Mānele? Or go annudah island?"

Shigeo felt his stomach twist. Two months ago Daniel had turned eighteen. He wanted his own place, but except for teachers' housing, there were no affordable apartment buildings on the island. Only fancy places for rich people or the old tiny tin-roofed houses in Lāna'i City—and those were all occupied by the families of former plantation workers. What the boy really needed was a private place where he could play his guitar. When Shigeo asked him "So what wrong wit' play down on da beach?" Daniel had rolled his eyes. "Dis da kine *electric* guitar, Dad. Got to plug in."

Shigeo knew well enough what kind of guitar it was. For years he'd urged the boy to learn to play slack-key acoustic, Hawaiian-style. "Like Terrance Benanua an' da Romero boys play . . . da kine dey like in da hotels." But Daniel would have none of it. "Dose old chalangalang kine tunes, Dad . . . so *uji!*"

Daniel liked bands with names like Wheezer and Metallica and Nine Inch Nails. On his sixteenth birthday he proudly showed Shigeo a Gibson catalogue from which he was going to place an order with the money he'd earned bagging groceries at Richards. "Dis a nice one," Shigeo said, pointing to a classic Les Paul teardrop model. That one wasn't cool at all, Daniel explained, then picked out a guitar that reminded Shigeo of a starfish with an extra-long deformed arm. When the guitar finally arrived, Shigeo discovered the problem wasn't shape but volume. "Got to turn da amp way up for really heah da music," Daniel claimed. When neighbors complained about the volcano noises shuddering through the walls of the Masuda house, Shigeo forbade Daniel to turn on the amplifier. None of the parents of Daniel's friends would allow him to play it in their homes either. So now the boy had an expensive electric guitar and no place on the entire island to play it.

"Who can tell?" Shigeo finally answered Vincente. "Now-time Daniel got dat inside-kine job at da Lodge. Carry da bags, clean up li'le bit. Strickly part-time. I tell him, you want da good-kine inside job, you got learn how for do papah work. Keep da books, be hotel *luna*, li' dat. But he no like dat kine job. Dat kine mean got to study, got to go back school. No, no more school for him. An' no want for just be Company man like all da rest dis island, he say. Mistah Indeependent got to keep all his options open." Too *boring* be like his faddah, Shigeo wanted to add, but didn't. *Daniel want be like you more dan you think*, Maria claimed. But Shigeo didn't believe it. How could Daniel want to be like him when he had also told his mother—only his mother—that what he really wanted was to fly to Maui with

Eiso Fujihara, where they would rent an apartment and look for jobs and find a place where they could play electric music and maybe start a band. Of course, the only instrument Eiso had was his voice, which reminded Shigeo of a turf shredder. Nobody Shigeo talked to knew of any jobs on Maui—and the rent for apartments was so high Shigeo wondered how anybody but rich people could live there. And O'ahu was even worse.

Suddenly Shigeo threw up his hands and said: "Mistah Indeependent think: Can do whatever he like."

Vincente nodded his head vigorously. "Dat da bes' kine choice."

"Hmmmph." Shigeo looked Vincente in the eye. "How Claudio been do on da Big Island?"

Vincente spread his hands wide. "Business not too good dese days. But he happy, dat da main thing." Vincente winked. "Got hisself one blonde haole girlfriend from Oregon. Her faddah high maka-maka kine guy in construction. Make da big bucks. I tell Claudio: Forget da girlfriend, marry her faddah."

Shigeo laughed, then drained his beer. "I got to go, ol' friend . . . Maria expecting me."

Vincente pointed his own bottle at Shigeo and said, "You one lucky Japanee, marry nice Pilipino girl. Keep you happy you whole dumb life."

Shigeo braced his hands on his knees and pushed himself to his feet. "I lucky all right." He paused for a moment, gazing at the grimy creases in Vincente's dark forehead. "Stay out da sun so much. Try wear yo' hat."

"Keep da greens green," Vincente replied. Then he took a long swig of his San Miguel, and his eyes grew vague and distant.

Outside, Shigeo sniffed the fresh clean pine-scented air. The red dust that once blanketed the high central basin of the island was barely a nuisance any more, now that the Company had paved all the streets in Lāna'i City and the big fruit-box-hauling trucks no longer rumbled along the wide dirt roads through the fields. These days the problem was smoke.

The dead fields periodically caught fire, sending stringy black clouds spiraling through the treetops of Lāna'i City, filling the air with a bittersweet scent that made people crinkle their noses. Last week another one of the old bench fields above Pālāwai had burned, and Sgt. Kamana suspected arson. Kids with too little to do, people said. A few whispered that it was Johnny Galang.

Shigeo hopped into the bucket seat of his new white Ford Explorer and drove south down Lāna'i Avenue, past the green corrugated iron walls of the old Dole Plantation machine shop and the rows of silent brown barracks. When Lāna'i Avenue bent west to become Kaumalapau Highway, Shigeo kept going straight, into the new Lālākoa subdivision. The houses in Lālākoa were tract homes, not plush like the new upscale condos overlooking Hulopo'e Beach or the bigger vacation hideaway homes creeping up the mountainside above the golf course at Kō'ele. But they were bigger and nicer than the little slat houses in the center of town, like the one Shigeo had grown up in. All the houses in Lālākoa had garages or carports and real asphalt shingle roofs, not iron or tin. For long-time residents who qualified for the new affordable mortgage packages the Company's developer offered, Lālākoa was a dream come true. Shigeo felt a tingle of pride as he swung the Explorer into the driveway of his banana yellow three-bedroom house at the end of Ohoha Street.

He found Maria in the kitchen, her back to him as she stirred a pot of what smelled like saimin with extra green onions and fishcake. Maria didn't care for saimin, but Shigeo loved it. That meant they were going to talk about something serious.

Shigeo paused silently in the doorway and gazed at his wife, who was wearing a faded blue cotton mu'umu'u beneath her gray apron. He could remember when Maria was as slim and willowy as his old girlfriend from high school, Maxine, who'd gone to the University of Hawai'i on O'ahu and become an attorney. A couple of years ago Maxine had returned to

Lāna'i with her husband, an investment banker, for the Class of '73's 20th reunion. Maxine had three teenage girls now, but to Shigeo's amazement at the reunion she looked even thinner than she had in high school. Slim-fast chocolate shakes and thirty minutes a day on the Power Rider, she explained. That was how you did it.

He watched Maria stir the saimin. He and Maria were both squishy people now. But, like old Ricardo Bilabong used to say, that just made everything more jiggly and fun.

I lucky all right, Shigeo thought, and slipped up behind her.

"Ho!" she yelped, then spun around in his arms. "Whassamatta you scare me li' dat!"

Shigeo raised his eyebrows.

"Oh no-no-no-no-no-no! " She pushed him away and braced her fists on her hips. The large spoon in her right hand dripped clear broth onto the black-and-white linoleum tile floor. "No foolaroun' time now. Got to talk about Daniel."

Shigeo sank into a chair beside the small kitchen table. He resented the fact that Daniel confided in Maria rather than him. But the truth was Maria knew how to talk to the boy, and he didn't. Daniel and he communicated best without words. When Daniel was younger, and something was troubling him, they would climb into Shigeo's old World War II vintage jeep and drive up the Munro Trail to a special place near the summit of Mt. Lāna'ihale, where they would sit and gaze out over the green quilt of the pineapple plain. Sometimes the boy's problem would simply dissolve right there in the cool moist mountain air. And sometimes it wouldn't. Shigeo sighed. There was still too much about his son that he just didn't understand. Especially his volcano guitar music. One evening a few weeks ago Shigeo had passed Daniel's bedroom and found him furiously hammering the unamplified strings of his Gibson with his bare knuckles while he listened to a CD with his headphones. Shigeo paused in the doorway and watched the violent musical pantomime, wondering if Johnny Galang did this sort of thing. Just as it looked like Daniel was going to bust the neck of the guitar with his fist, the song apparently ended and he sank into a sweaty heap on the floor. After a moment or two he noticed his father standing there, and slipped off the headphones. "You really like dat kine?" Shigeo asked. Daniel's eyes shone like morning as he replied, "Beddah dan anyt'ing." What you been listen to? Shigeo started to ask—then thought better of it, smiled awkwardly, and walked away.

Shigeo shifted his weight on the chair. "OK . . . I listening."

Maria dropped the spoon into the pot, turned off the heat, and sat down in the chair across the table from Shigeo. "Daniel needing for borrow some money."

Shigeo folded his arms across his chest. "For move Maui."

"Yeah. "

"What, no can sell his Samurai?"

"Can sell, yeah, but jus' would have to buy annudah car Maui. Got to have car for drive to work. Eiso no have car his own, you know."

"Eiso no have *job* his own," Shigeo countered. "Eiso too much like Johnny Galang. I no like Daniel hang around Eiso so much."

"Who you like him hang around wit?"

"I like him hang around his *job* more. If he no like da inside-kine job, get da outside-kine like me."

"He been ask me about your job, you know. How much you make, if you really like work for da Company all dese years . . . if it make you happy."

Shigeo frowned. "So how come he no ask *me* all dat?"

"Not so easy for boy ask his faddah some things. Besides, he already know you no would want him go Maui."

"No *any*kine job Maui." Shigeo closed his eyes for a moment and tried to picture Daniel playing volcano music in a cabin on the slopes of Haleakalā. He tried to imagine the pleasure of playing the electric guitar. But he couldn't do it. The volcano music was too loud and ugly. He couldn't hear the music in his head.

He reopened his eyes and looked at Maria. "You think he should go Maui?"

She sighed. "Not for me for say . . . But if he decide he going go, better he go wit' somebody, yeah?"

Shigeo didn't reply. He wasn't sure Eiso was better than nobody.

"Anyway, no can go Maui wit' nothing in his pocket. Got to have cushion, yeah?"

"How much he want?"

"Don't know . . . Main problem, he got to *ask* for it."

Shigeo nodded. "Yeah-yeah-yeah-yeah . . . I get da picture now. Mistah Indeependent got to ask Mistah Company Man fo' help . . . Not so easy, eh!"

Maria leaned forward; her eyes narrowed. "No talk stink. It no just li' dat. No just pride. I think Daniel li'le bit scare for move away. Same like you, if you was him."

Shigeo felt the muscles in his belly clinch. "So what I supposed to do?"

"Go talk wit' him. Tell him I say you should talk. But remembah, you no suppose to know nothing 'bout Maui. And no make him feel bad for ask for da money . . . OK?"

Shigeo leaned back in his chair and placed his palm over his chest. "No worry . . . Mistah Company Man got da big heart."

* * *

On Saturdays Daniel worked a ten to two shift at the Lodge. Shigeo decided to drive over and meet him there.

He drove back up Lāna'i Avenue to the northern edge of town, where the avenue became Keōmuku Road. Beyond the town spread the quilted gray-brown maze of the dead pineapple plain, a stunted forest of weeds and rotting crops stretching on out of sight. It was funny, Shigeo thought, how the identity of the island had changed over the years. For centuries Lāna'i had been known as the Island of Ghosts, inhabited only by evil spirits until they were all finally destroyed by a young Hawaiian from Maui named Kaululā'au. When Shigeo was a boy, old Mr. Kapano's stories of the Ghost Killer made Shigeo think of Lāna'i as a special, protected place. In his daydreams he pictured the ghosts of Lāna'i as dim gray figures moving through fog and mist.

As he approached the bend in the road, Shigeo slowed down and gazed out over the dead fields. The Pineapple Island. That was the Lāna'i of his youth. Most of the original field hands came here on work contracts from places like Japan and the Philippines. One of the early ones was Matsuro Masuda, his grandfather. For half a century Lāna'i was the world's largest pineapple plantation. But as Shigeo reached his manhood, competition from mainland and foreign producers began to kill the industry in Hawai'i. Hawaiian Fruit Packers on Kaua'i was the first to close, followed by the Dole plantation on Moloka'i. Lāna'i Plantation hung on longer than most, but Shigeo had always known the future wasn't pineapple.

Around the bend he let his eyes refocus on the road before him. In the gap between a double row of giant Norfolk pine trees glimmered the majestic copper roof of the Lodge at Kō'ele.

The Private Island. That's what the Company called Lāna'i these days, now that the two resorts had opened. In the old days, visitors were mostly ordinary people: hunters, honeymooners looking to get away from the crowds at Waikiki, relatives of long-time residents. They stayed at the old Lāna'i Lodge and bought cigarettes and crack seed from Lui's Dis 'n Dat Shop and rented jeeps from Oshiro's and Nishimura's Chevron stations. Today most visitors were rich—and sometimes famous. People who valued privacy and were willing to pay top dollar for it. At the Lodge at Kō'ele, Shigeo had seen with his own eyes Lee Iacoca, Heather Locklear, Jack Nicklaus, and Carl Sagan. On the golf course he'd seen Tom Selleck, Frank and Kathy Lee Gifford, Lee Trevino, and several U.S. Senators. Down at Mānele Bay he'd seen Suzanne Sommers, Dan Rather, and somebody called Bon Jovi.

Then there was Mr. Bill Gates.

Shigeo shook his head as he remembered driving out to the airport on New Year's Day, 1994, to pick up Uncle Toshio. The new air-conditioned terminal wasn't open yet, and when Shigeo arrived, people were crowded around the old chain-link fence separating the parking lot from the airplane taxiing area. Among the throng was Vincente.

"Claudio coming home?"

"Just for da weekend," Vincente replied. "Not dis plane, next one."

"So how come you don't wait in da shade?"

Vincente frowned and gestured toward the tiny open-air terminal. Near the baggage claim Shigeo noticed several porters from the Mānele Bay resort. But there were also a number of strangers: white-shirted men who looked like private security people. They seemed to be detaining a group of passengers. For some reason Shigeo couldn't pinpoint, the passengers didn't look like tourists. One, a slim middle-aged man wearing a khaki shirt, was yelling at the white shirts and gesturing toward the exit where three taxis were waiting.

"What going on?" Shigeo asked.

"One big mess," Vincente replied.

"Quarantine," Harvey Huerta corrected him. Harvey was a gardener at Mānele.

"Kennedy nevah quarantine Cuba li' dis," Vincente commented, but not too loudly.

"Reporters," Harvey added.

When Shigeo looked again, he recognized one of men from Channel Six. Most of the reporters looked like mainlanders.

"What dey do?"

"Come here for crash Mistah Bill Gates' wedding, dat what," Harvey explained.

Shigeo frowned. "Who Mistah Bill Gates?"

Harvey stared at Shigeo, then rolled his eyes. "Da second richest man in da U.S.A., dat who. Own Microsoft. Computah guy, yeah? He going marry his secretary o' somebody li' dat. I don't know about it."

Then Shigeo remembered the high maka-maka wedding Dave Selby had told him about. Dave and Shigeo had spent most of the previous week down at Mānele, helping Keoni spruce up the Challenge course for the wedding. The ceremony was to be held on the seventh tee, which sat atop a 100-foot cliff overlooking the ocean. "Why dere?" Shigeo had asked. "Privacy," Dave replied. When Shigeo asked what was so private about an outdoor wedding on a cliff, Dave explained that the height of the cliff made it impossible for anyone to view the wedding from boats. The grounds of the golf course itself were Company land, and reporters could be kept away.

Harvey gestured toward the white shirts. "Dey letting all da locals through, but da reporters, dey all got to leave."

Before he could ask "They can do dat?" Shigeo noticed Henry Palumbo and one of the white-shirted men questioning Uncle Toshio at the gate. Uncle Toshio was nodding vigorously and pointing in Shigeo's direction.

When Henry turned and saw Shigeo, he waved Uncle Toshio on through.

Vincente tugged on Shigeo's sleeve. "So who you? Mistah Bill Gates' personal friend?"

Over the following weeks, Shigeo gathered the news of what had happened. Some of it was in the papers. Some of it was whispered in Shigeo's ear by porters, landscapers, and desk clerks. To his amazement, Mr. Bill Gates had rented *all* the rooms at Mānele for his personal guests, one of whom was Mr. Warren Buffet, the first richest man in the U.S.A. Visitors not invited to the wedding had their reservations canceled.

"No nuff room at da inn," Uncle Toshio concluded as they poured over the Sunday *Honolulu Advertiser* the day after the wedding. "Dey had to kick out all da millionaires for make room for da billionaires."

The idea made Shigeo's head feel fuzzy and light.

Nevertheless, he stuck up for the Company. "No billionaires, no resorts maybe," he replied. "No resorts, no jobs."

Daniel raised his eyes from the newspaper, but said nothing.

The problem wasn't billionaires, Shigeo decided, but reporters. He hadn't known it at the time, but the reporters he'd watched being detained at the airport had been forced to sign "trespass warning" forms, which informed them that taking photographs required "prior written clearance" and that their own "presence and/or patronage was no longer desired on property owned or operated by Lāna'i Co." The only inland areas not owned by the Company were the airport and the police and fire stations. A few reporters tried to rent helicopters to fly across the channel from Maui and observe the wedding from the air. They found Mr. Gates had already rented every helicopter in the state with the range to reach Lāna'i. Reporters who had booked rooms at the Lodge at Kō'ele or the Hotel Lāna'i found their reservations had been canceled. When they demanded access to the public beach at Hulopo'e, just below the Mānele Bay Hotel, one of the white shirts claimed that reporters could in fact be barred from Hulopo'e because Castle & Cooke owned the beach and merely "sublet all the sand to the state."

"But all Hawai'i beaches public," Maria protested. "Everybody know dat. How can dey say dey rent out da sand?"

It turned out that they couldn't. When a reporter from Seattle sued Mr. Bill Gates and the Company for illegal arrest, Mr. David Murdock himself, Chairman of Dole Food, admitted that Lāna'i wasn't really a "private" island after all.

The whole affair had left a bad taste in Shigeo's mouth. But it was Daniel's reaction that troubled him most. Everyone who worked for the Company was reluctant to talk about Mr. Bill Gates in public. But Daniel refused to speak of the matter at all, not even in the privacy of their own living room. A few weeks after Mr. Bill Gates' wedding Daniel had begun to talk to his mother about moving to Maui.

Shigeo shifted in his seat as he steered up the road toward the Lodge at Kō'ele. Painted on the arch above the broad entrance was a giant ripe yellow pineapple. The pineapple was beautiful, like everything else about the Lodge. According to the Company brochures, the Lodge was constructed in the style of an elegant English country manor, including a Great Hall with slanted high beam ceilings and the largest natural stone fireplace in Hawai'i. On the lush green grounds were croquet courts, lawn bowling, a heated swimming pool and jacuzzi, a large fish pond, and paved walking trails leading through hillside gardens and gazebos to an English conservatory stocked with orchids. The Lodge was managed by Kurt Matsumoto, a local guy just like Shigeo. The very best inside-kine job, he thought.

Shigeo turned into the employee parking lot and pulled the Explorer into a stall right beside Daniel's red Suzuki Samurai. Before Shigeo could check his watch, he spotted Daniel emerging from the service entrance to the south wing. He wore the green and tan uniform shirt of the Lodge's maintenance staff with the deer logo on his left breast. Shigeo couldn't help noticing how his son had inherited his own square, squat build. The boy would have to watch his weight as he got older.

As Daniel drew nearer, Shigeo could see he was upset about something.

"How it go today?"

Daniel shrugged, then looked at his father suspiciously. "Somet'ing wrong?"

"No, just your muddah say we should talk about somet'ing on your mind."

Daniel raised his eyebrows. "OK . . . But no talk here. Can maybe go someplace private?"

In unison, their eyes turned toward the summit of the mountain.

"I drive," Daniel said.

"Cut through da golf course," Shigeo said as they climbed into the Samurai. "Faster."

As they drove past the new Club House and first tee, Shigeo sensed Daniel's growing discomfort. He felt it in the silence between them, saw it in the boy's white knuckle grip on the steering wheel. As the Samurai began to climb the winding path through the course and on up the mountainside, Shigeo wondered if he should say something to his son to break the tension. But what? Instead, Shigeo turned his head and studied the array of perfectly manicured fairways curling up the soft slopes of Lāna'ihale. Jack Nicklaus himself had designed the course down at Mānele, but Shigeo preferred Kō'ele. It was part of the mountain now. It was hard to imagine a human-made landscape blending so perfectly with a natural one, but there it was, right before his eyes. Sometimes he missed the gritty sweet smell of the pineapple fields. The golf course on the mountain smelled so fresh and clean it was almost antiseptic, like the pine-scented wood polish Maria used on the rattan furniture in their living room.

But pineapple was the past. Golf and tourism were the future. And the truth was, he had a far better future at Kō'ele than he ever could have had down on the hot dusty fields of Pālāwai. He only wished Daniel could see that too.

Shigeo waved as they passed a foursome on the fourth tee. He shook his head. Maintaining the golf course was so much more complex, so much more challenging than growing pineapple. The golf course not only had to be functional, it had to be beautiful. After his training on O'ahu, he'd worked on the Kō'ele course for two years before it opened for play. There was so much to know: soils, grasses, maintenance and renovation procedures. Machines: sod cutters, culti-packers, Meeker harrows, aerifiers, Turforaters, fairway spikers, Verti-cut machines. Back behind the shelter of the cart barn, Shigeo could hear the snaggle-toothed echo of the turf shredder as Primo Blanka's boy mixed soil, sand, and peat for top-dressing. How had he ever learned so much in so little time?

Quickly, they wound their way up the highest reaches of the course until the cart path emptied onto a short paved road that intersected the Munro Trail that would take them up the ridge line of Lānaʻihale. Daniel shifted into four-wheel drive as the paved road ended and they began a steep twisting ascent through ʻōhiʻa lehua trees and Boston ferns. To their left, the green mountains of West Maui loomed up across the channel. Shigeo looked the other way as the Samurai crawled up the rutted path of Hoʻokio Ridge, where a line of Norfolk pines had been planted to catch moisture from passing clouds. Shigeo noticed how badly the trail had eroded in recent years. Red crevices scarred each side of the ridge line. Too many vehicles squashing and uprooting the vegetation that secured the fragile earth. Many of the ferns showed signs of blight: brown, crumbling fronds. Even the great pine trees looked unhealthy, their limbs short and scraggly.

Just past a gnarled ʻōhiʻa lehua tree, Daniel turned off the main trail toward the arm of the mountain called Puʻu-aliʻi, their special lookout. No need for talk, Shigeo thought. Just look. But just as they reached the viewpoint, a cloud bank collided with the mountain, and the leaves of the pines and ferns and ʻōhiʻa began to sparkle in a veil of mist, as if their branches were strung with glittering jewels. A moment later the entire mountaintop vanished in a billowing gray fog.

"Sorry," Daniel said as he brought the Samurai to a stop at the end of the muddy trail. "Should have put da top up. No mean bring you up here for take a shower."

"No big thing," Shigeo replied. His shirt and pants were already soaked. Now what? He could see only a few feet in any direction. He reached over the side of the Samurai and plucked a small pie-shaped frond from a fern growing at the edge of the trail, and held it in his palm. The frond was about the same size as his hand. More than half of it was already brown, dying of blight. He looked over at Daniel, who was staring straight into the mist, lost in thought. Shigeo waited, watching his son's hands slide up and down the arc of the steering wheel, his fingers slippery and nervous, the way they'd been when he was six, when Shigeo had tried to hold his hand as they climbed up the windward side of the mountain on the stone footpath that rose from the ancient fish pond at Naha, built by the Hawaiians who came after the Ghost Killer. The boy refused to let Shigeo take his hand until he was too exhausted to take another step on his own.

All at once the cloud bank passed. Down the leeward slope of the mountain, the heart-shaped green of hole number five materialized, gleaming like an emerald reflecting pond beneath the returning sun. Below the green stretched the jagged pine tree skyline of Lāna'i City, and beyond that the rotting gray brown quilt of the pineapple plain. Shigeo felt a cramp in his right hand and discovered he'd tightened it into a fist. He unclenched it. In his palm lay an olive and rust-colored wad of debris.

"Eiso get one job today."

Shigeo turned to his son. "*Eiso*? What kine job?"

"Da Mānele kine van-driving job . . . . Full time."

"Eiso . . . working for da Company . . . ." Shigeo sank back in his seat and let it sink in. "Is dat what you wanted for talk about?"

Daniel stared at him with hard eyes, then slowly shook his head. "Nevah mind. I thought I need for talk about somet'ing, but I don't."

Shigeo studied his son's face, then took a slow, deep breath. "Listen: No need for be scared. Tell what on your mind."

Daniel looked down at the steering wheel and tapped it with the heel of his palm—once, twice—then turned back to Shigeo. "I was thinking, you know . . . Maybe I trade in da Gibson for one twelve string . . . acoustic." A tight smile stretched his lips. "Play chalangalang for da Lodge."

For a moment Shigeo did not reply.

'Course now I nevah know what it feel like . . .

"I give you one thousand dollar for move Maui."

Daniel reared back in his seat. "What?"

"Your muddah and me can spare dat much . . . maybe more latah."

Daniel's lips parted again, but he did not speak. He stared at his father like a hunter startled by the rustle of heavy brush in Kūahua Gulch, the approach of something large and unexpected. Finally, he said: "Why?"

Shigeo tilted his hand and let the remains of the frond slide off his palm over the side of the Samurai onto the exposed red earth of the mountain's crown. Then he grabbed his son by the wrist and looked him straight in the eye. "Go . . . Get off dis rock . . . Nevah look back."

LAURA IWASAKI

KAMIKAZE LOVE

The first time I heard the word *kamikaze*, I was watching an old World War II movie with my father. I asked him why all those guys wearing goggles and long white scarfs were crashing their little airplanes into the big American battleship.

"Are they doing that on purpose?" I wanted to know.

"They're *kamikaze*," he replied. "Suicide pilots."

And for the longest time, that's what I thought *kamikaze* meant, until someone—actually, it was my cousin Luke, who's an expert on that kind of cultural minutiae—told me it means "divine wind."

"That's what the Japanese called the typhoon that wrecked the Mongol invasion in 1281," he explained. "They figured the gods were protecting them."

"Oh," I said.

I was sure my father knew about that, too; he just hadn't bothered to tell me. When Luke went on to talk about spirits in trees and the souls of rocks, and how roads snake all over the place in Japan because certain trees can't be cut down and special rocks shouldn't be moved, I realized my parents probably knew a lot of things they'd chosen not to tell me about. They're great believers in science and Western religion. Everything happens for a reason, they like to say.

Which just goes to show that life doesn't always lie down and behave itself simply because we think it should. It's like taking a curly hair and trying to straighten it out with your hands. You can press it flat as long as you want, but as soon as you let go, it bounces up again with all its kinks intact.

I guess that's what's been happening to me. Because as soon as I touched down in Hawai'i, and felt that spooky voodoo boiling up through the soles of my feet, I forgot about Los

Angeles and the sensible person I'd become there, made in rational America. I leaped without a thought into a world of hard-headed ghosts, where mountains burn for love and the dead weep. It's a world I've carried around inside myself all along; I'd just forgotten I had it.

And then, there's Luke. I haven't seen him in years and I swear that long-lost blood of his is talking. Worse yet, I can't stop my own from answering back. For months, it has positively jumped and shouted. What it says to me on New Year's Eve has more to do with suicide pilots than divine intervention, but I listen anyway. It's homecoming in more ways than one.

* * *

We want to watch the sun come up on New Year's Day, so Luke and I agree not to sleep at all. We gather all the candles we can find and arrange them on the floor of the apartment, then light them carefully one by one, watching the flames flare pinkly through our hands as the wicks catch fire. The small room is barely furnished, nothing but bookshelves and a mattress on linoleum. A penitent's room, I thought at first, suited mostly to silence and solitary reflection. Now, hung with shadow tapestries and lit by a bouquet of yellow flame, it is warm and darkly rich, a place that makes me think of hearth fires and the sound of human voices telling stories.

We tell stories for revelation, not effect or disguise. With words, we cut past the glib skin, slip inside the brittle armor of our bones, and lay bare the hidden pages of the heart's mute history. It is a language made for truth, something I've never wanted to speak before.

And if I offer up more than is wise, and for all the wrong reasons—well, that possibility doesn't even occur to me. Second guesses are for the timid and the weak, not for heavenly sky divers like me.

Since I'm the one who asked, Luke goes first. It's a story about Otis, his younger brother.

"Otis"

All morning, Luke had been trying to shake Otis, but the little boy with the sun-bleached hair and mismatched eyes, one slightly smaller than the other, wouldn't leave him alone. It wasn't that Otis actually interfered; it was his mere presence that bothered Luke. Even when he tried to read, he could see Otis out of the corner of his eye, playing quietly in the middle of the room or just hanging around, watching him.

"Get lost," he told his brother with growing irritation. But Otis wouldn't listen.

Finally, after lunch, Luke stamped out of the house. If he couldn't be by himself, he at least had to get away.

"I'm going to play with my friends," he called to his mother as the screen door slapped shut behind him. He pretended not to see Otis, who had slipped out on his heels.

Luke ground his teeth together. He kept his head down as he walked the short distance to the house next door, counting under his breath each swift step taken by his slim, brown feet. His eyes, darker than Otis's, crackled angrily. Couldn't Otis understand? Sometimes he just wanted to be alone, to think his own thoughts unobserved, make faces in the mirror, or lie around looking at the ceiling. In those moments, he traveled as far as his imagination would take him—and these were distances both deep and wide—but he couldn't do it with Otis hanging on like a stone tied to the tail of a kite. He kicked at the grass as he made the turn into his friend's front yard. The change in direction brought him face to face with Otis.

"Go home," he hissed.

Otis looked up at Luke. He sat down on one of the large flat rocks that littered the yard.

"Please, Luke, I won't bother you," he said. "I'll just sit right here. Isn't that okay?"

Luke suddenly felt so angry he thought he was going to burst out of his skin in an explosion of unhinged molecules. Maybe then he could finally tear free and escape into the sky, away from Otis and all the other needy people who wouldn't leave him alone. He shoved his hands into his pockets to stop himself from hitting Otis and bent over his brother until their faces almost touched.

"No, it's not okay!" he shouted. "Now, go away!"

Otis's eyes filled with tears. Silently, he slid off the rock and began to walk home.

As Luke watched him go, he realized that his satisfaction was being spoiled by a nagging prickle of regret. Still, he let Otis disappear without saying anything. It wasn't so unreasonable to want a little time away from his brother, was it? Of course, it wasn't. If only Otis understood this, he wouldn't have to be so harsh. He would make it up to him another time.

* * *

Luke's face looks uncharacteristically apologetic as he ends his tale. "I always felt bad about that," he confesses. "I should have let him stay. He just wanted to be with me."

I nod, unsure of what to say. Like Luke himself, this story has left me with an odd sensation—as if I've suddenly stopped spinning while everything else continues to whirl around me—that I've already identified as love. At this point, it's too late to change my mind.

My thoughts shift to Otis, now fifteen, whom I'd seen in the parking lot out front a few days ago. Otis really is Luke diluted, I conclude, enumerating the details again. His fine hair has surrendered its blackness, accepting in its place a mild shade of sun-streaked brown. His eyes are warmer in color, almost amber; the angles of his face, more rounded; the mouth's uncompromising lines softened by frequent smiles. In contrast to Luke, whose posture suggests he resents both gravity and the weight of every earthly attachment, Otis slouches and, from the side, resembles nothing so much as an elongated question mark. I try to imagine him crying, but can't; then realize with sudden disquiet that I can easily envision Luke *making* him cry.

I eye my older cousin briefly through lowered lashes before shrugging the thought away.

"How old was he?" I ask.

Luke has forgotten his regret and is exploring my collarbone, skating a finger along the rounded ridge, down into the shallow valley, and back onto the bone again. He looks up at my question.

"I was nine, so he must have been about four," he replies. He returns to his fingerskating. "Now it's your turn."

Although Luke is usually the one who tells the stories, I've known from the start that this occasion requires a proper contribution from me. I think about it for a while, selecting and discarding many stories, before I settle on one that I believe to be either my earliest memory or a very vivid dream.

"It might not be real. Is that okay?"

He nods, and I begin.

"The Volcano"

The sky was black and the air was cold. I bounced restlessly in the back seat of the car as it inched up the narrow road to Kīlauea Crater. My mother sat in front of me, with Joyce, who was only a few months old. My father was driving. A single line of cars stretched ahead of us, taillights strung along the mountainside like a chain of tiny volcano mouths glowing red against the darkness.

I wore the red wool coat my aunt had sent me from Los Angeles. Because of its bright color and perhaps, too, because I can wear it comfortably only in the thin, chill atmosphere of the volcano, my parents call it "Lydia's Volcano Coat."

The whole island must be on this road tonight, I thought impatiently. I wished I could fall asleep, but I never fall asleep in cars. So I just looked out the window and watched the red taillights creep up the road.

After a long time, my father stopped the car and we got out. I slipped off my shoes and left them on the floor behind the front seat, but no one noticed. The soft dirt was cool under my feet and the sharp-edged chunks of lava rock didn't seem to hurt at all. I skimmed across the uneven surface as if I had no weight.

My father looked down at me and took my hand. "Lydia isn't wearing any shoes," he said to no one in particular.

We kept walking. My mother was behind us, carrying Joyce face-down against her shoulder. We had abandoned the line of cars to join a silent line of people who were slowly making their way up to the volcano. Although my eyes were level with everybody else's legs, I didn't feel small or confined. Instead, I felt protected, buoyant, exhilarated.

At the top, my father gradually zigzagged forward, guiding me into the spaces created by the shifting of the crowd. He had his hands on my shoulders and kept them firmly in place as we slid into an opening at the volcano's edge.

I saw the living world on fire.

Deep in the black hole at my feet, the earth

lay curled and knotted like any suffering creature. Its gnarled skin swelled and split, bleeding gold and red, as it sought relief from its internal conflagration. But there was no escape. Like all fevers, this one had been lit from within.

I didn't blink or move. My father tightened his grip on me as if he feared for my safety, but I was not afraid.

Then, next to me, someone began to speak. "You know, two people fell in there the other night."

"I heard they jumped," another person said.

"Jumped?"

"They were in love. They wanted to die together."

I closed my eyes and leaned back into my father's hands, suddenly off-balance. Then I looked down again, where the molten rock still twisted and groaned. The scorching light slid across my cheeks like a thin sheet of radiant tears. I wondered how it feels when human heat is wed to Pele's heat. And exactly what kind of devotion demands the sacrifice of life for love.

* * *

My task completed, I sigh and collapse onto my back. Luke, still propped on an elbow, regards me thoughtfully.

"Did that really happen?"

I shake my head. "I don't know."

Idly, he lifts a few strands of my hair in his fingers, then watches as they fall back slowly onto the pillow.

"The volcano erupted in 1952 . . . "

"When I was two. I know. And when I asked my parents if they had taken me there, they said they had, although they were surprised that I remembered it at all."

He leans forward on his elbow and arches the other arm across me, then, settling into a position just above and to one side, looks down into my face. I'm not distracted, though, because he's been thoughtful enough not to touch me, observing, perhaps, that my head is presently filled with volcanoes.

"I told them I remember it was dark, and they said we did go at night. When I mentioned I thought it took a long time to get there, they said it was very crowded because the old road was too small for all the cars. Everyone wanted to see it."

Bending closer, he lowers his face and whispers, "What about the two people?"

Still involved with my volcanoes, I answer, "My father says two people really did fall in there."

"They fell?"

"Or jumped."

But I notice he's no longer paying much attention to my words. At the same time, I become aware of the way his nearness, the almost-contact, teases and tickles my skin. The air is warm, but I begin to shiver.

"Another story?" I query, only half-meaning it.

"Oh no," he murmurs, smiling as volcanoes vaporize before his eyes, "there's plenty of time left before morning. Now it's my turn to choose what we're going to do."

They say we dream forward, look backward, and disregard every sign we pass along the way. Maybe they're right. For when a tiny voice whines a caution in my ear, I ignore it. I tell myself it's insect talk, mosquito quibbling, that it's too small to matter much to me. What significance could there be in the stories we've just told: his about the need for disentanglement, mine about annihilation in the name of love?

* * *

Hours later, when we drive out beneath the empty pastel sky, the entire island still sleeps. The smell of firecrackers lingers in the air, and their paper casings litter the street. When I first returned to Hawaii, I'd forgotten that firecrackers are used on holidays other than the Fourth of July, and I was surprised by the sparks and clatter with which the local people greeted the new year. Now it's another tradition I'll always expect, the smoky perfume of New Year's Day.

Our favorite beach is deserted. The tide has risen and fallen overnight, leaving behind white sand swept smooth by the obeisance of countless waves. We mar it with a double trail of footprints, from the dry dunes to the water's edge.

On the other side of Diamond Head, the sky is filled with portents of light. I step into the water. Still infused with the chill of night, it wraps its clear, cold fingers around my ankles. Luke tugs on my hand, and I take a few more steps, watching the ocean rise up and enclose first my knees, then thighs, in its limpid embrace. It's so clean it looks only inches deep; I can see my toes half-buried in the coarse sand on the bottom.

He releases my hand and angles into the water, in the direction of the reef and its crown of black rocks. I take a deep breath and follow, grateful that it isn't as cold as I feared. Always a graceless diver, I just curl in around my knees and sink toward the bottom, where I straighten out and begin to swim.

White slopes of sand drop away as I enter the deeper water around the reef. Stretching my weightless limbs wide, I peer into the infinite green haze until the sting of salt makes me close my eyes. I feel like I'm flying.

I think of love-crazed pilots floating through a black-and-white sky, their points of impact still far below. They seem pure and beautiful, like shooting stars who have given up eternity for one instant of blazing light. It makes a pretty picture. I don't look much further than that.

Fatal gestures charm me because I can't imagine dying; I scoff at wounds because I bear no scars. For now, I rule the air, fueled by illusion, faith, the promises of tangled blood in love with itself. I never even dream of a time when I will have to fall.

Across my back, I feel the sun split off from the horizon and blossom into the sky. The island's fierce colors deepen and begin to burn. I break the surface, moving swiftly with sure, even strokes. I know exactly where I'm going. Luke is already waiting for me on the rocks.

MILTON KIMURA

CORONATION

When the RK was only 12 and still known by his given name, Steven, he realized that rank in his Kāne'ohe cul-de-sac accrued to a family in direct proportion to the appearance of its property. Asphalt shingles, peeling paint, and unchecked weeds consigned one to the lowest caste while wood shingles regularly water sealed, vinyl siding from Sears, and an unbroken carpet of manienie brought drive-by smiles and over-the-fence compliments. Ever eager to do his share to raise the family status, which, one must be frank, was halfway down the left slope of the bell curve of Windward O'ahu family standings, the RK chose horticulture as his field of battle.

An afternoon's inventory narrowed the possibilities: Mr. Watanabe's orchids were unapproachable; Mrs. Fong's anthuriums were the envy of all; and Grandpa Kaikuahiwi's yard was lei maker heaven. So what was left? Well, there were plumerias and hibiscus, but anyone could grow those. Exuberant Singapore plumerias, their trunks blackened by mildew, guarded at least one quadrant of every yard. Leggy hibiscus, predictably red or yellow, sprawled over concrete tile walls with a frequency that defeated notice. Bonsai were a definite possibility, but it could be decades before the results would show. Delayed gratification had never been attractive to the RK. In a family of six children, one learned early on to grab and gobble; putting something aside for later never worked and frequently ended in fisticuffs.

Then it came to him: roses. No one grew roses. Oh, Mrs. Ferreira had tried but the bugs were too much for her. The RK could remember seeing Mr. Ferreira and Willy Boy pulling out the straggly remnants of Peace and American Beauty, their leaves more hole than whole. And Mr. Batchelor two houses down had made a spirited attempt but gave up when he couldn't get his soil to the right pH. The RK had heard Mrs. Chun Mui telling his mother that she had seen the lōlō haole come out after midnight and—here their long-time next-door neighbor had spied the RK hiding under the crown flower—well, *wet* the soil. Even that personal contribution had evidently not been enough. On a morning shortly thereafter, the RK had heard the garbage men swearing as they fed the rose bushes, sick and dying save their healthy thorns, to their steel-mouthed omnivore. But these failures were like bonus points to the RK. If he could grow roses, not only would they be the only roses in the neighborhood, they would also establish him as one who succeeded where others had failed. A broad smile slowly formed on the RK's face, puffing out his cheeks and nearly hiding his eyes in crinkles. He could already see the lines forming for garden tours and hear the envious gasps from Mr. Watanabe and Mrs. Fong, not to mention the begrudging praise from Mrs. Ferreira and Mr. Batchelor.

That picture carried the RK through the next months of careful planning and hard work. He held long after-school conferences with Mr. Koizumi at Kāneʻohe Farmers' Market. The old man was flattered that someone so young was interested in his favorite flower and even took notes while he talked. Acting on Mr. Koizumi's advice, the RK purchased 1.5-cubic-foot bags of organic matter and large boxes of soil additives to lower the acidity of the soil. After seeing the prices in the rose catalogues Mr. Koizumi gave him, the RK quickly realized the value of ohana. He called upon his aunt and uncle in Portland for sound rose stock, which they packed and weighted so it could be sent at book rate. And he thanked Hawaiian Electric for the street light in front of his house; it convinced the Japanese beetles that it was perpetually daylight, a condition most unconducive to chomping.

There was a reason for the failures of Mrs. Ferreira and Mr. Batchelor. It was not for lack of horticultural know-how or hard work that their roses failed to root, much less bloom. Had they examined the fine print on the wrapping around the root balls of their optimistically purchased plants, they would have read "Rogue River Nurseries" or "Willamette Valley Rose Company." These specimens were meant for overcast days, cool nights, and five months of winter. Plunked down in Kāne'ohe, they were as comfortable as the Mākaha Sons at the Golden Door Spa or a Matsumoto shave ice—kalakoa without azuki beans—in Kīlauea Crater. Not the whisper of a chance. Not the scintilla of a hope. But the RK was different. Not for him the blighted bushes and wormy buds, the neighbors' smirks and the garbage men's imprecations. While he knew no more and toiled no harder than his neighbors, the RK was different in one way: he was blessed. Some akua ex machina had her eye on him and cradled his family's 5,000 square Kāne'ohe feet in a micro-climate that his thoughtfully selected plants found salubrious. They loosened their root balls and stretched forth hungry fingers into the warm humus that the RK had pH corrected and nutritionally balanced. They put out tightly curled embryos that unfolded into leaflets of a hue that spoke of spring. They shuddered with pleasure in the gentle Ko'olau showers and reached up to the thin sunshine that came through the cloud cover. Had they voices, they might have assured one another that they must be, if not in the City of Roses, at least in a neighboring suburb.

The days became weeks, and the RK had all he could do not to shout for everyone to notice his changing garden. But there was one thing he savored more than the occasional word of praise, and that was the ringing cymbal clash of ultimate and undeniable victory. He could wait: That such a victory depended to a great degree on the element of surprise made him tend his plants casually, as though they were mere heliconia or red ginger. He slopped the garden hose about like an elephant playing in a river; he applied fertilizer in seemingly careless handfuls; he sprayed for bugs only after sunset when no one could make out what he was doing. It worked. Like one's co-workers when one returns from a precisely executed cosmetic procedure, the RK's neighbors knew that something looked different but weren't quite sure what it might be.

Some thought that perhaps the RK's mother had found her long-lost Miracle-Gro spray attachment while others merely nodded in the happy contemplation that this yard would no longer depress their cul-de-sac's property values. Difficult though it was to have his work go unnoticed, the RK endured the weeks without applause by imagining again and again the sweetness of that day when the scales would fall from his neighbors' eyes. And they shall see!

But not too soon. When buds emerged and began to swell their green capsules like bellies after a baby lu'au, the RK knew it was futile to hope that the transformation could be kept secret much longer. Surely Mrs. Ferreira or Mr. Batchelor, attuned to the comings and growings of roses, would realize what he was up to. If not they, then Mrs. Chun Mui, from whom nothing gossip-worthy escaped. It had been she who first got wind of Cindy Sakamichi's pregnancy—even before Cindy knew—and it was she again who revealed that Betty and Beulah Yap, the wealthy twin spinsters in the best house on the block, were giving away—as wedding gifts—the premiums they received by moving their savings from Territorial Savings & Loan to Honolulu Savings & Loan and then back again every six months. And in that Liberty House special wrap too. Shame.

But the RK's goddess again interceded and brought to the neighborhood news that blinded everyone not only to his roses but to everything else as well: the cul-de-sac was going fee simple. *Fee simple.* The words were like a UN food drop to a war-torn country. The residents fought for every shred of information they could grab. What they received from the neighbor on one side they masticated until it was transformed into something almost new that could then be fed to the neighbor on the other side. Question marks floated over the houses like egrets over an aquaculture pond: When would the conversion occur? How much would the Estate charge? Where would they get the money?

These questions so infected the neighborhood that the RK feared his roses might bloom and go without attracting any attention at all. Any day now all the buds would blossom (again, *pace* that cooperative goddess with her influence over internal floral clocks). But, the RK worried, no one would notice. He was wrong; for the last time in his life, the RK underestimated the effect he could create.

The day, a Sunday, came soon enough. In the pre-dawn, a sleepy Mr. Alfonso drove slowly home from his airport security job, the headlights of his pickup playing briefly over the delights in store in the RK's yard. A shama thrush serenaded Sonny Boy Kamaka as he ran from his father's van, leaving the *Advertiser* on doorstep after doorstep. There was a light on in the bathroom of the Sakamichi house where Cindy, just home from a night of contact sports at the Point After, was applying Clearasil to her hickeys. Other houses began to stir. Toilets flushed intermittently, and from kitchens came the smells of breakfast: Portuguese sausage and Spam frying, cinnamon buns baking, last night's fried rice reheating.

The RK opened his front door, picked up the newspaper, and tossed it back into the living room. He put on his slippers and stepped out into the half light. He made his way onto the front lawn, his feet leaving dark prints in the dewy grass. He breathed in deep and stopped. Like Sophie at her first sniff of the attar perfuming her cavalier's silver rose, the RK felt his knees go soft. He grasped the tether ball pole for support. What was that delicious scent? Even as he posed the question, he answered it: his roses. Throughout the yard hung that fragrance so ineffably fresh yet echoing ancient loves and disappointments. Through the gloom he could just discern the softly glowing circlets that hung on his plants. They had bloomed. Not just one or two, but all of them. On cue, the sun emerged from behind Waimānalo, its coral rays revealing the RK's handiwork. Along the low wall that ran the width of the front yard, a row of 14 identical Simplicity bushes were covered with myriads of uniform blooms, their clear pink suggesting innocence and youth. On either side of the walk leading to the front door, smartly trained examples of Touch of Class and Royal Highness—both All-America selections—stood like an honor guard, saluting those who passed with flowers of every shade of pink. Around their feet the RK had placed the miniature Willie Winkie, its tiny flowers perhaps a degree deeper in tint than those shading them. And framing the picture window and arching over the front entrance were prize specimens of the climber Viking Queen, its vibrant medium and deep pink hues set off against the green leaves and white siding. The RK was overwhelmed; he felt at once proud and humble. He had created a bower, a refuge from the ordinary. But would his neighbors appreciate what he had wrought?

He didn't have long to wait. "Hooo, da nice, your flowers, Steven," Mrs. Chun Mui called as she approached, parting the mock orange hedge separating her yard from his. "What you wen do? And when you wen do 'em?" she asked, delicately freeing the skirt of her faded mu'umu'u from the hedge. "Ay, Mr. Batchelor, try come look," she called. "Steven stay make like he the king of the roses." She had said it: "The King of the Roses." The RK looked at her. He was startled yet tempted, but he quickly looked down at his feet, modestly shaking his head.

Hearing Mrs. Chun Mui's summons, Mr. Batchelor stood up from retrieving his paper and walked over in his bathrobe, the cuffs of his pajamas soaking up the dew. He studied the splendor before him, slowly pivoting in a half circle to take in each section in turn. At last he looked down at the RK and shook his head in amazement. "Why, Steven, this is wonderful! You know that I tried to grow these myself, but I could never get the hang of it. You must tell me your secret." Here, he reached over and patted the RK on the shoulder. "Mrs. Chun Mui is right," he acknowledged, "you *are* the Rose King." Feeling the weight of the hand on his shoulder and the crown on his head, the RK again demurred.

Then the Sakamichis, on the first of their morning circuits of the cul-de-sac, stopped in front of the yard. Mrs. Sakamichi's mouth hung open and Mr. Sakamichi whistled softly in wonder. Before they could say anything, the Ferreiras, on their way to early mass, pulled up in their Galaxy station wagon. Willy Boy, in white shirt and necktie, rolled down the back window and exclaimed, "Who wen do this to your yard, Steven? You guys must be buying your fee simple if you making 'em that special. Look like one palace, this place." Here he paused and addressed the RK: "And you the king of the palace."

And a third time the RK refused the proffered title, holding up his hand in denial. "Nah, Willy Boy," he answered softly, "I only wen plant some roses."

The parade continued, for news travels fast once Mrs. Chun Mui gets hold of it. And for everyone in the neighborhood, the RK's feat assumed a different value, unvaryingly high but flavored by the personality in question. For Willy Boy Ferreira, it was like batting three for four with Derek Tatsuno on the mound. For Mr. Batchelor, it was like getting from Kāne'ohe to UH through rush hour traffic in only 20 minutes. For Mrs. Chun Mui, it was like singing "Alika" with the Royal Hawaiian Band and holding the high notes even longer than Genoa Keawe. For Betty and Beulah Yap, it was like answering the door and finding a camera crew with Ed McMahon, check in hand. For the Sakamichis, it was buying Cindy's clothes in the right order: wedding gown first, maternity dresses second.

And for the RK himself, it was like being elected Most Popular in the 7th grade hoss election and getting free Milk Nickel from the cafeteria manager after school and being chosen first when Danny Ho and Eddie Tamanaha picked teams at recess and . . . no, it wasn't like any of these. It was better. It was like being the Rose King, of which there was only one. The RK assumed the mantle.

JEANNE KAWELOLANI KINNEY

REDRAWING THE BIG ISLAND

Pele, the Hawaiian Goddess of fire
has no use for black sands anymore,
decides to magician it back into hot lava,
headstrong and sullen, she has summoned
the town of Kalapana back into her arms.
At night, the island glows, grows past
the boundaries of old *National Geographic*s,
cutting maps into useless paper
adding latitudes and longitudes
into brand new numbers.

The houses have burned into land.
The crowds gather, their silent eyes
watch the muscle of heat shift
and create, inch the island bigger
than yesterday, smaller than tomorrow.
This growing is patient, moves beyond
the atlas that tries to confine land to books,
beyond the way tourists try to take pictures
of something they think they see—
I was there when the volcano erupted!

Hawaiians know how useless it is
to tame eruptions onto film,
the eyes of our hearts say, don't
just look, *see*. We know new land
is unruly, an adolescent blowing off steam,
slamming doors to emerge centuries later
smooth-skinned with lines intact,
filled out, and smiling through

wild orchids and passion fruit.

No National Park can contain this woman
who scribbles self-portraits red and black
against the earth, holding up her work
to say *here is more for you,* ignoring
the critics and agnostics who miss
the point of fire. *Let this burn a hole
into your memory,* she says,
I am too busy with revisions to be stilled.

PETER C.T. LI

A FIRE IN THE FIELDS

The wooden fence around Mei's two-room plantation house on the Kalihiwai Sugar Plantation was faded and gray with years of water stains etched on its splintered panes. The rusty hinges of the gate creaked like the delicate sounds of crying as she opened it and walked into her yard.

"You did good, Mei," her husband, Hung, said. "Everything going be fine now. We not going get trouble from dah luna now."

"Think so?" Mei asked. The wooden steps gave a little as she walked up to the front door. A small hexagon-shaped Taoist mirror used to ward off evil spirits shook above the doorway, reflecting only darkness as though it had lost its protective powers against ill fortunes.

"No worry. I know what best fo' us," Hung said.

"I lie fo' you tonight only cuz you my husband, you know," Mei said.

"Whatevahs, you wen do dah right thing fo' everybody."

She stared at Hung under the starlit night, his sunburned face dark against his red palaka shirt. "Not fo' Mrs. Oshiro and her daughtah," she said.

"Mei, you Chinese or what?" Hung said. "What is one Japanese girl compared to dah entire Chinese camp?" They entered the house and he slammed the door shut behind them and lit the oil lamp on the square table at the center of the living room. The numerous Chinese calligraphies and paintings on the wall danced to life as the light cast benevolent shadows around the confined room.

"One too much already," Mei said. "Dah luna was wrong to do that to her."

"Eh, listen," Hung said and pounded his fist on the table.

The shadows on the wall flickered then disappeared for a moment. "Remember where you wen come from. If not fo' me, you still going be in Canton walking knee high in mud in dah rice paddies and raising chicken fo' your stupid family."

Mei's mind raced randomly with no will of her own as her husband scolded her. She was feeling the same emotions of worthlessness now as she had when she first married him eight years ago as a picture bride from China. She was only sixteen at the time and he was twenty-eight. He was the eldest son of the Wong family and worked as a hāpai ko man for the plantation, and she had been forced to marry him against her will. She had thought things would change between the both of them and that Hung would come to care for her like a true wife—one that had married out of love. But things had not changed, and at moments like now, she had doubts about their relationship and felt things had gotten worse over the years. There was nothing she could do to try and make things better. She just listened to his words and said nothing. There was nothing she could say.

"No stare at me li'dat!" he told her. "Go boil dah water fo' take a bath. I tired."

The blocks of wood cracked and popped in the stone stove behind the plantation house as Mei scooped water into an iron pot from the large wooden barrel next to the stove. The mid-January air was cool and the heat from the fire felt good and refreshed her with strength. Sounds of crickets and geckos spoke to one another and sang songs only the night understood. Mei felt at peace.

"Hi, Mei," she heard Onnei yell from a window at the house next door. "How the meeting wen go tonight at Takeda Cafe?"

Mei walked over to her small vegetable garden beneath Onnei's bedroom window. "I nevah wen say not'tin."

Onnei leaned out the window. "Nah, fo' real you nevah wen say not'tin. You must wen say something," she said.

"I wen tell them I was at home wit Hung wen they wen find dah Japanese girl in dah field," Mei said.

"Why you wen do that fo'?" Onnei asked. "Why you wen lie?"

"I had to listen to Hung. He say that if I wen tell'um that I wen see dah luna rape dah girl, dah plantation own'nahs going make pilikia for him and everybody else. Hung no like me bring trouble for him and his friends."

"Why you listen fo'? You know bet'tah than that," Onnei said.

"You know why," Mei said. She bent down and plucked one of the bug-eaten leaves off a bunch of choi sum. The tiny yellow flowers of the leafy green Chinese vegetable glowed like jewels in the soil.

"This not China," Onnei said. "Was me, I go tell'um everything and help Mrs. Oshiro and her daughtah. I no care what my husband think. He only like go fishing and drinking all dah time. Men, they all the same, no mat'tah back in China or ovah hea. Hung no different, I tell you. Only want face from everybody and be one big man on dah plantation."

"He not that way. He tell me he know what best fo' dah both of us," Mei said.

"You know what, Mei? Stop letting him treat you like one stupid woman. No let him boss you around just because he wen bring you to Hawai'i."

"What you mean?" Mei waited for Onnei's reply but there was a sudden commotion in Onnei's house. Mei heard Onnei's son screaming something desperate.

"What's going on?" Mei asked.

"I think you bet'tah go back inside your house and get Hung," Onnei said.

"Why? Something wrong?"

"That Japanese girl you saw, Yumiko, she wen go kill herself. They found her hanging on a mango tree in Mrs. Oshiro's back yard. She probably wen do that wen everybody was ovah at Takeda's tonight. Poor girl."

Mei went bone-white as the blood drained from her limbs to her stomach. She felt like throwing up. "No. No can be. Why? Why she wen go do that?"

Mei did not hear Onnei's last few words as she went spinning to the ground and banged her head on the rocks that surrounded the choi sum patch. "Mei!" Onnei cried. She left her house and ran out to Mei's yard.

"Onnei," Mei said from the ground. "Why she do that? Was my fault, my fault . . . ."

Mei felt the life drain from her body as she lay there with the side of her head bleeding. Images of a hundred faces with a thousand laughters and tears flashed through her mind in pulses. She heard and felt every single vision pulling her away, robbing her of control over her mind and body, like the dragging of a dying corpse. They told her truths and lies about who she was and how she should behave. They showed her the happiness she had had with her five brothers and three sisters in their small village in China. They recalled the horror she'd felt when the Ching Dynasty was overthrown and everything was in chaos, her family broken and lost in the birth of a new China. It was a China that Mei had had to escape from. It was a China where she became a picture bride.

"This is a picture of your future husband from Hawai'i, the land of the Sandalwood Mountains," Mei's father had told her. She remembered it clearly now. "And when you marry, you must listen and be good and not let your husband and our family lose face. Causing the loss of respect is the worst thing you can do."

"Ah-bah! Ah-bah!" Mei called out to her father as his image faded away and was replaced by Yumiko's as she passed her in the field.

Luna Williams was there also. He was dragging the kicking and punching Yumiko into the sugar canes. "Help me, help me!" Yumiko screamed as the two of them disappeared and visions of Mrs. Oshiro begging on the floor of the Takeda Cafe appeared. "Help my Yumiko, help her please, no lie, tell them what you wen see," she cried. Mei wanted to, but her husband was there. "I love you. No say not'tin. You my wife," Hung said to her. Then all the voices yelled at Mei at once. "No say not'tin. You liar. Help Yumiko. You are a Chinese wife. You must obey. Don't let our family lose face. This is your husband. I love you. No say not'tin. No say not'tin." Mei fought for her sanity and screamed as loud as she could. But the images and voices kept coming faster and louder into Mei's mind like a thousand firecrackers going off in a kaleidoscope of blurred madness. Mei screamed to fight back. Fought to hold back the pain. There was nothing Mei wanted more now, even for a brief moment, except for empty blackness and silence. Then it stopped.

"Mei going be okay?" she heard Hung ask the doctor.

"It's not serious. She should be fine. Have her rest a while," the doctor said. He wore a white shirt and a gray pinstripe vest with a black ribbon tie.

"Hung," Mei said from her bed. She felt the pounding of her head as she watched Hung speak to the doctor with Onnei standing next to him. A slight breeze blew the window curtains and the morning Pacific sun broke through into the small room and warmed her face and eased her pain.

"Thanks," Hung said. He shook the doctor's hand and walked him out of the bedroom.

"Onnei," Mei called out. She lifted her hand and reached for Onnei's layered cotton work dress that protected all hoe hana women from the razor edges of sugar cane leaves.

Onnei walked over to the straw mat lined bed. "How you feeling?" she asked.

"My head so'ah. What wen happen?"

"You wen go faint last night and wen sleep until now."

"Yumiko," Mei cried. She remembered what had happened the night before.

"It's okay." Onnei held Mei's hand and gave her a hug as she stroked Mei's black hair.

Hung returned to the bedroom. "You okay?"

"Was my fault," Mei said. "Yumiko wen die cuz I nevah wen say not'tin fo' help her."

"Was not your fault," Hung said.

Mei began to cry. "How you can say that? Yumiko wen die. Her mahdah wen ask me fo' help and I nevah wen help."

"But you not dah one wen hang her. She wen do that by herself," he said.

There was a knock on the Wong's front door. "Godfunnit," Hung said. "I go see who at dah door."

Mei lay motionless and watched the wet vision of her husband leave the room. "Onnei, who you think at dah door?" Mei asked. "What if that's Mrs. Oshiro? How I going tell her that I nevah wen say not'tin cuz Hung no like trouble? How I going tell her that saving face for him was more important than Yumiko's life?"

"Mei, we friends, right? I tell you something now. Go tell Mrs. Oshiro the truth. Tell'um what you wen see. Never mind what Hung wen say. Do'um fo' youself."

"Onnei, I dunno."

Hung came back into the room and pointed at a woman behind him. "This Mrs. Bickman."

"Hello, Mrs. Wong." Mrs. Bickman's hair was blond and she wore a tan dress with little white cross-shaped prints. Her hair was tied up in a bun and she stood about a head taller than Hung. "I'm with the Hawai'i Sugar Planters' Association. I'm here to investigate what happened two days ago. May I ask you some questions?"

Mei stared at Hung and back at Mrs. Bickman again. "Guess so."

"As you may already know. The workers here at Kalihiwai have accused Mr. Williams of raping one of the women workers. I got a letter from a Mr. Takeda that said you saw everything that happened. Is this true?"

Onnei gave Mei a little push on the arm. "Go tell'um," Onnei whispered.

Mei looked up at Onnei. She saw Hung watching Onnei

and then quickly turned to Mrs. Bickman. "She nevah wen see anything," he said. "We already wen tell'um."

"I am aware of that, Mr. Wong. But I need to verify your wife's story for the meeting tomorrow."

"What meeting?" Mei asked.

"The HSPA and the owner of the plantation are having a meeting tomorrow night in front of the sugar mill to settle complaints between the workers and the plantation concerning Mr. Williams. If he is found guilty, the HSPA will bring in the authorities and have him arrested."

"So you need Mei to tell you what she saw?" Onnei asked.

"Shud'dup Onnei," Hung said. "She nevah wen see not'tin."

"Why you no let Mei tell the truth?" Onnei said. "Why she gotta lie fo' you?"

Mei grabbed Onnei's hand and looked her in the eyes. "Onnei, please," she said.

"What?" Onnei yelled. "It's dah truth. No let Hung boss you anymore."

"If you my friend, quiet okay?"

Hung picked up the small Buddha from the sandalwood dresser carved with Chinese mountains and clouds, and pointed it at Onnei. "Eh, Mei, tell your friend shud'dup before I put this in her big mouth."

Mrs. Bickman stopped Hung's arm in mid-air. "Is she telling the truth, Mr. Wong?"

"I dunno what that crazy woman is talking about. And if you get sense, you bet'tah not listen to her. She lōlō, like old crazy Mr. Chang up dah street. She just like make trouble."

Onnei pointed her finger at Hung and waved it like a pistol. "He dah one wen go lie. Mei wen see everything and he no like her tell. Mei, go tell'um you was deah dah ot'dah day." Onnei nudged Mei's side. "Tell Mrs. Bickman you wen see everything."

"Please, I no can," Mei said. "Just stop it, okay?"

"Mei, I'm warning you!" Hung yelled. "Tell your friend shud'dup." He pushed Mrs. Bickman aside.

"Come on Mei, tell'um," Onnei repeated.

Hung threw the little Buddha across the room at Onnei, but it missed and shattered against the wall next to the bedroom window. Ceramic fragments exploded onto Onnei's foot.

"You dah lōlō!" Onnei yelled. "Mei, how you can protect one selfish guy like that? He no care about you."

"That's enough, Mr. Wong," said Mrs. Bickman. She grabbed onto Hung's shirt sleeve as he tried to rush towards Onnei. "Leave this room now or I'll get one of the luna to drag you out."

"Why. This my house. You dah one gotta leave."

"I'm warning you, Mr. Wong."

Hung pounded the wall and then stomped out of the room. There were sounds of furniture crashing into one another and against the walls of the living room. When he became tired, he yelled profanities and cursed everyone in the house and then slammed the front door shut and left.

"I need to speak to Mei alone," Mrs. Bickman told Onnei. "Could you wait outside please."

"Yeah, sure." As Onnei looked at Mei, she tilted her head a little to one side and made her brows rise and her eyes widen. "Tell Mrs. Bickman everything," she said through clenched teeth and narrowed lips.

Mrs. Bickman closed the bedroom door and then looked at Mei. "Now, tell me everything that happened."

"I no can."

"Why? Your husband is not here now."

"You no understand. I just cannot. Hung going lose face."

"Lose face? What?"

"He going lose honor if I make trouble for him."

"That's silly," Mrs. Bickman said. "If you don't tell what you saw, Mr. Williams is going to get away with what he did?"

"Not silly. You no understand. I really no can."

"Look, if you tell them tomorrow what you saw, you'll be giving your husband face."

"No, no face," Mei replied. "You not Chinese. You no understand. I just going bring him trouble."

"You're right. I don't understand you people. A girl hung herself because Mr. Williams raped her and all you care about is your husband's respect?"

"No, I care Yumiko too," Mei said.

"Then tell everyone what you saw."

Mei did not reply. She turned away from Mrs. Bickman and stared blankly out the window. She wanted to tell Mrs. Bickman what she knew. She wanted to tell everyone. But she could not do it for the sake of fulfilling the promises of marriage to honor and respecting the wishes of her husband. If Hung didn't want her to do something, then she wouldn't. If she was to be a good Chinese wife, then things must be this way. It was how things were traditionally. But Mei was beginning to feel trapped and wished that it wasn't. "Sorry," she said.

"I see," Mrs. Bickman said. "But please consider what I have said. Tell everyone tomorrow what you saw."

Mei watched Mrs. Bickman open the door and leave the room. "Onnei!" she yelled.

There was no answer. Mei lay in her bed for a long time and thought about Mrs. Oshiro and Yumiko, about Mr. Williams, but most of all about her marriage with Hung. Was it worth it? Was the imagined honor of a man she'd been forced to marry and did not love so important that a life could be traded for it? Was Onnei right? Was her husband selfish? Did he care about her as much as she thinks she did about him? At times Mei felt more like a servant than a wife. But she was a picture bride and she owed Hung for the life she had now. The rules of marriage would be simple if she wasn't. The answers would be simple—she would tell everyone the truth. But she was a Chinese picture bride, and little would change that and her feelings of being trapped in traditional marital obedience with no independence of her own. With no will of her own.

Mei lay in her bed until the noon sun rose and the heat of the afternoon mixed with the cool trade winds from the West to stroke her to sleep. For those brief moments Mei found escape and peace away from the plantation. Away from everyone she knew. But most of all, away from Hung, and his insistent command for her to lie.

It was night when Mei heard the front door slam shut and saw the lamp light in the living room glow bright. Mei could see a dark shadow move across the living room wall like a black serpent slithering and searching for its prey. Furniture crashed about and Mei could see her husband stumble over a fallen chair. She lit the lamp on the night stand next to her bed as Hung entered the room. The orange glow of the light revealed his drunken red face and he seem almost demonic. "What you looking at?" he yelled. The alcoholic spit from his mouth sprayed like venom.

Mei felt paralyzed in her bed and didn't know how to respond. "You wen go drinking?" she asked.

"What if I did. All cuz of you." Hung took a couple of steps but stumbled to his knees. "Why you no listen fo'? Why you gotta get diarrhea mouth and tell Onnei you saw it?"

"I sorry. Dah thing just came out wen I wen talk to her after it happened."

"Now I going get all kine trouble from dah luna."

"I nevah know you no like me say not'tin. How I going know?"

Hung pulled himself up and stood next to the bed. "Everybody at the plantation blames me for dah extra work and hassles that the luna all giving them. Now they all no like talk to me and give me stink eye. And your friend Onnei, she going around telling everybody stink stuff about me. Telling them I boss you around cuz I marry you from China." Hung slapped his palm through the air in front of him. "I like slap her."

"Sorry, Hung," Mei said. "I go ovah and tell her stop it." Mei sat up and planted her foot on the floor in front of Hung.

"Too late already," Hung snapped. "It's all your fault." He slapped Mei hard in the face and sent her flying onto her side, back into the bed.

Mei felt the pain cut through her face and saw the blood from her nose splatter onto the embroidered sheet. "Hung. No. Please. I sorry." She began to cry.

Hung moved closer. "It's always your fault."

Mei climbed to the other side of the bed. "Stay away," she warned. The blood from her nose dripped over her lips. She could taste its sweetness. "Get out or I going yell."

"You not'tin but bad luck fo' me," he said. "Even heaven punish me because of you. All these years we marry and you no can even make me one son. What kind wife you. You think you so good. You broken that what I think."

Mei picked up a piece of the shattered Buddha that Hung had broken earlier and pointed it at him. "Move away, I like go out." Mei walked towards the door and Hung moved in front of her. She could smell the alcohol from his sweating body.

"You know, your fah'dah wen marry you off fo' dah money," Hung said. "That mean you mine. Not because I wen marry you, but because I bought you. So you bet'tah listen to me because I know what best fo' you."

"Onnei was right," she said. "You only care about yourself. Know what best fo' me. You only know what best fo' you. I going tell'um everything tomorrow," she said.

"You bet'tah not. Remember where you came from. You one picture bride. I own you!"

"I going tell'um everything," She turned and ran for the front door and heard Hung fall to the floor behind her.

Mei ran out of the house towards Onnei's house. "Onnei, Onnei," she called as she pounded on Onnei's door.

The door opened and a crack of light lit Mei's bruised face. "What wen happen?" Onnei cried. She pulled Mei inside. "How come you bleeding?"

"Hung, Hung," she repeated with broken breaths. "He wen hit me."

"Why he do dat fo'?"

Mei began to cry. "He wen come home all drunk and mad."

"Look up," Onnei said. She wiped the blood off of Mei's face. "What you going do now?"

"I don't know Onnei. I don't know."

The workers at the Kalihiwai Plantation had been arriving steadily back to the sugar mill since pau hana time, when the labor train returned from the field and the mill whistle blew at four-thirty in the afternoon. The yard in front of the sugarmill was now nearly filled. A number of workers that had come late climbed up onto crates, wagons, trees, and whatever else they could find that would provide them with a good perch to view from.

Mrs. Oshiro and Mr. Takeda sat on the front row of a couple of makeshift wooden benches next to a long picnic table. Mr. McCorduck, the plantation owner, and Mrs. Bickman with two other representatives from the HSPA sat behind the table. Meanwhile Mei and her husband sat next to one another on the second bench. Neither of them spoke a word to the other, nor did they look each other in the eye. They sat like the strangers they had been when they were first married and listened to Luna Williams as he gave his side of the story.

"I wasn't on that side of the field that afternoon," Luna Williams said. The afternoon sun had changed his red hair to orange and it made him look like a six-foot tall match stick as he stood in front of the officials. "Just ask Robert Barlow from the Filipino camp. He'll tell you that I was with him fishing down by the landing."

"But Mrs. Oshiro insists that her daughter was raped by you," Mrs. Bickman said.

"Where's your proof that I did? Barlow will tell you I

didn't." Luna Williams smiled and heard the plantation workers behind him go into a commotion.

"But we have proof," she said. "According to Mrs. Oshiro, Mrs. Wong saw you in the field with Yumiko that afternoon."

Luna Williams gave Mei a cold gaze.

"Mrs. Wong, stand up and come over here," the man next to Mrs. Bickman said.

Mei stood up and began to walk towards the table, but Hung caught her hand and stopped her. "Let go," she said.

"I sorry Mei," Hung whispered. "I was drunk and nevah wen know what I was doing last night. I promise I nevah going hit you again. Remember we husband and wife. Remember I love you."

Mei pulled her arms back. "I no like be your wife anymore. I no like be your picture bride," she said. She broke away from Hung's grasp and stood in front of the table.

"Mrs. Wong," said Mrs. Bickman. "Mrs. Oshiro and Mr. Takeda said you were in the field at the time Yumiko was raped. We have a witness here that said you carried some sugar cane to a wagon that was nearby a little before Yumiko saw you. Is this true? Were you on that side of the field?"

Mei stared at Mrs. Bickman but made no response. Her fingers were shaking. She rolled the ruffles of her skirt between her fingers and squeezed them and felt the crisscross texture of the cotton. She turned and looked at the crowd behind her, then at Hung, then at Mrs. Bickman.

"Mrs. Wong, were you on that side of the field or not the other day?" asked Mr. McCorduck loudly. His white shirt and fedora hat glowed under the crimson dusk sky.

"Yes," Mei answered. She looked at Hung and he was motionless except for his lips which parted slowly as if to say no.

"Did you see Yumiko in the field?" Mrs. Bickman asked.
"Yes."
"Did you see Mr. Williams that afternoon?"
Mei hesitated. "I did."

The talk in the crowd grew louder and everyone became restless. Torches were lit and the darkening sugar mill burst into a dance of light as the godlike shadows of the officials were etched onto the wall behind them.

"Quiet down, please," commanded the HSPA representative next to Mrs. Bickman.

The crowd grew silent, and there were only scattered comments.

"On that afternoon you were in the field," Mrs. Bickman asked. "Did you see Mr. Williams drag Yumiko into the canes then rape her?"

Mei opened her mouth a little as though to speak. She stopped. Her lips slightly parted. She turned and looked at Hung one more time. "I don't know," Mei answered in a broken voice.

"What do you mean, you don't know?"

Mei turned again and saw Hung staring back at her. She felt she owed Hung a part of herself regardless of how he had treated her. Despite whether it was the right or wrong thing to do, she felt a debt owed must be paid, and she was going to pay Hung for all the good he had done for her. Not because Hung was her husband, not because she was his wife, but because she was simply herself, Mei.

"Did you or didn't you?"

"I don't know."

"Did you see Yumiko being raped."

"No. No, I nevah!" Mei cried out, then she dropped to her knees. She began to cry like someone trying to hold back a great pain. "I nevah wen see not'tin."

"Are you sure? Are you absolutely sure?" Mrs. Bickman asked one last time.

"Yes, yes. I sure. So please, please no bahdah me anymore," Mei implored the HSPA officials in front of her. Her face was stained with red dirt as she tried to wipe the tears from her eyes. She heard everyone yell profanities at her. They didn't understand. She had to lie one last time. Not for Hung. But for herself.

Mrs. Oshiro charged from the bench. "How can you hang my daughtah a second time?" she screamed. She kicked Mei in the stomach and started pounding Mei's back with her fist until Mr. Takeda pulled her back to the bench.

Mei saw Hung get up and run over to her. She felt his arms lift her and knew it was the last time they would touch as husband and wife. Mei had decided she was no longer going to be his picture bride. She had lied to the officials to pay the debt she owed Hung. To her, he was now someone who had helped her escape China. Not someone to obey. Or to save face for. Or to love.

"Everything going be fine now," Hung said. "They not going bahdah us anymore. Our life going be back normal." He brushed Mei's hair aside and off her face.

"Let me go," Mei said. "Things not going be same. I not going be your wife anymore."

"Why you wen lie to them den?"

Tears began to flow out of Mei's eyes again.

"Right now you don't know what you saying," Hung said. "We talk about it la'tah, when you mo' calm."

"I know what I saying." She pushed him. "Things all different now."

"Where you going go? Back to China? They going laugh at you. You going be one disgrace. Picture bride running away back home. Nobody going take you. Not deah. Not hea."

Mei turned without saying another word and started to walk away.

"You wait, you going come back to me. No mo' place fo' you to go. You no can leave. I like see you try. You mine."

Mei heard Hung laugh as she pushed her way through the crowd of workers. Hung was right. There was no place for her to go, and divorce was unrealistic in a Chinese picture bride marriage. She wanted to cry, but had no more tears. She had chose to walk this path of independence that she had discovered for herself. And though she had little left of what her life was before this entire incident, she felt no regrets. The only thing she had left was her life and one last debt. It was time to pay Yumiko.

Mei watched the plantation workers go into an uproar as Mr. McCorduck and the HSPA officials announced there was no case against Luna Williams. She saw Mr. McCorduck, Mrs. Bickman, and the rest of the HSPA officials disappear quickly into the safety of the sugar mill as a mob of angry workers chased after them. The workers wanted justice, and they wanted it now, as did Mei.

Mr. Takeda, Mrs. Oshiro and a group of Japanese workers armed themselves with several torches and began to hunt after Luna Williams. Meanwhile other workers caught up in the anger and rage wanted the sugar fields burned as payment for the injustice done against Yumiko.

"Mrs. Oshiro and Mr. Takeda them going to burn Luna Williams and the sugar field," yelled Onnei after she broke away from an angry mob marching past Mei. "We bet'tah go quick before the luna come back with guns."

"Which way Mrs. Oshiro them wen go?" Mei asked.

"They went to dah west fields."

"*Doh je*," Mei said as she thanked Onnei in Cantonese for a last time. Without saying another word, Mei turned away from Onnei and ran. She fought her way through the rushing mob and headed for the cane fields on the west side of the plantation. By the time Mei reached the field, it was already burning.

"Mrs. Oshiro!" Mei called into the dense gray smoke that guarded the flames. "Mrs. Oshiro where you stay?" Mei tried to listen for voices, but all she heard was the thunder of exploding cane stalks as the fire burned its way across the field.

Charred remains were snapping to the left and right of her as they fell to the ground. The smoke from the burning leaves rubbed against her eyes, irritating them, teasing them to close with tears. She dodged one of the hot cane, but the razor edged leaves from another cut her arm. The hot air numbed her wound and she ignored the pain. Suddenly, something burst out of the smoke. It pushed her to the ground. Mei felt the heat from the heavy object. It was too large to be sugar cane. It was Luna Williams.

"Quiet or I'll break your neck," he snarled. The blood on his burnt arm trickled down his hands.

Mei felt his hand cover her mouth. The mix of smoke and salty sweat on his fingers choked her and she bit them.

"Dammit," he cried, and he slapped her across the face.

"I saw you here the ot'dah day," Mei told him. "I saw you rape Yumiko."

"You should have told them back at the mill," he said. "Get up, you're gonna be my way out of here." Luna Williams stood up and then pulled Mei up by the hair.

Mei tried kicking Luna Williams to try and free herself, but he punched her in the head and she went crashing to the ground. She felt her eye lid split and the warm blood flow down her face.

"Try that again and . . . ."

Suddenly, Luna William's body crashed down on Mei and smashed her into the ground a second time. Mei opened her eyes and looked up. Mrs. Oshiro stood above the both of them. Her eyes were wide and red as the reflection of the fire in them grew brighter. She wielded a hoe in her hands. The blade, chipped and worn from years of cane cutting, now dripped with blood. "He wen kill my Yumiko," Mrs. Oshiro said. "I going take revenge for my Yumiko."

"No!" Mei said. She pushed Luna Williams off and stood up. "They going put you in jail if you do. Who going visit Yumiko's grave if you in jail?"

Luna Williams tried to get up. The blood on his ripped back had soaked through his torn shirt.

Mrs. Oshiro began to cry and raised the hoe into the air,

it's curved blade a shadow against the glowing smoke. "I kill him, Mrs. Wong. I kill him. Don't let him get away anymore."

"Stop!" Mei grabbed the hoe and pulled it away from Mrs. Oshiro.

"He die, he die," Mrs. Oshiro repeated, as if in a vengeful, hypnotic trance as she watched Luna Williams get up onto his knees.

Mei held the hoe tight in her hands. *It was her decision.* She raised the blade high into the air. *Not her husband Hung's.* And drove the hoe down. *She wasn't going to be trapped anymore.* The air snapped against the crackling sounds of exploding echoes and the blade ripped through flesh and bone as if they were sugar cane. *She had found the path to her freedom.* She thought of her parents, her brothers and sisters, her husband, Hung, and finally, Yumiko. Mei said nothing. Her face showed no emotion. She had found peace.

Luna Williams' body dropped in front of Mrs. Oshiro as an offering. It convulsed like a headless chicken reluctant to become the object of retribution. Mrs. Oshiro screamed as Luna Williams' head rolled across the ground and onto her foot. His eyes and mouth were open in a permanent silent scream as his head was drenched in a pool of sacrificial blood.

Mei dropped to the ground, her hands still holding onto the hoe. "Go home, Mrs. Oshiro, before dah fire comes."

"Why you—"

"For your daughtah," Mei said. "For Yumiko."

Mei watched Mrs. Oshiro run towards town as the flames grew red, orange, yellow, then white behind her. The fire and smoke grew stronger with each cane it consumed and seemed to have a life of its own. The fire in the field swirled like a thousand spirits ascending to heaven in the midst of destruction. Purifying and vindicating the land, the field, and all the pains it held. Mei saw the beauty of the fire come and felt the warmth of the flames bathe her as she embraced them. She was truly free now. A picture bride no more.

SHIRLEY GEOK-LIN LIM

Excerpt from AMONG THE WHITE MOON FACES:
AN ASIAN-AMERICAN MEMOIR OF HOMELANDS

Prologue

The first time I heard Shakespeare quoted, it was as a joke. Malayans speaking pidgin English would dolefully break out into Elizabethan lines, "Romeo, Romeo, wherefore art thou, Romeo?" before bursting into chortles and sly looks. *"Aiyah! Dia Romeo, lah!"*—"He's a Romeo!"—I heard said over and over again of any number of men, including my father, Baba. "Romeo" was a name recognized equally by English, Malay, Indian, and Chinese speakers. As a child I thought it meant the kind of thing men did to women; not so much in the dark that no one could see it, but sufficiently outside the pale that it was marked with an English word. That thing was a male effect—erotic heat combined with suave flirtation, distributed promiscuously, promising a social spectacle and unhappiness for women.

"Romeo" was both an English and a Malayan word. "Hey, Romeo!" the young men said of each other as they slicked Brylcream into their glossy black hair and preened before mirrors. The performance of the Romeo was their version of Western romantic love. It had nothing to do with tragedy or social divisions, and everything to do with the zany male freedom permitted under Westernization. It included a swagger, winks, laughs, gossip, increased tolerance, as well as disapproval and scandal. The Romeo dressed to kill, a butterfly sipping on the honey of fresh blossoms, salaciously deliberate about his intentions. Although there was a Romeo around every corner for as long as I could remember, I did not learn of Juliet's existence until I finally read the play at fourteen. By then, my imagination had hardened over the exclusion. For me, there were no Malayan Juliets, and sexual males were always Westernized.

This was Shakespeare in my tropics, and romantic love, and the English language: mashed and chewed, then served up in a pattering patois which was our very own. Our very own confusion.

I didn't know about Juliet, but I knew my name. On my birth certificate, my name appears as Lim Geok Lin, a name selected from the list that Grandfather had prepared for his sons' children. It is a name intended to humble, to make a child common and same, like the seeds of the hot basil plant that puff up as hundreds of dandelion-whirly-heads in sugared drinks. The significant name, appearing first, belongs to the family, its *xing:* Lim. There are millions of Lims on this planet, spelled Lin, Ling, Lum, Lam, Leng, and so forth, depending on the anglophone bureaucrat who first transcribed the phoneme. Drawn as two figures for "man," a double male, formed from the hieroglyphs for two upright trees resembling two pines or firs, the Chinese name is the same despite its English-translated differences.

To be sure of my existence, however, Baba gave me other names. So everyone would know that I was from the female third generation of Grandfather's line I was named "Geok," the second name giving descent position. Every granddaughter wrote her name as "Geok," the Hokkien version of that most common of Chinese female names, "Jade." Tens of millions of Chinese baby girls over the millennia have been optimistically named "Jade," the stone treasured above all stones, smooth as deep running water fossilized in a moment of alchemical mystery, whose changeful colors, from greenish white to leaf-gold to the darkest hue of rich moss, were believed to signal the health of the wearer.

My name birthed me in a culture so ancient and enduring "I" might as well have not been born. Instead, "we" were daughters, members of a family that placed its hope in sons. Something condescending and dismissive, careless and anonymous, accented the tones in which we were addressed. Girls were interchangeable. They fetched, obeyed, served, poured tea, balanced their baby brothers and sisters on their hips while they stood in the outer circles of older women. Unnecessary as individuals, girls need concern nobody, unlike sons, especially first sons, on whose goodwill mothers measured their future. My girl cousins and I, collectively named Precious Jade, were destined someday to leave our parents' homes, claimed by strangers, like jewels given up to the emperor of patriarchs. No wonder we were valued generically as girls and seldom as individuals.

Like my cousins I received a personal name, my ming. So as not to confuse me with Geok Lan, Geok Phan, Geok Pei, Geok Mui, or any other Geok, I was named Geok Lin. All my girl cousins answered to their Chinese *ming*. Ah Lan. Ah Mui. Ah Pei, But I was always "Shirley" to everyone. "Ah Shirley," my aunts called me.

Shirley, after Shirley Temple. Because we both had dimples. Because Baba had loved her in the movies in the 1930s. I knew the story of my name. "It's your dimples," Baba told me from the beginning. "You look just like Shirley Temple." I thought Shirley Temple was an untidy child, burnt brown, with straight black hair, a Hollywood star whose fame ensured my own as a Chinese girl.

The first time I saw the child actress in the 1934 movie "Bright Eyes," decades later in a television clip on New York public television, she was tap dancing in shiny black patent leather shoes, her ringlets bouncing to the music. I know the details now: golden hair, blue eyes, Mary Janes on her feet. We could not have been more different as babies and little girls. But growing up I was assured that I was like Shirley Temple; a child star, reborn in Malacca, the glory atoms just the same.

It remains a mystery to me what strange racial yearnings moved Baba to name me after a blond child. I'd like to think he was not tied to the fixities of race and class, that this presumption was less colonized mimicry than bold experiment. Looking at the dozens of nieces duplicated for a domestic future; did he revel for me? Although, unarguably, he had written in his neat English script my Chinese name on my birth certificate, he never called me anything but Shirley, a Hollywood name for a daughter for whom he wished, despite everything his heritage dictated, a life freer than his own.

I was confused when I first went to school and the Irish nuns called for "Geok Lin," For the first few years I had to remember that I was "Geok Lin" in English school and "Shirley" in my home. It did not occur to me then that my scrambled names were a particular problem. Language mixes and mix-ups were Malayan everyday reality. Your own name tripped on your tongue, a series of hesitations, till you stopped noticing the hesitations, and the name flowed as yours, as a series of names.

When I was baptized at the age of eleven, Father Lourdes said I had to choose a Catholic name, the name of a saint. Baba had shown no interest one way or another when I told him that I wanted to become a Catholic. He signed a form agreeing to my baptism with no discussion; it could have been a form for participation in a School Day parade. The looming question that almost turned me away from the moment of baptism was, what would I call myself? Unlike Baba I knew that baptism intended a serious change of identity. At eleven I didn't know who I wanted to be. Saint Martha? Saint Lucy? Saint Bernadette? Saint Josephine? If I was going to change from Shirley to Martha, I wanted to know what I was exchanging my star status for. Who were these saints and what kinds of lives had they led?

In the sales annex of the convent school, I looked through the holy pictures, glossy cards which featured images of sainted women on one side and brief biographies on the other. The nuns' favorite presents to successful students, these holy pictures showed white women in long robes clasping their hands upward with piteous expressions. The stories were equally unvarying: saints died to preserve Christianity and their virginity. I chose Agnes, a virgin condemned to be devoured by lions because she had refused the seduction of a Roman tyrant. Agnes had a young noble face cast toward a stream of sunlight, and she rested her hands casually on the manes of a couple of lions who lay by her sandaled feet like overgrown house cats. I knew no one named Agnes in Malacca. It would seem a difficult name for my aunts to pronounce: Ah Agnes. For a few months after my baptism the nuns called for Agnes, had to call for Agnes again and again, before I recognized it as my name.

Then in a year there was confirmation. "You must choose a confirmation name," Father Lourdes said. More sophisticated, I checked out the Hollywood actresses whose looks I liked. Jennifer Jones matched with a Saint Jennifer, but Jennifer Jones had breasts, dark hair, a sultry look. Unlike Saint Jennifer of the holy picture, she was a moving image, a woman larger than life on the screen in the Rex Cinema. I wrote my name down as Agnes Jennifer on the cover of my school exercise books. Jenny was a friendlier version, but I already knew of at least three Jennies in Malacca; it would be too confusing to take their names.

I tried writing my names down: Shirley Agnes Jennifer Lim Geok Lin. But after months of trying one or another, only Shirley stuck. It was the name Baba had given me out of his fantasy of the West, what he saw when he saw me for the first time, his only daughter, with dimples, in a Hollywood halo. Shirley was Baba's version of the beloved girl-child, played back without the Mary Janes, without the blue eyes and golden ringlets, without anything Western in it for a Malayan daughter except the language of the West.

Whether I have had too many names or never received my right name still isn't clear to me. Malayans, imagining Romeo as a comic outlaw, transformed the play into a comedy of sexual manners because the tragedy of naming was so much a part of everyday life that we could not see it. Names also stuck on us: Chinese names, Malay names, Tamil names, English names, Portuguese names, Dutch names, Hollywood names, Roman names, Catholic names, Hindu names. They stuck, and they peeled off, became tangled like string of DNA matter. Too many names, too many identities, too many languages.

But it was never certain that this confusion should lead to comedy or tragedy. For my mother's people, the peranakans—a distinctive Malayan-born people of Chinese descent assimilated into Malay and Western cultures—mockery and laughter accompanied our mélange of Chinese, Malay, Indian, Portuguese, British, and American cultural practices. Laughter acknowledged we were never pure. We spoke a little of this, a little of that, stole favorite foods from every group, paid for Taoist chants, and dressed from Western fashion magazines, copying manners we fancied. One of the earliest peranakan writers in English, Ee Tiang Hong, titled his first book of poems I of the Many Faces. He meant the title as an angst-loaded lamentation, but angst also is one of the many stances of the peranakans, one of their elaborate cultural plays between Chinese and Malay, Asian and Western. They, we were neither one nor the other: true peranakan copies, mixes, looking like nothing else in the world that ourselves.

I begin my memoir in the United States at a moment when a female heroic of autonomy and resistance seems to have lost some of its persuasive edge. Perhaps that is why now more than ever we need to reconsider Virginia Woolf's plea that women think back through their mothers. For many of us, it is the story of our mothers that makes a female heroic so necessary, yet also so impossible. In my first life, growing up as a Malaysian woman, I only could write of Asian women whose identities intertwined with mine: mother, aunts, cousins, rivals, and friends. In my second life as an immigrant Asian American, I find that Western women have also helped me plot my life, as I write forward: women of all colors—workers, neighbors, colleagues, mentors, and sisters. This book is for all these women in my life.

Chapter Seven: Outside the Empire

For almost two decades, politicians had argued first for home rule, then for nationhood, and finally Tengku Abdul Rahman, a Malay prince, presided over the separation of the Federation of Malaya from the British empire. In 1957, when I was twelve, the Federation of Malaya received its independence—Merdeka—and joined the Commonwealth of Nations as its eleventh sovereign member-state. Throughout the peninsula thousands of people cheered, had dark thoughts, prepared their passports for departure, sighed, felt relief that they were finally able to protect their rights from alien newcomers, checked their identity cards and citizenship papers. Thousands others never knew it was happening, made love to someone of a different race, brought a pagan to mass, washed their feet at the water tank before entering the mosque for prayers of thanks, held meetings to secure financial holdings, checked their identity cards and citizenship papers, talked about multiracialism, wondered about the status of the English language, ate *chapatis* and mutton curry for lunch and *rendang* for dinner, proclaimed the Chinese would own the country, worried about the departure of the British Army, checked their identity cards and citizenship papers. Thousands argued about the rights of the sultans, and assumed everything would remain the same, only better. The terms of the debate for those in English education were rhetorically reassuring—a constitution, national identity, citizenship rights, a parliament, a judiciary, free elections. The British Empire was dead. The British Commonwealth was alive. The new university graduates, setting the course for a multiracial, multicultural, pluralistic democracy, set bold topics for our English papers and our debating teams— What is a democracy? Who should run the country, the army or the civilians? Which should we value more, the individual or society? Is free speech ever wrong?

A young student, I was not so much apathetic as complacent. British education had trained me for the privileged ranks of the Civil Service. Hungry and ragged or socially disgraced, I never doubted that my talents placed me in a meritocracy. The empire promised impartial evaluation under the socialist standards of the civil bureaucracy that the British prime minister, Harold Wilson, had established in defense against communist criticism of capitalism and entrenched class interests. With high grades validated from Britain, earning me respect where none else existed, I believed that scholarly excellence alone would decide my professional life.

I was a resident in that sheltered elite village, the University of Malaya, from 1964 to 1969. But the changes taking place in the political and social fabric of the new nation were causing rifts even inside the campus gates. Little was expected of the undergraduate except folly, frolic, and academic obedience. Lecturers were lofty men, chiefly white, to whom we were uninteresting children of the Asian masses. I signed up for history, geography, and English in the first year, but all that remains vivid are the weekly English tutorials, composed of five randomly selected freshmen, to whom were assigned a young lecturer newly arrived from Cambridge.

Tall, gangly, and awkward, as if his arms and legs had grown too remote from a center of command, Mr. Preston was shy about women but voluble concerning Shelley, Byron, Keats, Yeats, and other assorted English poets. At our first meeting, he handed us a mimeographed booklet for the Practical Criticism course and asked us to analyze an anonymous poem, "Ode to Limestone." I recognized the style as Auden's. Unriddling the poem's structure and intertwined themes was the kind of thing I did when I had turned to poetry for consolation during my years in the cramped Malacca house. At the end of the third meeting Mr. Preston returned my essay without a grade. "You are supposed to write this without any help," he admonished me. "Which reference did you use in the library?"

"I wrote this myself," I protested, alarmed and flattered

that he thought I had cribbed my essay. But he ushered me out of his office disapprovingly.

The rest of the tutorials, however, went by without a fuss. He never questioned the originality of my essays again. They were returned with comments and grades, and I looked forward eagerly to the weekly meetings when, for the first time, it seemed to me, I was able to talk freely about language and ideas with someone who understood and shared my pleasure in both.

Academic standards for the bachelor's degree in English literature were ensured by a form of quality control, with the English department operating under the anxiety of Britain's shadow. Back issues of *Scrutiny* were required reading; external examiners from Cambridge and Oxford scrutinized our exam papers for softening of intellectual rigor in the department's offerings. The English department was notorious for its emphasis on standards, a term which seemed synonymous with British upper-class culture, and the university, which had separated from Singapore University in 1965, had never awarded a First Class in English.

During the mandatory Chaucer, Shakespeare, Augustan, Romantics, and other traditional survey courses, listening hard but not hearing, students diligently copied every word the lecturer uttered. In my three years as an undergraduate, I had only one woman lecturer, a British medievalist who taught the great mysteries of Middle English. All my tutors were male. Mr. Lark crammed his hands in his pockets and jingled the coins throughout his hour-long peroration. Mr. Hughes prowled from microphone to blackboard to locked door before taking off his shoes and sitting on the desk. Dr. Wismal stood very straight and lectured from note cards which he turned over meticulously after each point. Their presence really didn't matter; afraid to miss a syllable, every student's head was down. Above the air conditioning's hum and the lecturer's drone, usually only the slur of note paper turning and the skittering of ballpoints were audible.

But even within the anglophile offices of the English department the world was changing. In my final year, an eccentric visiting French professor offered electives on the Continental novel. He held late-night showings of avant-garde films by Alain Resnais and Francois Truffaut, during which the students tittered politely. He gave parties in his apartment in Kuala Lumpur where he grumbled as we gulped down expensive French wine as if it were sugar cane juice. "Sip slowly!" he urged as he ogled us.

Mr. Farley, the first visiting Fulbright professor in the department, introduced us to Mark Twain, Ralph Waldo Emerson, Walt Whitman, and Henry James. The United Sates appeared in my imagination for the first time, from a literature more mysterious than that of Victorian England. A New Englander, very tall, gray, and stooped, Mr. Farley was also the first professor to encourage me unstintingly. His formal kindness offered me a glimpse of teaching as a nurturing relationship that the years of British education had disavowed. After I received a tutorship with admission to the master's program at the university, he urged me to apply for a Fulbright fellowship to complete a doctorate in the United Sates. Whereas the British lecturers had questioned my legitimacy in their subject, he serenely assured me that my future lay in American literature.

In contrast to Mr. Farley, when Mr. Hughes called me after the final exams results to tell me that I had achieved a First Class Honors, he did not congratulate me. Instead, he added, "Of course, you know you were fooling us in some of your papers. But remember, you can't fool all of the people all of the time." The British lecturers consistently warned me against studies in English literature. Even as I fervently memorized "Tintern Abbey" and long passages from *The Prelude*, they shook their heads and advised, "You cannot hope to understand Wordsworth unless you've been to the Lake District."

This British superiority had always grated on me. I wondered why they were teaching us what they believed we who were not English could never possibly appreciate. Besides, I didn't believe them. The physical sensation of expansion in the chest, even in the head, as I read a profoundly beautiful or mindful poem was conclusively and possessively subjective. The literature may have been of Britain, but my love of literature was outside the empire.

A Malayan professor, a dark Eurasian of Sri Lankan descent, offered us as countercurriculum a course on "Commonwealth Literature." Undergraduates were intimidated by Dr. Wismal's air of stern reserve, perhaps a mask for his struggles against both British and Asian racism. From Singapore University Dr. Wismal had gone on to receive a Ph.D. from Leeds University. His ascendancy to head of the English department appeared as a triumph of local merit against British expatriate snobbery, for it was generally agreed that his publications in Victorian literature had gained him the position. But we knew also that the new government had determined to replace Britons in positions of power with local professors. His appointment, therefore, mirrored the shift in Malayan society from colonized to national culture.

Together with Amos Tutuola's and Chinua Achebe's novels from Africa and the works of West Indian writers, including V. S. Naipaul and George Lamming, we finally read a few Malayan writers in Dr. Wismal's course. Studying the poems of Ee Tiang Hong and Wong Phui Nam, many of which lamented an alienation from Malayan society, I saw the contrast between their concerns and those in Wordsworth's poetry. From my position of undergraduate superiority I was pitiless in my criticism of these poets' separation from their national landscape. While their simple act of writing against colonial disparagement was to be admired, I puzzled over their images of displacement. Truly I loved the hibiscus bushes that bloomed all over the campus; I never tired of the delicious foods sold in the night food stalls all over Petaling Jaya, the suburb that had sprouted around the university, and even the steamy afternoons brought their own keen sensations of tropical languor and heightened sensuality. In contrast, in the poems of these pioneer English-language writers, Malayan identity was of something absent. I wanted to write a literature like Wordsworth's *Prelude,* but overflowing with native presence: writing should be an act of dis-alienation, of sensory claims. If we were not Malayans, who could we be?

As a concluding paper, Dr. Wismal asked that we each write a short story. The night before it was due, I wrote my first short story, a brooding imagining of an abortion witnessed and abetted by the young unknowing daughter. The pleasure in writing the story, which flowed unforced, confirmed my belief in the vital connection between the English language and the breathing emotions that ran through my body. Dr. Wismal later included it in the first published collection of English-language Malayan short stories, many of which had been written as assignments for him.

Dr. Wismal's readings directly contradicted the exclusive claims on English that British lecturers like Preston and Hughes had repeated. His course was part of a struggle to extricate a valuable sense of self-in-language from the colonialist's etymological grip. We had grown up in a compulsory language system, but, as if to strip us of all language, we were constantly reminded that this language did not belong to us. Depriving us of Chinese or Malay or Hindi, British teachers reminded us nonetheless that English was only on loan, a borrowed tongue which we could only garble.

Closeted within my love of the English language, I did not hear the increasingly hostile language debates breaking out all over Malaya till it was too late. In 1967 my joy at being admitted into the circle of English literature was pure, naive, and tainted at the source, for, of course, there could be no easy future for "Englit"—Britain's canon of great English works—in the context of postcolonial politics.

In 1964, in my first year as an undergraduate, many university students were heady with optimism toward a new kind of human, the Malaysian. Meeting on the common ground of multiracialism and multiculturalism, politicians of all races had seemed to agree to the formation of a new political unit, composed of island pieces colonized by Britain in Southeast Asia: the Federation of Malaya, Sarawak, and Singapore. One evening I followed the crowds in Malacca to Coronation Park, now renamed Merdeka Park. A lean Chinese man dressed simply in a short-sleeved white shirt and khaki pants addressed the milling audience from a plain unadorned platform. "We have to make sure everyone has something," he shouted into a microphone. "When people own things, they don't riot. When they see a riot forming, they run home and they take their motorcycles inside their houses and lock the doors." He was Lee Kuan Yew.

But Lee, prime minister of Singapore, offered an economist's vision of Malaysia, the view of a pragmatic Chinese immigrant generation. It did not succeed in assuring the Malays who feared their claim to indigenous ownership eroded by precisely the kind of materialist striving that he urged. By 1965, the racial divisions in the region had become clearer in the polarities that finally led to the dissolution of the Malayan-Singapore union.

That weekend in Singapore when I was embarked on my mission to rid myself of my virginity, Uncle Charlie called me excitedly to watch Mr. Lee's address on television. Tearfully, pleading for calm, the distraught statesman spoke of finding a separate destiny for Singapore. The Malaysian prime minister, Tengku Abdul Rahman, perhaps acutely accepting the increasing electoral tensions between Chinese-dominant Singapore and Malay-dominant Malaya, had summarily expelled Singapore from the union. Jostling the lines at Customs as I crossed the border at the Johore Causeway, I felt fearfully sad. The meaninglessness of my sexual encounter—the physical rupture in my body—with Rajan, the stranger I had chosen to initiate me in bed, appeared enlarged by the violent meaningfulness of the political split between Singapore, the city I was just beginning to know through my mother's residence, and Malaysia, the country I implicitly loved.

My second year at the university was filled with continuous debates on the cultural future of the country. More and more, the term "Malay" appeared where "British" once stood. The "Malaysian," that new promise of citizenship composed of the best traditions from among Malays, Chinese, Tamils, Eurasians, Dayaks, and so forth, seemed more and more to be a vacuous political fiction, a public relations performance like those put on for Western tourists at state-run cultural centers: a little Wayang—traditional theater and puppetry—some Malay candle dances, a Chinese ribbon dance, Tamil dramatizations of the Ramayana, and the national anthem concluding the evening. One group's empowerment appeared to lead to another's oppression. As a thoroughly English-educated mind, emptied of Chinese racialized sentiments, I was a mold into which the idealism of a progressive multiracial identity could be poured. Chinese chauvinism offended me as much as other racisms, for, although of Chinese descent, I was usually treated by Malayan Chinese speakers as foreign, alien, and worse, decadent, an unspeakable because unspeaking, degenerate descendent of pathetic forebears. But Malay chauvinism was no better.

In the face of competition for dominance between Chinese and Malay elites, I was attracted contrarily to Eurasians and Indians, a romance of minoritism, as a way out of the fixedness of race identity. Tentative about my social position, I was most comfortable with those who were on the outside. Frequently mocked as different, they did not suggest there was something wrong with you simply because you were different. To many xenophobic Malays and Chinese, Eurasians and Indians were always the wrong race. Eurasians were jibbed at as "half-breeds," "mongrels," white-lovers, loose, unambitious, the disintegrating fragments of a dying race. Indians were mocked as the wrong color, communalistic, quarrelsome: they smelled, used coconut oil, and worshipped strange gods. Chinese and Malays were equally dogged by negative stereotypes, but, larger in numbers, many of them also asserted a palpably contemptuous superiority from which I cringed.

In my second year, I refused to return to Third College. Its regime of gossip, regulated hours, and enforced women's company was, after all, only an adult version of what I had thought I had escaped in leaving the convent school—the pettiness of schoolgirls. I bought a Honda motorbike, rented a room in Petaling Jaya with another defiant undergraduate woman, and became engaged to Ben, a Eurasian student a year my senior.

"Going steady" had seemed the only alternative to risky independence, and Ben's devotion was balm to my sense of physical damage. He was more than devoted; he was sentinel and guard, for I was in his company every evening. I was always a little bored and a little flattered in his company: half-asleep by eleven or midnight, I would beg him to leave, then watch his slow retreating back with confused emotions, not quite able to figure whether the slight depression I felt was remorse at my relief that I was finally alone or regret at his leaving me alone. Nagged by a sense that there was something more important than simply walking or making love, I had no idea what this more important thing could be.

Being without him was grievously lonely. In my small sad room my roommate, whose boyfriend had just broken up with her, sulked because I wouldn't stay still. Attending lectures, going to the library, and returning to the room was an intolerable routine which I could only escape with Ben's help. With Ben I could stay out late; I could avoid the endless small talk of university women. With Ben, I needed never to return to Malacca; instead I stayed in his parents' home in Penang at every university break. There I shared a room with his sister, and his mother politely ignored me.

I was always braver with him, even at night, even riding without a license, even when a sudden police block stopped us on the Federal Highway. Tall, brown, and gentle-spoken, Ben repelled unwanted male attention either with a twenty-dollar bribe to the police or with an aggressive stare at jostling strangers. I was secure with him, and he played on that, calling me his lamb, his little one.

Although he was a geography student, Ben wanted to paint. In his home, his doting mother had set aside a room for his studio. Through the university breaks I sat in the airless room reading aloud from the *Encyclopedia of World Art* while he painted. In between passages on the pointillists, Duchamp, Matisse, and Chagall, we discussed my supporting him. As we stretched his canvases together, I thought I would be muse to his talent. His canvases showed a facility with figures and landscapes, a restlessness with colors, and growing obsession with abstraction. He was sure he had talent and could become a famous painter, given money for canvas and oils and time. He spent his money on expensive magazines like *Artforum* and introduced me to Penang artists whose batik-style paintings that sold well to tourists he excoriated. It was true that he could produce paintings just like those but chose not to. Yet he was conflicted between his love of painting and his desire for security. I was proud of his intransigence, his apparent contempt for money, and his belief in art, but after twelve hours in his studio, he wanted only a good time.

Also, it seemed to me that Ben's love for me usually led to his comfort rather than mine. He insisted I come up to Penang, but I stayed indoors all day beside him while he painted. For my twenty-first birthday he brought me a rose and a basket of tinned Western delicacies—mandarin oranges in syrup, deviled ham, soft-centered chocolates, smoked almonds. I was pleased by his thoughtfulness, but he ate the delicacies. When I returned to Third College to concentrate on the examinations that would decide my degree in my final years Ben, who was teaching in Penang, called me every night. The calls were a loving reassurance, but it was impossible to stay out late without having to account for my absence. I had to be back in the

College and waiting by the dormitory public telephone every night by nine.

I couldn't understand my restlessness and grew more passive with him, as if I were deliberately disinheriting that bad and dangerous child within me who kept wanting to run away. After I took on the position as tutor in the English department, Ben moved down from Penang, found a job teaching at a Malay college in Petaling Jaya, and brought lunch to me at the university every day. When I began having tea with the other tutors, he came by each afternoon and sat glumly through our giddy conversations.

I was flushed with success. The boring hoop-jumping of exams had given way to the disorienting freedom of independent studies. Tutors read alone in their library carrels to produce a master's thesis at the end of two years. Any famous writer was fair study: Gerard Manley Hopkins, Eugene O'Neill, Anthony Burgess. Out of the unyielding structure of the exam system, I found myself in the unsupervised zone of graduate studies. You could die in a carrel and it might be two weeks before your body was discovered. Certainly you could work on a master's degree, and it would be two years before anyone discovered your thesis was missing. I alternated between happiness at the unaccustomed absence of surveillance and despair at the anomie of graduate work.

Similarly, I zig-zagged between valuing the claustrophobic security of Ben's possessiveness and acting on a growing confused discontent. Moving to Petaling Jaya, Ben had given up painting. His life seemed to be devoted to waiting for me, for he didn't enjoy teaching. While I read in the carrel, he played billiards for hours. I was sometimes particularly tender. He reminded me of Father in the way his life drifted along shallow currents of desire and pleasure. More often I quarreled with him in order to feel an emotion sharper than pity or boredom.

Each master's student was assigned an adviser. I was

intimidated to have Mr. Hughes, he of the prowling peregrinations during the lecture hour. He had just returned from sabbatical in England, wore black turtlenecks, and smoked a pipe which entailed a great deal of fussing—unscrewing a tin of tobacco, knocking off the ash and cleaning the bowl, stuffing it with a careful measure of the brown shredded leaves, striking a match and holding it to the bowl while clamping strong white teeth on the stem, sucking on it attentively, and finally succeeding in blowing clouds of smoke over the head of the person before him. I was attracted to such little-known women poets as Edna St. Vincent Millay, Elizabeth Jennings, and Laura Riding, and wanted to write my thesis on selected women poets. Mr. Hughes frowned on the proposal. "You have a problem with being scattered," he said, "and should work on fiction which will provide you with external structure." I had just read *The Lord of the Flies* and was drawn to its gloomy Christian aesthetics, so much like my own experience with colonial Catholicism; it was simpler to acquiesce and to turn to William Golding's novels for my master's thesis.

We met a couple of times to discuss my progress. Materials had to be specially ordered by the library or requested through international interlibrary loan. Everything took at least three months to arrive. Researching the history of allegories and Augustinian theological treatises on free will and determinism, I was pleased to be learning curious things, the way a hermitic scholar hidden away in a cell was supposed to do.

During the same period, as I teetered between an idea of adulthood that appeared ever more removed from myself and the passive sexualized adolescence that I was locked into with Ben, a group of fellow tutors began gathering in the Senior Common Room in the afternoons, smoking furiously and drinking beer. Mr. Hughes came to sit with us for hours, smoking his pipe, his long legs pulled in along the low rattan chair. No longer a remote lecturer, he reveled in our excessive drinking and frivolous talk.

A few months later, he asked me to his office to discuss

my work. The English lecturers' offices on the fifth floor were little visited except during tutorial sessions. "Come in," he said when I knocked, his voice calm and professional. The usual cloud of pipe smoke filled the small room. Through the windows tinted for privacy, one saw only empty sky. As I shut the door, he put down his pipe and came up to me. Putting his arms around me, he muttered, "I love you, I love you." He was trembling and very warm in the air-conditioned chill. His words ricocheted in my mind, shocking because of their seeming finality. He had always appeared so much older and superior. An English man, married with two children, he had never entered my imagination as a sexual person. In that brief moment, he had moved, flatteringly, from teacher to lover.

Speaking with lowered voice, he said, "I have to see you alone. Will you come? I'll get a room at the Station Hotel for Saturday. Please come at eight. I'll be waiting for you." Through his thick turtleneck sweater I could feel his heart pounding. His face was distraught, and he clutched at me almost impersonally, as if with despair.

What should I have done on this occasion? Sometimes, reminded by debates on sexual harassment in the universities, I ask this question. I did not think of him then as a harasser, although his actions then and later clearly had the effect of harassing me. I should have refused his request and discreetly asked for a different adviser, so ending the matter right there. But in the dim tobacco-scented room crowded with books and papers, I was intrigued by his passionate clumsiness and the dangerous secrecy of the encounter. Above all, I felt a sense of power, that unwittingly I had been able to reduce this superior man to frantic begging.

Telling Ben I was ill and had to stay in bed, I rode on my Honda to the Station Hotel. The hotel was a Victorian fantasy of Indian Islamic architecture that the British had constructed early in the twentieth century to mask the bleak functionality of the railroad tracks that carried them, imperial transients, up and down the peninsula. It was not a place I had ever visited. I was grateful for the tropical dark. The Moorish-style towers and arabesque porticos deepened my mood of fatal romance. James, for that was how I was beginning to think of Mr. Hughes, had placed a note with simply the room number written on it in my mailbox. Avoiding the front desk, I kept to the far walls of the cavernous reception room, took the elevator, and rode to the fourth floor.

James had brought a bottle of red wine. Light from a street lamp below the window steeped the room in shade and shadow. He was jubilant, moody, depressed, and talkative. I reminded him of his first love, another high-strung graduate woman who had died in an accident after an argument. He was in pain in my presence. As he made love to me on the stark white hotel bed, I wasn't sure he was aware of me or of that long-lost spirit. Even his endearments sounded like a soundtrack from a British film. I left the hotel room as dumbly as I had entered.

James was dazzled by my personality and completely uninterested in me as a person. I had no history for him before the moment he fell in love with me. Immediately I regretted the affair. When we met at the Senior Common Room, which was almost daily, he threw quick significant glances at me, and paused extravagantly as he uttered philosophical abstractions that the other tutors listened to with awe. Enmeshed in his melodrama, however, I was conscious only of paranoia. I was afraid Ben would suspect James's feelings and that James's wife would discover our night at the hotel. Fleetingly, I imagined marrying James and running off to England, but I dreaded a future in the company of his academicism, in a cold country I didn't wish to live in, saddled with his history, the dead woman, the abandoned middle-aged wife and sweet children. After a few more clammy embraces in his office, I warned him of Ben's suspicions and asked that we stop meeting before Ben confronted his wife.

It was true that, as I grew more unhappy, Ben became

more jealous. When I house-sat for a German professor and would not tell him where I was, he went to James's home to find me. Later, he followed me to the house. Finding it locked, he broke in through the bathroom louvers. He refused to accept my need to be alone. Since I didn't have another boyfriend, he argued, I was merely confused. That Christmas break, acceding to his demands, I accompanied him to Penang, where I slept for more than fifteen hours each day. Groggy and depressed, I woke up in the afternoons, took slow subdued walks with him, then fell into bed exhausted.

Back in Petaling Jaya, living in a spartan room intended for servants which I rented from a wealthy Malay family, I received no visitors except Ben. His overpowering daily presence constricted me. I felt I could not live without him and yet I did not want to live with him. In a poem I described the position of Daphne as she attempted to escape Apollo: dreading him and yet unable to win the race, she metamorphoses into an olive tree, a bitter ruckle, whose leaves the god ironically takes as the symbol of victory. One night, I took out the bottles of tranquilizers prescribed after my accident which I had saved for just such a moment. I closed the door and swallowed all the little white pills, then fell asleep.

I slept for more than twenty-four hours; but when Ben finally succeeded in rousing me, I had suffered no more than a bad headache. Remorseful, he promised that he would accept my wish for more privacy and my desire to be with other people. We would remain engaged, but he would stop hounding me. Feeling I could breathe again, I moved to a married tutor's house, where I spent evenings washing my hair and discussing literature with her. Ben stopped by only on some evenings.

One afternoon, while I was buying cigarettes at the Senior Common Room, Iqbal, my brother's colleague in the history department, came up from behind and commented on my taste for mentholated cigarettes. Iqbal had just returned from a five-year fellowship at the University of California in Berkeley, bringing with him a veneer of American sophistication. He was casual where Ben was pretentious. Dressed simply himself, he seemed to like my usual costume of blue jeans and print shirts. One afternoon, early in our relationship, he took me in a taxi to the university apartment he had just moved his things into to give me a well-washed work shirt that he had brought back from Berkeley. We both knew the gift was a symbolic act of cultural and sexual claiming. The next month I moved into the apartment. At the same time, Iqbal asked that I keep a room in Petaling Jaya, warning that if his traditional Punjabi mother should ever visit him, I would have to move out for the duration of her stay.

Later, when Ben found out that I had been seeing Iqbal, he wondered at my terrible taste. Iqbal was the ugliest man I could have picked, he said. Not much taller than I, inclined toward fat, with a mass of unruly black hair that looked greasy even when clean, and wearing thick glasses that gave him the myopic popped-up glaze of a goldfish in a small bowl, Iqbal charmed by more tenacious routes than the body. Fresh from the Berkeley Free Speech Movement, he brought to the decaying British tradition of the university an irreverent intelligence and institutional skepticism that caught me completely.

For a month, over afternoon tea, he listened to me talk about my confusion over Ben. When he first asked me to leave Ben, I refused. Then he invited me to a party. I was intrigued as the taxi drove through an expensive Kuala Lumpur suburb that I had never visited. Patting my hand confidently, Iqbal said, "Just stick around, baby!" The evening was full of older professional people whose interests I didn't share; someone remarked snidely that Iqbal was cradlesnatching. As the taxi took us back to my rented room, Iqbal's flippant Americanism echoed in my head. "Just stick around, baby!" I was tired of scenes, tensions, the heavy inertia of my relationship with Ben, like living in a sack with its neck slowly drawn closed. Iqbal's patience, his

American past, even his older Malaysian professional circle, seemed desirable, an alternative to Ben's emotional dead end.

Ben was waiting in my room when I came upstairs. "You were with another man, weren't you?" His anger was blazing even as I was unable to feel anything except weariness. I could no longer ignore the contrast between Iqbal's intimate liveliness and Ben's stultifying rage. "I won't let you leave me, I'll kill myself first!"

The threat usually brought on a rush of guilt and pity. I would find myself anxiously smoothing his hair, consoling him, with tears of frustration in my eyes. Tonight, Iqbal's casual offer, "Just stick around baby!" played jazzily against Ben's words. "I don't care," I murmured, amazed I was actually saying it. Suddenly it was clear to me that I really didn't care. I wouldn't miss Ben if I never saw him again.

"I'll kill you before I let you leave me!"

I felt strangely calm, immutable: I couldn't bear to be with him, my unhappiness was intolerable. "I'd rather be dead than be with you."

"All right," he said. His voice was stricken. "I want you to keep the ring. Tomorrow, we go to Chee's house and tell all our friends our engagement's off."

That last afternoon with Ben was also my last afternoon with the friends we had made together as undergraduates. None of our mutual friends, who usually gathered at Chee's home for dinner, appeared surprised at the news, although I knew they blamed me for the break. Leaving Ben was leaving the community I had known for the last three years. I went home to Malacca to gather my thoughts and called Iqbal from the Arts Concourse public telephone as soon as I returned to Kuala Lumpur. "Wait there," he said, and came in a taxi to fetch me to his unfurnished, waiting apartment.

What I loved first about Iqbal was the openness of movement he offered. For the first few months he spoke continuously of Berkeley and the United States: the Indian student naked under her wrapped sari; the hundred-dollar steak dinner his adviser had bought him; driving over the Golden Gate Bridge and seeing San Francisco from the hills; the secondhand bookstores and the good cold beer. Chain-smoking, with my long unkempt hair, faded dungarees, motorcycle, and obsession with literature, I was like a fragment of Berkeley he had dislodged from the backwaters of Kuala Lumpur.

However, except for the straight-arrow American literature course a year ago, I had no interest in the United States. I was ambitious about my writing; I wanted to be a Malayan writer, and walked around somewhat askew, looking for materials. I began a novel, wrote poems, completed a few more short stories, and worked on my thesis on Golding.

I thought Iqbal's simplicity ravishing. He refused to have a telephone or a television in the apartment, and would not learn to drive. Living with him held a lightness of being, an improvisational spontaneity that made each day fresh and mobile.

After a month of eating muesli and milk, Iqbal bought me a copy of *The Joy of Cooking*. We shopped together for a roast beef, and with extreme anxiety I found myself alone among the gleaming untouched kitchen counters. I had never cooked in my life. I had never faced such a large mass of beef. The roast had shrunk to a dark brown butt by the time I served it. Sitting in solitary grandeur at the dining table, Iqbal cut into it. "You will have to learn to cook if you want to live with me," he said as I stood, crushed, by the kitchen door. Resentfully I returned to the kitchen to wash the dishes. Why was he smiling and why wasn't I, I wondered. The kitchen door between us seemed to me an ominous sign of something already wrong with our relationship.

But I applied myself to learning to cook. It was a new challenge. Besides, Iqbal began throwing elaborate dinner parties. On my Honda I carried home bunches of orchids, fresh plucked chickens, yogurt, anchovies, pineapples, spinach, *garam marsala*, bottles of red Wine. I worked all Saturday arranging a bountiful display, then slipped in and out of the kitchen door serving the lecturers, the visiting fellows, the U.S. embassy people he favored. Occasionally I followed a fascinating conversation; more often I glowed in Iqbal's social success. After weeks of such parties, I began to resent the work, the unsatisfactory uncompleted sentences as I served the salad and the dessert, removed the dirty dishes, and brought out more wine bottles.

One afternoon, Iqbal saw me at the university. "I've invited two more for dinner tonight," he added casually. "You'd better make sure there will be enough food."

I rushed to the market and shopped furiously for another chicken, they stood in line at the supermarket for a frozen Sara Lee cheesecake.

"Did you buy wine?" Iqbal asked when he returned to the apartment later that afternoon. "We can't have only beer!"

It was raining as I set out once again on my motorbike for the six-mile round trip to the supermarket. As the rain pelted my hair and soaked through my clothes, I cried at my own submissiveness.

That night there was just enough cheesecake for everyone except me. The American woman Iqbal had invited with her handsome husband was a green-eyed blond whom he seated beside him. Gulping glasses of wine, she laughed drunkenly at his jokes. I was sullen and silent, and Iqbal fell asleep without noticing my anger. But I did not speak to him of my resentment: I could no longer imagine a life without him.

One morning I woke up to hear someone crying in the living room. When I went out in my pajamas, I saw an elderly woman in a sari crouched on the rattan sofa weeping. Knotting his sarong around his waist, Iqbal came up behind me and whispered, "That's my mother. You have to leave."

Numbly I took some clothes out of the closet and rode off to the room I had rented and that I had never slept in. The Chinese family who took my check monthly stared to see me in the house. I sat on the bed, gazing through the window at the other small working class houses with their tattered front yards and bare concrete driveways. It struck me that I was homeless. Iqbal's apartment was not my home. I was like the live-in Malay maid whose place in the apartment was functional and without rights.

Iqbal told me I could return two days later, after his mother left, still weeping over his taking up with a non-Punjabi woman. "My mother will never change," he said. "She will never be able to accept a Chinese daughter-in-law."

The next time I heard her crying in the morning I didn't wait for him to tell me to leave but dressed immediately and left him still sleeping while she moaned in the living room.

I was desperately jealous of Iqbal's mind.

Our first week together, he gave me Kahlil Gibran's *The Prophet* and asked me to read it. I was amused by its pretentious profundity. It wasn't as good as Fitzgerald's translation of the *Rubb'iyat*, and I told him so. His vast look of approval signaled that I had passed some kind of test. On weekends he read Wallace Stevens and William Carlos Williams aloud to me. He had a caressing deep voice which made "Sunday Morning" sound gorgeously musical.

He was the first person to convince me he was intellectually superior. He publicly corrected my pronunciation. Visiting the father of his ex-girlfriend, he was angry that I had mispronounced "pediatrician." Together we had unpacked his boxes of books from Berkeley. In the yellow highlighted pages of Theodore Dreiser's *Sister Carrie*, Henry James's *The Golden Bowl*, and dozens of other college paperbacks, I glimpsed a different kind of mind from the *Scrutiny* essays that I had so scrupulously copied.

He took me to an expensive French boutique in a new shopping mall full of Western stores. Choosing a white pleated skirt and emerald green knitted top, he told me I had to stop dressing like a shop girl when he took me to social events like play openings and embassy parties. At these gatherings everyone had just come from Europe or the United Sates. They talked about how difficult it was to find graham crackers in Kuala Lumpur, how hot Washington D.C. got in August, and how cheap wine was in California. I was Iqbal's girlfriend, and they talked to him around me as if I were only a penumbra of his body.

Before Professor Farley returned to New England, he asked me to apply for a Fulbright scholarship. "The university needs someone permanent to teach American literature," he told the head of the department. He had met both Ben and Iqbal and had been attentive and kind equally to both, but unlike the other Americans Iqbal and I knew, he was chiefly concerned about my future. "Be sure to take the GREs," he had told me. "Massachusetts is a lovely state with a wealth of resources. You will be able to visit Harvard." Each time he met me on the campus, he would lean down with twinkling eyes toward me and say, "I hope you are considering going ahead with your Ph.D."

Iqbal didn't like Professor Farley, but he said nothing as I sat for the General Record Examinations (GREs), then was interviewed for the Fulbright fellowship, dressed in the sedate white and green outfit from Paris that he had chosen for me. Of course, my first choice of graduate school was the University of California at Berkeley. Then, checking the college guides at the United States Information Service Library, I read about Irving Howe at Brandeis University and put Brandeis down as my second choice.

I was perversely persuaded in this choice by the first open disagreement I had with Iqbal. In June, soon after we began living together, we argued about the significance of the Seven Days' War. I was convinced that the efforts to destroy the Jewish state were anti-Semitic and historically related to the Holocaust. Iqbal, arguing that Israel was a territorial aggressor, rebuked me for my position. For once I refused to back down. The hostility I felt at his criticism of Israel was strangely personal, as if it threatened my own being. The prospect of studying with Irving Howe at Brandeis appealed to me as a strenuous counter-Americanism to Iqbal's Berkeley laissez faire.

The GREs were amazingly easy. They were my first multiple-choice exams, and I was surprised to find that the answers were provided on the question sheets. You merely had to identify the correct answers. Compared to the onerous strategies of arranging masses of memorized information to shape comprehensive yet original thought, these pencil-dot responses were nonintellectual exercises.

The interview for the fellowship seemed similarly undemanding. With the local Fulbright director, a visiting neurosurgeon, and Professor Farley, on hand, I assured them that besides reading I enjoyed cooking and long walks, and that if there were no publication resources in Malaysia after I returned from the United States, I would begin my own journal. The Fulbright director was very excited at my GRE results which had impressed even Iqbal.

Soon after, I was offered both a Fulbright and a Wien International fellowship at Brandeis.

Iqbal said nothing as I went through the application processes. Since he had said nothing about marriage, we were both silent about my future.

At university parties, acquaintances began to have conversations with me. In winning these fellowships I had become visible, a person separate from Iqbal. But my public excitement about leaving for Massachusetts was forced. I had not yet accepted the fellowships because I was wretched at the prospect of leaving Iqbal.

As unhappy as I was, my attachment to him was total. In the apartment I sat quietly beside him while he smoked, read, and listened to music, observing the fine black hairs on the backs of his hands or his small fingers tapping with the hypnotic tabala accompaniment to Ravi Shankar's sitar. He had put on weight. I loved the little brown roll of fat around his waist.

When we walked together, I felt an emotion of completion akin to bliss. Alone, I suffered keenly from a sense of emptiness. With him, the present was vivid.

When the English department placed an advertisement for a local lecturer, my relief was enormous. With the best academic record among the tutors, I was certain I would get the position, and then Iqbal and I would manage together as we had been doing for over a year. But the university administrator was cold and contemptuous as he interviewed me, and Dr. Wismal was quiet. The position was offered to Karmal, a Muslim male colleague.

The official rumor alleged that the selection committee believed I would accept the fellowships and leave the country. Months later a visiting professor at a party said that the university administrator had described me as an opinionated woman. I believed that the university preferred a male and a Muslim over a Chinese woman. For the first time I saw that the prejudices I had believed the product of small-town religious bigotry were systemic in Malaysian society. Worse, it became clear to me that merit was not the main criterion for professional status. In Malaysia, I would always be of the wrong gender and the wrong race.

Still pressing was the unavoidable moment of choice between accepting the fellowships or staying with Iqbal and leaving the academic world forever. Professor Farley was leaving Kuala Lumpur in February. Seeing me with Iqbal in the Senior Common Room, he spoke with concern about my delay in accepting the fellowships. "You'll have to decide soon," he warned. "Brandeis has to hear from you before March. Otherwise, the university will give the fellowship to someone else."

Iqbal and I were both silent as we walked back to the apartment. The late afternoon was warm. With the academic year over, the road was empty. Plodding along the dull road, I felt the heavy tropical foliage recede, as if I were already hovering over the scene, looking back on it as past.

Glancing at my pensive expression, Iqbal said, "Let's get

married! I don't want you to leave." Whimsically, he added, "I'll buy you a washing machine!"

I knew I should have been glad; I did not want to leave him. But I also knew I wanted to continue with graduate studies. I wanted to teach at the university.

Married to Iqbal I would be a faculty wife, one of those women on the outer circle of every university party I had attended, who sat with folded hands, like low fires banked for the night. Their demeanor was, in fact, even less open than the convent nuns who had tried to train me, as if I were a vine to be contained by wire and clipped. I could not bear the prospect of sitting in that domestic outer circle, excluded from the interesting talk, the arguments and jokes and important information.

At faculty parties, men abandoned their wives to cluster with each other, forming inner circles, tight groups sharing beers and Tom Collinses. Their company was charged; explosive laughter ripped through them, and low exchanges, loud interruptions.

I wanted to circulate in this talk, not circle outside it. I wanted not only Iqbal, but also myself.

When we arrived at the apartment, I sat on the bed and said miserably, "I can't marry you. I need to grow." More than my present misery, I saw that I would be infinitely more unhappy sitting in Iqbal's shadow. Giving up the fellowships, I would be giving up my hopes to write, to learn more, to spend my life with books. I would be only Iqbal's wife. I passionately wanted to be both, but felt offered only one or the other.

Ironically I was more devastated than Iqbal by my decision. Tearfully, for weeks, hating to have him out of my sight, I intensely and tensely negotiated each moment. Counting the days till the flight to Boston, I begged him to spend more time with me, but he subtly withdrew. In the apartment he became morosely preoccupied. When he found me in tears, he was impatient. "I can't live at this level of intensity that you want me to," he said, and turned to his books. He accompanied me to farewell parties and glumly denounced my friends as immature or as windbags and bores.

I was frantic as he pulled further and further away from me. He began to play mah-jongg all weekend and stayed out till late at night with different groups of people. At first I went with him, and sat beside him as he played. One evening, after he had been playing at a friend's house for hours, I walked out of the pleasant suburban home into the cool walled garden. The sun was close to setting. Impulsively I climbed a low branching tree. Perched on a fork I looked out at the green watered lawns and red tiled roofs of the exclusive housing estate. I was twenty-four, but finding myself in a stranger's home, waiting for Iqbal as he gambled with his friends, I remembered the Malacca childhood hours hidden in the mango tree branches. I was still waiting, still dreaming, still unhappy.

Once the decision was made to leave, events rushed onward as if without my volition. To pay for warm clothes, I taught evening courses at a private school which offered tutorials to students preparing for the A-level exams. I hated teaching the class. We were reading Shakespeare, and the students sat dazed through the hour, understanding nothing in the text and very little of my explication. Macbeth meant nothing to them, and their blank gazes forcefully conveyed to me the truth that English literature was meaningless in Malaysia except to anglophile freaks like myself.

On Friday May 13, we read the witches' scene, which in demon-haunted Malaysian society reads like a child's caricature of evil. "Tail of newt" and "eye of toad" were comic trivia beside what Malaysians whisper of blood-sucking *pontianak* and entrails-flying *hantu*. Doubly disturbed by this vision of my future career in English literature in Malaysia and by my confusion about leaving Iqbal, I stopped at the corner gas station. As I was pumping gas into the Honda tank, the attendant came up to me. "You better hurry home," he said.

All the street lamps were going out. I sped up the hill,

wondering about the uncanny darkness that had fallen over Petaling Jaya. Iqbal hugged me as I came through the door. "I was so worried about you," he said. "Didn't you hear? There's a curfew on."

All we had was the radio; without a telephone, we were cut off from news for the five days of the curfew. Over the radio, we heard that Malay counterdemonstrators, brought in from the *kampongs*—their rural villages—to protest against a Chinese postelection victory march, and armed with *parangs* and knives, the report said, to defend themselves, had turned violent. Much later, first through rumors and then through foreign news reports, we learned that streets of Chinese shop houses in Kuala Lumpur had been burned down and hundreds of Chinese killed. Later estimates placed the number at about two thousand massacred. The army was called in, but the Malay soldiers had been slow to stop the race riots and had allegedly shot at Chinese instead.

During the next few volatile days, to offer us some protection should the murderous attacks of ten miles move closer, a Malay professor and his white wife in the apartment below invited us to stay with them. She spoke passable Malay with a broad Irish accent, and among his small-boned mother and sisters shyly hanging back in the kitchen, she carried her fair babies like a Nordic giant. No one discussed the curfew. "Aish, the soldiers! They'll take care of things," she said carelessly as she brought out the domino set. I wondered at her concentration on the game and her lack of self-consciousness among her nervous sisters-in-law.

Two days later, the curfew was lifted for a few hours. Iqbal refused to leave the apartment building, but I was worried about Second Brother and insisted on riding to Chien's rented bungalow. He was safe with his wife and baby girl and scolded me for taking risks. Speeding back through the deserted streets, however, I knew that hiding out was not security. No place in Malaysia was a refuge as long as racial extremists were free to massacre and burn.

A palpable tension hung over the university community. The Chinese students and lecturers who usually did not mix with the Malays were even more visibly segregated. Miriam, the daughter of a Scots mother and Malay aristocrat, who was also completing her master's degree in the English department, said exultantly in one of those moments I carried with me for years like a scriptural passage, "We Malays would rather return Malaysia to the jungle than live with Chinese domination." She was simply expressing the strong racial antipathy to the economic success of Chinese Malaysians that was suddenly orthodox among Malays. To the question, how will Malaysia succeed without Chinese industry and labor, she replied, "We don't need the Chinese. We will be happy to sit on the floor if that's what it means to do without the Chinese!"

I looked at her angular features, surely inherited from her Celtic ancestors, and marveled at the ironies in her position. A tough, hardworking woman who was outspoken about her social snobbery and wealthy background, she appeared an unlikely voice for those protesting Malay poverty and dispossession; indeed, in an earlier age her aristocratic connections would have separated her from a parvenu like me. However, even after achieving independence, Malaysian society had remained structured on the meritocratic policies that Harold Wilson had implemented for Britain then, and on capitalist competition. Miriam, already poised high among the elite, had more directly to gain than less well-situated Malays in the change from democratic multiracial competition to Malay or Bumiputra privilege, presented as a kind of affirmative action carried out through strict quota systems and governmental preferential treatment.

In the process of the formation of a Malaysian elite, the May 13 riots provided the bloody revolution that changed Malaysia from the ideal of a multicultural egalitarian future—an ideal already tested by hostilities over power-sharing—to the Malay-dominant race-preferential practice in place today. Listening to Miriam's unrestrained words, even as I swallowed the humiliation of my position—to be informed that I was not an equal citizen, that my community was a "problem" and that race massacres were an appropriate way of dealing with that problem—I rebelled against the notion that I would have to submit to such attitudes. Sitting dumbly before Miriam, I thought that I might never return to Malaysia.

Almost twenty-five years later, I am still not certain that I made the right decision. Miriam was speaking from the blood victory of May 13; I was suffering the cowed paranoia of the defeated. It seemed easy then to walk away from a violated dream of a national future which included people like me—people not tied to race-based ideology, who were looking to form a brave new nation. Hundreds of thousands of Malaysians have also emigrated to Australia, Hong Kong, Singapore, Britain, Canada, and the United States. A young Malaysian, young enough to be my son, living in Oxnard, California, recently asked me to write of the pain of this aborted community, of the anger of people who unwillingly leave their country because of laws that discriminate against them. Yet now I understand that this story is only one part of the political narrative. The other story to which Miriam was speaking is of people who perceive the justness of their claim for special rights in an original homeland.

As I was struggling to make sense of the May 13 riots and of my ambivalence about leaving Iqbal, I was also trying to complete my thesis. With five chapters on Golding's novels written and only a few footnotes to write up, I handed the thesis to James. He had followed my break-up with Ben and attachment to Iqbal from a sardonic distance, permitting himself heavy-lidded glances and an occasional unsympathetic comment. At the same time, he remained friendly, if removed. The structure of the master's program did not encourage interaction between adviser and student, and, aside from reminders that I should be writing, he maintained little contact with me.

A few weeks before my departure, he sat across from me

in the Senior Common Room. Tamping tobacco into his pipe, he said, "Your thesis is very good!" A grateful relief washed over me. The anxiety of writing the master's thesis together with the messiness of leaving Iqbal had been dreadful.

"It's really quite brilliant," he continued. "In fact, it is publishable." I did not process this statement; all I could think was that he would approve the thesis and I would leave for the United States with the degree completed.

"Of course," he added, "it should be published in both our names, as I gave you most of the ideas and you merely followed up on them." Stricken, rising from my seat, I fled the room and ran into Iqbal who wondered why I was so upset. Later, I refused his advice to complain to Dr. Wismal about James.

It is easy now to see James's behavior as harassment from which I should have been protected. More difficult to explain is my refusal to ask for that protection and my silence since then. What is it that shapes women like me to forbearance in the face of bullies and oppressors, to flight and silence rather than justice in struggle and speech? Perhaps my parents' physical and emotional abandonment had led to my despair, to my profound distrust of any available protection. My childhood education, illuminating powerful adults as unloving, unjust, and violent, had driven me underground to avoid further damage, exchanging the hurts of trust for the hurts of futility.

I never finished those footnotes for the thesis. I carried the five chapters to the United States, and they lie unread in a file cabinet, a material sign of my abandoned academic future in Malaysia.

In 1969 I saw myself as a passive and innocent victim of the conflict between elites and races. After May 13, most events in Malaysia, whether public or domestic, were, and possibly still are, inevitably charged with a racialized dimension, whether in civil service or private business, whether professional or personal, economic or literary. However, even after this violent rupture, I held on to the necessity of art as aesthetics; the notion of living in a society where every aspect of one's life was unavoidably cathected in the political horrified me. I wanted social justice without having to struggle for it, a position I see now as available only to those already privileged.

After May 13, thousands of Malaysians like myself withdrew into mass depression. The censorship of news accounts, the compulsory black-out of commentaries and analyses, and the consequent governmental revisions of parliamentary rule to enact Malay domination only confirmed our paranoia. Twenty-five years after this trauma, however, millions of Malaysians of Chinese descent still resident in the country, and thousands more in a global diaspora, continue to bear witness to the ideal of an equitable homeland for all Malaysians.

Weeks before my departure for Boston, Iqbal had asked me to leave the apartment. Withdrawn and moody, he did not want to deal with either my tears or his feelings. The national anguish after May 13 echoed inside our own domestic division. I was leaving him voluntarily at the same time as I was unwilling to break up the relationship. My unhappiness could not be magnified further, and I enlarged on his failures, hoping that these would dissolve the bonds of dependency that made my leaving so fearful. Although I recognized that love was not a sufficient vocation and understood that a career held more promise for satisfaction than marriage, this strong feminist vision did not lessen the intensity of sexual and emotional attachment nor the hysteria at its loss.

Too proud to plead with Iqbal for shelter, I stayed with Karmal and his roommates, young Indian men who tried to cheer me up and saw that I ate occasionally. A few nights before my departure for the United States, I had a nightmare. At first I imagined I was lying on a cement floor which was borne up in the air by a layer of clouds. I felt simultaneously the cold hardness of the floor and the soft fleeciness of the clouds. Then the strongest fear came over me—the fear of being alone. I could not wake up out of this fear. As I whimpered in my room, Karmal heard me. "Hold me," I begged him. "I'm afraid." He must have held me for a long time. The total panic was like an accumulation of the pains of abandonment that had crowded my life, till I no longer understood the difference between abandonment and love, between the abandoned and the abandoner. Gradually, Karmal's thin warm body woke me out of the dream and the panic seeped away. So I have learned to ask for help from strangers.

Boarding the Boeing jet in Kuala Lumpur en route to Bangkok, then to Frankfurt, Amsterdam, London, and Boston, I was numb with misery. Iqbal had not come to the airport to say good-bye, and among the many friends who were there, there was no discussion of when I would return. In the airport lounge, gazing at the batik decorations intended for tourist consumption, I felt already the disconnection of the stranger. I would never see Malaysia again, except through the eyes of a traveler.

MARY LOMBARD

THE FINE ART OF COSMETOLOGY

Haven decided to get a haircut the day she saw herself in a hardware store window. She had been rushing down the street in her usual flurry when suddenly her reflection appeared through the letters of a home improvement sign. How apt, she thought.

A few years ago she would have laughed. Now she stopped to let the sight sink in. She wasn't a poet, obviously, though she had tried to be. She was nothing as lively as a hula dancer or a free spirit off the beach without a pair of scissors to her name. She was, simply, Woman with Hair. No wonder her students snickered.

Haven was late that day. A gust of wind picked up her denim skirt and blew her hair in front of her face. Vowing to get the hair cut soon, she loped on down the street. She was supposed to be sitting in the dentist's chair at the very minute she'd stopped to gawk, at herself, no less.

Not that she was trying to flee her image, but first things first, as her mother always said, and right now that was teeth. She ought to make a list. Teeth, eyes, breasts, grades, eggs and bread. And brakes. What else? Hair. This seemed easy, but like teeth, hair required an appointment. You had to plan, clear the way, call, mark it on the calendar, be prompt. And while you were marking time, time passed. She would do it, though. Soon. After groceries.

She made a mental note to call about the hair. As soon as Dr. Lum finished her bridgework. As soon as she had this batch of exams corrected and the summer stretching before her. She would wash it herself to save the shampoo charge. She would color it also. Then she would call. Or maybe she would whack it off herself.

But Haven had lately formed the habit of busyness. She had no time for her secret passion: writing poetry; no time for her secret indulgence: watching late night horror films. She had to catch up on her committee work and finish a report due at the end of the spring term entitled: "Committee Recommendations for Community College Developmental Voc-Tech Courses Submitted for Articulation for Entering High School Students." She had to review a pile of textbooks, as yet uncounted, and take turns driving to the university with another teacher from the windward side of the island for a class in holistic grading methods for college instructors. The course involved two texts totaling 1,105 pages, theory, research, reams of handouts, reports, a major paper. Haven was exhausted before the end of June.

She had already been applying many of the principles without calling them "holistic," and the professor, who had come from the mainland as much to soak up the Hawaiian sun and edit proofs of his new anthology as to teach, presented his material in a dry, superior manner and seemed incapable of taking into account the teaching experience of his fourteen mature students.

As a result, Haven felt stupid. She was tempted to let fall the fact that she had published nine poems, but when the opportunity appeared, she said nothing. She was reluctant to write a paper for this Yaley, so she put off her research, and then she had to ask for an extension. By this time, she was teaching a second summer session in American Lit and pinch-hitting for someone else in business English. Despite the fancy grading course, she was marking papers the same old way. She was giving out inflated grades and couldn't stop herself. I'm in a rut, she thought.

To make matters worse, she couldn't find the time to scout garage sales for decent used furniture. Except for shelves and books, Haven had tossed out all her living-room furniture along with everything that belonged to her mother and to her daughter. This happened last year after she lost her mother.

One month to the day before her mother died, she had lost her daughter. Both deaths came with the same terrible swiftness as the click in the back of Haven's head when they brought her the news and which she thought was the sky cracking open. The first from a four-car freeway collision at the Punahou Exit. The second from heart failure.

Regretting her hasty action, Haven wanted everything back that she had so thoughtlessly given away, especially an old rocker her mother had painted a rich, electric blue. She had complained of the color, accusing her poor mother of sitting in the chair so that she wouldn't have to face it, and would have thrown it out long before if she had not been vetoed by her daughter. Now that it was gone, however, she missed it, longed for a glimpse of that same vulgar, blazing, glorious, neon blue and had even begun to look for it, stopping to stare in stores or odd places, filling her eyes with various near blues, but never the blue, the glaring splash that was her mother's particular blue, the same blue her daughter declared "articulate." Because it was impossible to get the rocker back, and because duplicating the color in another chair was unthinkable, Haven lived in the kitchen, using the empty room only for her collection of grocery sacks full of aluminum cans and newspapers.

The summer was hot. At the end of the term, when everyone most needed clear heads and she was groggy from lack of sleep, the air-conditioner conked out. She had to take her students to the cafeteria for their finals where two fans kept the air moving, if not cool. Watching them bend over their papers on that day, Haven could not help but notice that even on the muggiest day of the year the men as well as the women looked clean-cut. They looked chic in their hair.

Haven could no longer put off the hair. She got as far as the yellow pages, but her head swam at the list of beauty salons, which she found outnumbered churches. Bars and restaurants also outnumbered churches. Gas stations outnumbered both churches and schools, but schools outnumbered beauty salons. This information seemed significant.

Once, late at night, inspired by a TV actress with chopped hair, she clipped a few wispy ends, but then she stopped. The house was absolutely still. Only the sound of snip, snip in her ear. The scissors were dull. They felt heavy in her hand. She had to put them away.

Growing her hair seemed the obvious solution. She had tried doing this once before in the sixties along with a brief attempt at marriage, but by the time the hair had reached her shoulders, she had given up on both. In those days her hair was a soft brown. Now it was coarse. The gray coiled like wire. It sprang up from her part as if born to fly. It was easy to forget about the hair.

Suddenly, the summer was over. She had to organize classes while writing up her research notes, and weeks passed before she called the Hare Parlor, finding the number only when she realized she had misspelled "hare." Then, just as she was about to ask for an appointment for the following week, she was flustered to hear the woman on the line say, "Now."

"You mean right now?" she repeated, feeling stupid. "Well, I suppose so, let me see," she said, stalling, noting busy voices in the background, the ring of the cash register, the speaker's comment to someone else about a cake in the fridge. "It'll take me half an hour. Hello? In half an hour?"

"You come in now, I take you because of the cancellation. Next week even I am booked."

Now was better than another time, of course. Next week she had a faculty meeting, and the hair was getting heavy. It fell forward when she corrected papers or chopped carrots. Bobby pins slid out and loose ends drifted into her eyes and fell all over the bathroom floor, eluding her when she tried to reach them with a wad of toilet paper and blowing under things and gathering dust so that by the time she got around to sweeping them out, they had formed balls. Balls of hair. "I'll leave now," she said. "Why not?"

Thirty minutes later, a plump man in silver hair and a black tee-shirt with the sleeves rolled high on his arms gestured at the chairs in front of the window. "Ursula'll be out in a jiff," he said.

Haven sat next to a table strewn with torn magazines. The Hare Parlor had been recommended by her neighbor, Mrs. Ohta. "Be sure to get Roger if you want style," she'd advised. Now Haven realized that she hadn't asked for Roger. Ursula was to cut her hair. The man at the desk would be Roger. She glanced away from the bright hair curving like a rat's tail over his shoulder.

The place smelled of chemicals. An open room with barber chairs ranged along two walls, each one facing a mirror. A reception desk opposite the door. The chairs occupied by women who chatted with the beauticians and each other like old friends, their banter rippling easily back and forth. A functional room, modest and conservative. Haven had gone to a beauty parlor once before, without knowing it featured "creative" cuts, an intimidating place of black walls, chrome and mirrors, and she had ended up with the back of her head shaved from her ears down. But this place looked friendly, like a neighborhood salon. She picked up a magazine.

Nearby, the man leaned against the reception desk arranging his silver tail and laughing with two women. The one with red hair was talking about furniture. Despite a knowing manner, she looked young in black tights and loose shirt. That's exactly the kind of outfit I need, thought Haven.

"He goes, 'You want it, hey, name it,' so I do and in it comes, this bookcase, which, to get it home, he has to go and rent this truck, and it keeps coming, chairs, lamps, yesterday this cute koa desk, every few days something else, and what I can't get over, no labels, no one keeping track."

From outside, two solemn children munching doughnuts stared blindly into the window. Haven returned to her magazine.

"The best part, he get time and a half for overtime, double for nights. You ought to get Calvin to apply down there." Their laughter rose. The woman shook her head so that her hair flared out. "Hey, is this red or not?"

"Comb it with your fingers," the man said. He poked at the hair, shoving it upward. "Use your palm. No, way-way-way, yah?" That beautician needs a diet, Haven thought. She watched the hands fussing with the hair, the blunt fingers. The young woman smiled dreamily as he pushed her limp head this way and that. "If we all had hair like yours there would be no problems in the world," he said.

The bell at the door tinkled, and the two women walked past the window. Haven didn't see the children. She wondered if they belonged to the woman with the furniture. She wondered how such a young mother could appear so perfectly at ease with herself in this complex world.

"Ursula'll be right out, I'll get her," the man said to Haven. He left through a curtain into a back room. Immediately, snatches of argument came from the back room.

Just as the thought occurred to Haven that she might slip away unnoticed, the curtain moved and a tall woman appeared. A vision in white. Dressed in gauzy white blouse loose over a full white skirt that floated about her ankles, the vision strode directly to the reception desk and draped itself over the appointment book. Blonde hair wrapped in a fat, gleaming braid about her head, like a careless halo, unstudied, artful. If I grew my hair, Haven thought, maybe I could wear it like that, a darker version.

"Someone, no name, at 11:45," the woman said, staring at the book.

The sudden feeling of a mistake came to Haven. Her stomach fluttered. "Oh, I think I neglected to leave my name."

"Rog will cut you. Today, I am errand woman." The vision swirled through the door. The bell tinkled.

The man appeared. He led Haven to a chair, fastened a white cape around her neck, and stared from behind her into the mirror. "Hm. You're growing it."

"Not really. I usually wear it short, but I've let it go. Yes, short. Whack it off, by all means."

"I thought you wanted a trim." He looked at the green watch on the inside of his wrist.

"If you're rushed . . . "

"Nah. I'd rather cut hair than eat lunch. It's the way I am, I love cutting hair, so don't worry, we aren't going to let you go yet. Turn that way." His silver hair glistened in the mirror. His face looked doughy, pallid under the brown skin. The thought occurred to Haven that if she touched him, her hand might sink into his flesh. "This wave real, yah?" He plucked at her hair. "'Kay, wet or dry? I don't like to do it dry, dry's bad."

"Oh, wet by all means."

"You keep saying 'by all means,' but we'll just do it wet, 'kay? "

"OK."

"First, we wash. This way. "

"Wash?" Haven felt foolish.

"Yah. We only do clean hair here. Nah, I'm kidding. It's the rule, though, you know what I mean? You never can tell."

"Of course," Haven said. She had washed her hair early that morning, but she would cut out her tongue before saying it now. She followed silver tail to a sink. Lying back with her neck in the groove, she thought of a French guillotine and wondered if she smelled bug spray or cologne. To avoid staring at the plump face so close to hers, she closed her eyes as he scrubbed. I'll rinse it out when I get home, she thought.

"Relax, 'kay?" he said.

In the barber chair, Haven sat with wet hair combed over her eyes while the beautician answered the phone and then washed his implements. In the mirror, her staring face above the white cape looked sallow. She looked old. Next to the mirror a certificate announced in Gothic script Roglio Kauikeaoulinui Pua's degree in cosmetology. "With Distinction," she noted. Closing her eyes, she wondered how much to leave for a tip. The woman in the next chair was talking about adding onto her lanai. "It's either that or eating in two shifts," she said. Haven's hair was now almost dry.

"'Kay, where were we? Oh yah, short." He was studying the mirror. While lifting his lip to suck on his teeth.

She watched his reflection, realizing with a little shock that she had expected to see tattoos under his black sleeve, that his arms looked naked without them. "I thought, a simple frame. With hair in back. I don't want a shaved neck."

"I'll go this far." He indicated the place below her ears. "Your hair grows way down low on your neck, but. Relax, kay? We'll try. Relax now, I won't shave you, no whacking."

Haven flinched slightly at the first snip.

"Hey, I'm not going to cut your neck."

"I'm sorry," Haven said. "I wasn't ready, I guess."

The beautician sighed heavily and put his scissors down. He combed her hair straight back, smoothing it firmly with his hand. "You have split ends," he said.

"No doubt."

"'Kay. Here I come with the scissors. You ready?"

"Yes."

"This your first time here, right?"

"Right."

"I can tell because you're stiff. Try relax."

"I've been trimming it myself, lately."

The snip came close to her ear. She felt the knot tighten in her throat. "I've been so busy lately, I . . . " Her eyes stung. They filled with tears. She wasn't thinking about anything in particular and suddenly the room blurred. She gripped the arms of the chair. How stupid.

"Lots of people hate to get haircuts," he said. "It's like they getting a vital part cut out. I can relate. But afterward, they look."

Haven clutched the Kleenex pressed into her hand and dabbed at her eyes. "I don't know what's come over me," she said. "I'm just tired, I'm OK now, really, I'm sorry."

"Nah." He began to snip again, in the back, slowly. "You

remind me of my Aunty Aulima," he said. "I can't help it, you do."

"This is ridiculous!" Haven blew her nose. While this man sucked his teeth and pushed her head around, the tears kept welling up, they kept rolling down her face and into her neck and under her shirt, and she couldn't stop them. She wadded the Kleenex into a ball and dabbed and blew and nothing stopped it, the flow became a stream, a flood, and she couldn't get up, she couldn't move.

"My Aunty Aulima," he was saying. "The dancer, yah? My hanai aunty. Her hair coming down to her waist, she will not even go get the ends singed. Come in, I tell, your ends frayed, you need a line, I'll fix you up free. But no, she like dancing, the ends all split and flying. She goes, 'I like it, my hair like that, whirling all round me, coming big, it's making my hips little.' 'Kay then, I tell to her, do what you want but stay outta the wind. The wind's bad."

"I'm not used to coming in, that's all. My mother used to do it and . . . " She broke off to breathe.

The spasms from deep in her chest were now little gasping sounds. The hardness there was growing, and she couldn't seem to contain it. It spilled out and filled the room and came back into her lungs hot and moist as she sat here fighting for air, drenched in sweat, swelling, drowning. Her chest, her head, her skin, every breath, hurt, and this man, his touch, every tug of his fingers, every clip, hurt.

She felt his fingers pressing into her forehead now and moving in hard little circles down the back of her head. The rumbling sound came from him. He was bending over her with his hard knuckles and humming. She could feel his voice box resonating. He was speaking low and she didn't know what he was saying. A Hawaiian lilt, his words flowing, incomprehensible. "What?" she said. "What?"

"Funny thing, my mom used to cut my hair too, in Waipahu. Five kids, 'as why, the cost."

That seemed to be what mothers did, along with a few

other things. If you took all the mothers in the world and counted the ones who cut hair, her mother would get the prize for fussiest. She would comb it out between each snip and do a lot of kneading. She would comb it up and down and stand back and squint and measure and snip and either rap her on the head or knead it like bread, depending on her mood, and snip and comb and comb. She was always trying to make a curl in front.

"She goes, 'Eh, you lōlō, sit still or I'm going to poke out your eye. She tells this in church, too. I am the kolohe in my family, but. My talent, my gift I get from this amazing woman, who got it from her mom. My kupuna wahine, yah? Like it's pass' down, skipping my aunty, all my sisters, landing on my shoulders so I have to carry it. Not the poking part though, I never poke my clients. I don't mean that like it sounds, yah? It's sculpting I mean, styling. Right now, I'm making a line here, under your ear. A line. You'll get used to it, we all do. Time, yah? And the back, shorter. 'Kay, nice and easy, now."

It wasn't always her mother. Sometimes her daughter would cut her hair. Her daughter was always in a hurry. Slow down, her mother used to say, you're not mowing the lawn. Now look! It's uneven in the front, let me do it. And she would have to sit under the towel blowing hairs out of her nostrils while her mother took a turn and her daughter commented. Her daughter always laughed at the way her mother had to use that silly ruler, and the other two always caught it. Oh, the way they would stagger around that kitchen laughing! Just laughing and acting silly.

He had rubbed something from a tube into her hair, and now he was clipping again, the sound muted, as if it came from far away. Closer was the rumbling motor at her head, the hand tilting her chin. She could hear him breathing, feel his warm breath in her ear, his words moving, his gentle pidgin rhythm. English words, local, Hawaiian.

She would cut her mother's hair, her daughter urging her to get on with it as she paused over the fragile pinkness of the scalp. Her daughter's hair was harder to cut; it was wild, thick, stubborn. She knew every whorl, of course, every bump and cowlick, the tender place at the part, the tiny bald spot over her left ear, the way her hair flashed on like a light when she walked in the sun.

Her daughter was the one with the gift for style in their family. Haven never had to think about such things, the child would tell her whenever her hair needed perking up or something. A "frame" she called it. Haven could hear her clear voice all over the house— time for a new frame, Mama. Time for a frame.

"I'm creating, 'kay?"

Clipping faster, he answered himself: "'Kay 'den." He was talking about his aunty now, a different aunty, the musical aunty who was so intent on making a good impression the first time she sang a solo that she swallowed the bug that flew in her mouth without missing a beat. Humming his words, crooning, he held her hair up between his fingers and snipped and told her about his cousin with thirteen kids who was desperate for one more. Clip, clip at her temples, the sides, the back. Handing her a Kleenex, he sprayed her face and hair with cool water and combed her ends out, snipping at the barest tips and talked about one of his sisters, the sister who got up every day at 4:00 a.m. to write stuff before going downtown to work as a paralegal. His hands stopped for a moment while he stared in the mirror. "It's like a drug the way she gets really cross if she cannot make her poem every single day."

She sat like a lump of clay under his probing fingers while he pressed her head against his warm paunch, clipped some more and, taking his time, massaged downward, her forehead, her neck, her shoulders and up again, harder, gouging, using the heel of his hand, his knuckles. "'As better," he said, turning her chair. "Loose, the bes' way. Ta da!" With a flourish, he whipped off her cape and held out a mirror. "How's it look?"

Haven swung her head and felt the coolness against the nape of her neck. He smiled at her from the mirror.

"Feels light, yah? 'Kay, every six weeks now. Ask for Rog." All business, he flapped his hand when she tried to speak. "Just keep outta the wind," he said. "The wind's bad." He whisked her off, led her to the desk, instructed her to comb her hair back when wet and forward when dry, recommended vinegar rinse and super-hold spray gel, told her she was doing good to stay away from peroxide and, as the phone rang, waved goodbye.

Outside the Hare Parlor, Haven paused to listen to a child whistle a familiar tune. She saw her daughter in the window. And she saw her mother. And then, finally, she walked away.

WING TEK LUM

POEMS AFTER WANG WEI

Empty Ridge

The din does not cease though no birds appear.
Atop this ridge the sun slants through pines
shadows swallowing the fractured light.
On the ground needles scatter in a dapple glow.

Returning Home

Through the valley, wind swirls treetops overhead.
Foragers follow the stream for kindling and berries.
In the surrounding ocean I know night approaches.
I take one last look at the aimless clouds.
Along my path are drooping ginger
and the pale hibiscus in its momentary bloom.
It is summer, and fledglings are learning to fly.
At my door I falter; sorrow bleeds through my heart.

Leaving the Island

At the pier we share dumplings.
You wonder if we will ever return.
Giving up, you say—
those blood red fields lead only to the grave.
Then go, never turn back,
though in this vast sea its waves roil white.

NOEL ABUBO MATEO

LAPU-LAPU IN NEW YORK, NEW YORK

Lapu-Lapu
killed Magellan
Lapu-Lapu got a fish
named after him
the others are small fry
tilapia and bangus
are little fish
in the big sea of Mactan
Lapu-Lapu
is the only one
with two names

like New York, New York
a city so nice
they named it twice

it wasn't exactly for being nice
that Lapu-Lapu got named twice

Magellan wished he was Columbus
better to be lost
and not be able to find
his ass from a hole
the size of India
than to be right
and end up getting beheaded
by a kris wielding
pissed off Pinoy with two names

Lapu-Lapu
a warrior so fierce

Magellan stuttered
and cried in tears

Lapu-Lapu was a badass
he did not negotiate

the dutch were lucky
they might not have bought
Manhattan for quite so cheap
if Lapu-Lapu was in charge
he'd have told them
to go fuck themselves (like a true new yorker would do)
twenty four dollars my ass
you dutch have always been cheap
no wonder they named
having your date
pay their own way
"going dutch"

the city would not be called
New York, New York today
it would be Lapu-Lapu instead
a city so nice
they paid for it twice
with their lives

Magellan tried to pull that shit
Lapu-Lapu said ah-ah
ferdinand circumnavigated his own neck
his head spun around so much
it flew off its axis

Lapu-Lapu
they named a fish after him

MICHAEL McPHERSON

THE LONG SWIM

Dark waters of evening blue
as we clear Pier 14, industrial
dock, round Aloha Tower and motor
slowly from under these high glass
and stone spires of the waterfront.
The low drone of the city is left
in the wake, replaced by this single
diesel and lapping sea against our bow.
There to port is the spot we called Flies,
named for the incinerator, a secondary left.
Not great but rideable, best at high tide.
Now we pass the better of Waikīkī's waves,
spindrift of a late spring swell.
Our course is toward the greatest of all,
Castle's, seldom seen to break these days.
Passing Public Baths and the Natatorium
a set rides under the hull, rises and
pitches over the reef known as the boneyard.
The long concrete seawall ashore marks
this spot we anchor. Petrels wheel in
the calm evening sky, drift down and light.
Brother shuts down the engine. I the elder
son take the calabash from my mother, unwrap
ti leaves and under the growing orange sky
pass my father's ashes through my fingers
out over these rolling waters. Papa, I say
to him watching him dissolve and become one
with the sea, guarantee tonight come big.
We leave for him garlands of ginger,
puakenikeni and pink plumeria, his mother's

favorite flower, watch as he drifts
with the current. Over the towers
of our city in the grey dancing light
next dawn, over the farthest reefs
first break Waikīkī, the summer waves
are huge, long and tall and green.

MICHAEL MCPHERSON

THE MAYOR OF ALA MOANA

The sweetheart of my reckless youth
phones me today and asks after you,
recalling your grace on green waves
we rode through those shining summers.
She and I speak once or twice a year,
and her voice now raspy with hard travel
sends memories tumbling forward in time.
The lines hum and I remember all of us young,
her stunning beauty captured in photographs,
the shot of you in the first *Surfer* magazine
extended like a hawk on a white Pūpūkea crest,
and once you came home so fat from Aspen
none of us knew you till we saw you ride.
Even forty pounds overweight you made us all
look bad, in the hot glare of high tide
afternoons you were smoothest of the best
in your own distinctive old Waikīkī style.
Our signature rider Joe Kolohe, effortless
prince of surfers and yours truly Buddyboy,
holding court on the rusty transformer box
and ever dapper waving a good bottle of wine.
But this time I must tell her some jogger
found you dead next to a loaded dumpster
at dawn in a chilly California beach town,
sitting upright in an alley behind a grocery
where paint peeled on the wall next to your head.
Santa Ana wind tossed scraps of black plastic
into cold corners of your final audience
among mangy stray dogs with protruding ribs.
Summer waves are gone to distant shores,

and our sad awkward silence on these wires
cannot carry us anywhere nearer you now.

MICHAEL MCPHERSON

TAPES

I've received your phone messages
and kept them all, years worth.
This archive contains voices dead
and dear, and much I've traveled
far to forget. Today I foolishly
played it all from start to finish,
lavished this afternoon on my back
listening to hear a long gone brother
of my heart, and the father I lost
last week. I find that in between
there are women. I must admit
there are lots of them. They call
for chocolate ice cream, for damaged
cars, cigarettes, directions, boyfriends
who've betrayed them, to hear how I am.
One offers a haircut. Another waits
on the bar. It's eerie.
I admit I find it easier
to love the dead. It's a mistake,
this electronic snooping on the past.
Voices in prison, voices grave,
streams of promises and forget me
nots, urgent requests,
cries against this restless
tide of our years toward what
we cannot know—Hello. I'm here.
Still waiting for your call.

WENDY MIYAKE

WONDER WOMAN AND MY JUNIOR PROM

My mother wanted a normal girl. One who dressed in pink ruffle dresses and played nicely with her Donny & Marie Osmond Barbie dolls. As a five-year-old, I was more ambitious. I would parade down our quiet street in red rain boots, a red flannel slip-on robe buttoned around my neck in cape fashion, plastic clip-on earrings and crayola decorated paper crown and power bracelets. I thought Wonder Woman was a fascinating character to live in but the neighborhood boys thought it was odd. My mother thought it was very odd. I guess sleeping in the costume was too much for her. Needless to say, I outgrew the Wonder Woman attire but I failed to outgrow a certain backwardness of my ways. Even something as traditional as a junior prom turned out unusual. Now that I look back on it, it was downright embarrassing.

In our narrow high school world, there were certain pre-prom scenarios that were acceptable. For example, boy meets girl, asks her friends to ask her to the prom, and then exists in eternal bliss and relief. My scenario unfolded into girl buys dress, earrings, shoes, gloves and bids in pure optimism of snagging a date. Unfortunately, in my mad rush to purchase all these items, I had forgotten about the existence of the Hierarchy of Social Greatness. Basically, this system worked if you were very skillful with pom poms, exuded a consistent aura of perkiness or were born with incredible bone structure, you sat in the coolness of this pyramid's summit. Few made this level. Few strayed from this level. I was somewhere in the middle of the pyramid where it was starting to crack under the weight. Although this would severely limit my choices, I told myself, "I am not worried."

I leisurely dialed the number of one of my guy friends.

He was a good Japanese boy: intelligent, tall, and a lot of fun. Notice the past tense verb. I thought he was all these things until I heard the tactful version of "no" spelled out to me over the phone. He said he was scheduled to work. Right. I wished I could have ripped off my golden truth lasso and squeezed his pudgy body until he fell over begging to tell the truth. However, in the spirit of optimism, I told myself, "I am not worried."

A few days later my best friend Eileen called. Ryan, another decent Japanese young man and our mutual friend, did not have a date yet. Wonderful. Unfortunately, Ryan means "No, don't ask me" in some distant European language. He said he didn't think it would work out. I wasn't looking for a four-month commitment but rather a fun night. Was it a part of my anatomy—too small here, too large there? What? The questions kept coming. Could you choose a part? Pinpoint the problem. At this point, I buried my nose into Leo Buscaglia "love yourself" books to keep my self-esteem up. I mumbled to myself, "I am not worried."

As the days dragged along, my dress began to sag in the closet as if trying to empathize with me. The bids were crinkled from my constant fingering of the pages. Now my father, my brave father, was disgusted at seeing me deep in the trash barrel of life. He asked me, "Do you want me to ask Scott?" I was on the couch staring blankly at the darkened television screen. I turned to him with red, swollen eyes and said:

"I don't know." This was my dream to avoid the heart wrenching rejection and all I could say was "I don't know" because at this point I did not care. My father took that as a "yes" and marched over to our neighbors, the Marumotos, like a determined superhero. As I watched him approach their rust house on the corner, I saw his shoulders droop as if all that super power had been sucked out of him by the impending deed. Scott was watering the front yard. "Hi Mr. Iwamoto."

"Um . . . ya . . . hi . . . uh I don't know how to ask you this . . . and he he . . . and . . . uh I-I don't usually ask these uh questions.. but . . . well, you see . . . " His voice trailed off and he began wringing his hands like an intimidated child.

"Yes, what is it?"

"Well . . . my daughter . . . y-you know the one who lives in my house. Yah, well . . . she uh bought this beautiful white dress, see, and ah . . . these bids you see . . . and I-I'd hate for it to go to waste and . . . ."

"I'd be glad to take her."

"And she has these pretty gloves that go with the dress . . . and oh I don't know how to say this . . . "

"Mr. Iwamoto, I'll take her."

"You will?" my father's eyes were wide like a child's at Disneyland.

"I'll give her a call later, okay?"

"Thank you. Thank you so much." And with that my father practically skipped all the way home. He pushed open our front door and said, "Praise Buddha." I knew that he had said "yes."

Scott was twenty at the time and he had been very popular at Mililani High School. He sat atop that pyramid with all the other nice football players. He did not gain his popularity by being a rebel or a major athlete but rather he gained it by his gentleness toward women. He's been a gentleman all his life. In fact, I do not remember him laughing at my Wonder Woman costume when I was young.

That night when we stepped into that enormous ballroom, people looked and they smiled. I smiled back. Scott smiled. The place looked like a wedding reception with candles, peach napkin fans and tons of flowers. It made me wonder if anything could be this blissful in my entire life. We ate, we danced, and the whole time we were the life and energy behind this night. We even led the whole dance floor in a rendition of square dancing.

When we drove home that morning, a cool aura draped over me like a shawl. For the first time in my high school life, I could feel the cool breezes of the pyramid's summit. I may have mistaken the air conditioning for this feeling but even in the warm morning air, I felt like I had reached this peak. We got to my front door. Scott stood holding my hands. "My Wonder Woman," he said as he kissed me lightly on the lips. I smiled, covering the peephole with my hand. My mother wouldn't need to know he kissed me again.

WILLIAM STARR MOAKE

MEMORIES OF A PLACE CALLED THE SEVEN

*"The past is a foreign country.
Things are done differently there."*
—L.P. Hartley

Uniquely beautiful places haunt the memory like a dream that happened to someone else in another time. You can choose to leave such a place, but it never really leaves you. It remains a part of your internal landscape, the perspective from which you judge all other places, and it changes you forever.

For me the turning point was Nāhiku, a tiny and remote jungle community above the northeast coast of Maui in the Hawaiian islands.

Perhaps it was serendipity that Nāhiku had been a center of learning celestial navigation in ancient Hawai'i. Nāhiku means "the seven" in the Hawaiian language and refers to the Seven Sisters constellation of stars by which Polynesian sailors navigated the Pacific Ocean.

In hindsight it's easy for me to believe I was unconsciously following some kind of star the first time I saw Nāhiku in the spring of 1972. I was on leave from the Air Force at the time and, on the advice of a friend, I rented a car at Kahului airport and began driving down the narrow and winding Hāna Highway.

I was positively awestruck by the scenery: jungled valleys and steep lush gorges rising out of the sea in a staggering profusion of tropical vegetation, with waterfalls cascading into pools at nearly every turn. The intense greenness of the landscape was almost blinding as the sunlight flashed strobe-like through breaks in the dense canopy. I recall that my mouth hung open for such a long time on that drive I actually got a sore jaw.

This was the Hawai'i I had always dreamed about, but was never sure really existed. I wanted so much to live there I could practically taste it. But at the same time I couldn't imagine any possible way I could make such a miracle happen, which evoked an odd sense of nostalgia for a place I was seeing for the first time.

Nāhiku itself was a rather unobtrusive scattering of houses strung along the Hāna Highway just before the road descended to the coastal lowlands leading into the village of Hāna. I hardly took notice of Nāhiku that day, thinking it had nothing to do with me. First impressions can be that wrong.

* * *

As luck or fate would have it, the impossible dream came true two and a half years later.

After reading Thoreau for months, I made the most momentous decision of my life. I decided to chuck the security of a steady paycheck and trade it in for a freer life in the wilds of East Maui. I quit my reporter's job at the Maui News, packed everything I owned into a jeep station wagon, and headed down Kīhei Road.

On the way out of Kīhei, I stopped off at a store to get some beer for the drive. An old man named Gus was sitting on a folding chair outside the store.

"Looks like you're moving," he observed.

"That's right," I said.

"Where to?"

"Nāhiku."

"Well," Gus said with a big grin. "Don't rust."

As I drove away from sunny Kīhei, I knew exactly what he meant. They didn't describe Nāhiku as a rainforest for nothing. It started raining even before I reached the windy part of the Hāna Highway. I turned on the windshield wipers and began thinking about my situation as I steered around the curves.

When I gave my notice at the newspaper, some of my

fellow workers treated me as though I had suffered a nervous breakdown. They spoke in funeralistic tones about my future. I didn't know whether to laugh or weep or get angry. However, one understanding friend at the newspaper had secured a temporarily free house for me in Nāhiku. She saved me from attempting a Waldenesque escape to the uninhabited back side of the island, which I am convinced would have been a huge mistake.

The closer I got to Nāhiku, the harder it rained. Although I had directions, I could barely see the road and drove past the house before I realized I had missed it. I doubled back and pulled into a short driveway between two houses. In the garage I could see two men, one sprawled under a jacked-up truck with an arc welder and the other watching him work from a squatting position.

I dashed into the garage and introduced myself nervously. The older man crawled out from beneath the truck and lit a cigarette.

"You're the kid from the newspaper," he said.

I was 30 and hadn't been called a kid for some time, but I nodded anyway.

Even wearing a baseball cap, Carl Polk looked like a soldier. I learned later he had been a Green Beret lieutenant colonel in Vietnam, and had a battle scar under his chin to show for it.

The other man was a part-Hawaiian named Glen. He offered me a beer and said: "You're gonna love it out here, brah. The bush is the best place to be. I wouldn't live anywhere else."

The colonel pointed to the old house on the other side of the driveway. "That's your place over there," he said. "It ain't much, but at least it's dry."

When I complained about the heavy rain, they looked at each other and laughed.

"No more rain, brah," Glen told me in pidgin English. "It's da kine liquid sunshine."

That night I drank too many beers at Colonel Carl's house

and met his diminutive wife, Lan, who spoke with such a thick Vietnamese accent I hardly understood a word she said. Sometime after midnight I borrowed a flashlight and staggered through the driving rain to the old house next door. I stripped my wet clothes off and went to sleep naked in a bed that had been made for me by total strangers.

* * *

One of the first things I learned about my new home was that it had been built by the very same man who supervised the landscaping of the Hāna Highway during the 1930s. This did not seem like a coincidence to me. There I was living in the house of a man whose wizardry with tropical plants cast a spell over me in 1972. I began to believe I was destined to be in Nāhiku.

But my new-found faith was sorely tested as it continued to rain every day and all night long for the first three weeks I lived in Nāhiku. Without pause the rain fell straight down when there was no wind and blew horizontally when the wind kicked up. The four-foot overhang on the roof was no protection. Inside the house I watched the driving rain seep through the window panes, drip down the wall and form little puddles on the floor. I mopped up with a towel and stared helplessly as the water pooled again in seconds.

Every time I went outside I was soaked to the skin before I could reach the car. I draped my wet clothes over a line in the house only to see them sprout white mildew by the next morning. A feverish mix of desperation and depression overwhelmed me as I sloshed around in the mud outside, waiting for the rain to stop. I wondered if I would have to grow gills to be able to continue breathing in this climate. I asked myself what in the hell was I doing there.

And then something totally unexpected happened. It sneaked up on me ever so slowly, like a cane spider creeping down a wall.

For some reason I actually began to enjoy the rain. At first

I didn't want to admit it to myself because it went against my upbringing. Where I came from, people were supposed to dread the downpour and pray for sunny days. But then I started to notice how soundly I slept each night with the rain drumming on the metal roof. Nobody ever dropped off quicker or got a better night's sleep than I did listening to that mesmerizing drone. It was like a sleeping pill from Mother Nature herself. (I actually suffered a bout of insomnia one time later during a rare drought.)

I was surprised to notice that very few people ever wore raincoats in Nāhiku. That's because the residents had their own way of dealing with the wet. If it was raining and you had something to do outdoors, you simply went outside and did it—then came back inside and changed into dry clothes. Chances are you would never feel cold if the task required any kind of exertion. The rain was always fairly warm and body heat counted for a lot in Nāhiku.

The tempo of life in that part of the island seemed to be tied somehow to the squall lines that rolled in endlessly from the ocean. Everything occurred (or didn't) on a happenstance schedule known as Hawaiian Time: yes meant maybe, and maybe meant much later or possibly never. It all sort of depended upon the weather and daily prospects for fishing or hunting.

Many haoles (whites) can't handle Hawaiian Time, but I took a philosophical view of it from the beginning. Why beat your head against a brick wall? Besides, I discovered it was fun living on Hawaiian Time once you get accustomed to it.

The rainy weather gave Nāhiku the moodiest atmosphere of any place I have ever lived. The brooding clouds were a perfect reflection of the dark mango trees and guava thickets that dominated the jungle landscape.

But on those rare sunny days in Nāhiku, when the clouds evaporated like a parting of veils, no place on earth could look so brilliantly beautiful. That's when I felt like a pilgrim who had stumbled into the holy land of his dreams.

* * *

Even though the free house lasted much longer than I expected, I was dismayed to learn that rental houses were as scarce as droughts on that side of the island. After eight months of living "inside," as the locals referred to it, I faced the depressing prospect of returning "outside" to that other world at the opposite end of the Hāna Highway.

I had given up looking for a rental and was already saying my farewells when I was contacted one day by a Hāna man who was a stranger to me. He wanted to know if I would like to rent his deceased relative's house in Nāhiku for $100 a month.

Saved on almost the last day! I couldn't believe my good luck. As it turned out, however, luck had nothing to do with it. I discovered later the house was offered to me through the intervention of a Portuguese family with whom I had become friends.

I had met the owner of the house shortly before he died. His name was also William, and he was reputedly the descendent of an American Indian sailor who had jumped ship to marry a Hawaiian lady. William and his wife had homesteaded the place until death took them within a short time of each other.

It was an old ramshackle house on two and three-quarter acres of land between a stream and a small bamboo forest. A single story wooden structure, the house had four bedrooms, a combined kitchen/living room, one bathroom, a large workroom and a carport.

The front yard was fenced and covered with the kind of mowed weeds that passed for a lawn in Nāhiku. The back yard was something out of a fairy tale: a riot of flowering plants and banana trees half swallowed by the encroaching jungle, rabbit hutches and pig pens cloaked in sweet potato leaves, liliko'i (passionfruit) vines dangling everywhere. The land sloped down to the edge of a dense forest that stretched for a mile to the cliffs above the ocean.

On my thirty-first birthday I moved into the house with the help of a couple I knew from "outside" and a young woman I had met recently in Nāhiku. We cleaned house all day and then shared a home-cooked meal and some good wine to celebrate. They stayed overnight to help me feel at home in my new residence. It was probably my happiest birthday ever.

As a lifelong city dweller, I made some stupid mistakes in those first few months of learning how to homestead. For one thing, I found out it was foolish to try to clear much acreage with a machete. I settled for a modest vegetable garden next to the pig pen. With advice from my neighbors and very little work, I was able to harvest a surprising amount of vegetables every couple months.

I soon discovered that a homesteader's work is never done. There is always something to fix or some new problem to deal with. The moment you think you have everything running smoothly at last and smugly congratulate yourself on a job well done—that's inevitably when all hell breaks loose.

Like the time I was wrestling with my girlfriend in the living room and my foot suddenly crashed through the floor.

"My God, I think we have termites," she said.

Another friend had no doubts at all. "This isn't a house," he said. "It's a bunch of termites holding hands."

I didn't care what anyone said. I loved that funky old house more than any place I had ever lived, and I wasn't going to soak it in poison as everyone recommended. Instead, I made a sort of peace pact with the termites in my own mind: if they ate only nonessential parts of the house henceforth, I would leave them alone. The termites never bothered me again.

The house had the only good television reception in all of Nāhiku, but even so I watched very little TV. After being a night owl for years, I quickly got into the habit of going to bed early and rising at dawn. With the physical labor I was doing every day, it just came naturally to me and felt like a normal cycle of life in the tropical rainforest.

Necessity may not be the actual mother of invention, but

they are close blood relatives when you live in a place like Nāhiku. The house had large propane tanks for the stove and water heater, and when the Hāna supplier stopped making deliveries, I tried cooking on wood campfires in the carport. That got old fast and I finally bought a kerosene stove.

Since I no longer had hot water in the house, I decided to bathe in the stream pool at the lower end of the property. At first the water seemed too cold, but I reminded myself that the original Hawaiians managed to survive quite successfully without hot water baths. Eventually I got used to the invigorating chill and to this day cannot stand hot baths or showers.

Of course there was another reason to bathe in the picturesque privacy of nature. The surrounding scenery looked so much like paradise I always left my outdoor bath cleansed in spirit as well as in body.

* * *

I remember the residents of Nāhiku as the most diverse group of people I ever encountered in one small place. When I close my eyes and think of them now, I see a kaleidoscope of colorful and eccentric individuals who seem larger than ordinary life.

The Medeiros clan traced their Nāhiku land holdings back to the Prohibition era when their forebears sold home-brewed alcohol for fun and profit. Because of that, elder Frank Medeiros displayed a forgiving attitude toward the young longhairs who grew marijuana in Nāhiku for the same reasons.

Skippy Young came from Hawaiian and Chinese ancestry, and his father owned a big chunk of land in Nāhiku. Nicknamed "Pineapple" when he was in the Army, Skippy later sold pineapple-laced hamburgers to tourists from a stand in front of his place. After tasting his burgers myself, I was sure this was a sneaky kind of revenge for the nickname.

Several other haole paradise-seekers besides me made their home in Nāhiku. Among them were surfer Mike, whose brother Pat and four other men were lost at sea; Chris and Tim, two southern Californians trying to escape from that rat race; Juanito, whose family hailed from Puerto Rico; a cowgirl named Susie who raised pigs; an aging hippie named Rainbow, who bought land right down the road from Colonel Carl.

And then there was Bully, a pure-blood kanaka Hawaiian whose family had lived for countless generations in the village of 'Ula'ino below Nāhiku.

A mountain of a man in physical stature, Bully came close to being a living legend in that part of Maui. His given name was Solomon. Bully was the nickname he got as the "bull" or strongest kid when he was a student in Hāna school. Once, when I questioned his claim to strength, he deadlifted the rear end of my jeep two feet off the ground and laughed at my astonishment.

Yet I have never met a kinder man than Bully. With a smile missing some teeth, he was always ready and willing to help anyone who needed help. As big and strong as he was, the most noticeable thing about Bully was the size of his heart.

* * *

"Hāna is a state of mind, an aura. As
soon as I get to Ke'anae, I want to
slow down and look at the flowers.
How do you explain paradise? You can't.
You just have to go out there and feel it."
—former Maui Mayor Hannibal Tavares

Early on I heard about a special place called the Muliwai. People spoke of it in hushed tones, as if they were protecting a secret. My curiosity led me to discover that the Muliwai was a waterfall and pool about a mile below the house I had rented, and was so named because of the peculiar blue color of the pool water.

One day I got directions from a neighbor and started walking through the bamboo forest. The vertical cluster of bamboo trees made me feel dizzy, but I was soon under giant mango trees trying to follow a trail that seemed to disappear at every turn.

Along the way I kept telling myself it was impossible to get lost in Nāhiku because there were basically only two directions—uphill to the road and downhill to the ocean.

In no time I was hopelessly lost on the flattest piece of ground I had ever laid eyes on. My hiking boots were caked with mud from the previous night's heavy rain and I couldn't tell which way was up or down. I sat on a rock to contemplate the possibility of spending a night in the bush without food or drinking water.

Then I noticed the rock I was sitting on was actually part of a rock wall, what looked like the remnants of a house foundation. The sight of it made me feel safe again. If people used to live here, I told myself, I can't be that lost.

When a beam of sunlight broke through the canopy in the distance, I followed it until I heard the familiar sound of waves. A moment later I emerged from the trees and found myself standing on a cliff overlooking the ocean.

Remembering the directions my neighbor had given me, I took the switchback trail down the cliff and ran into a rock slide that had buried the path. I was too close to turn back, so I turned to my left and started making a new path through tall grass. At one point when I was walking directly downhill I stopped for some reason and made a wide circle to the left before proceeding. A few seconds later I discovered I would have fallen twenty feet from a hidden ledge if I had continued on my original path.

Feeling lucky to be alive, I descended at last to a boulder beach and there it was: a waterfall cascading into a pool only a few yards from the pounding ocean surf.

The pool water truly was a strange color of blue, and I noticed watercress growing up the cliff wall. I stripped naked, dove into the pool and swam beneath the falling water. It was so cold it took my breath away. I climbed out of the water and tasted a sprig of watercress. It was bittersweet and slightly hot.

"Excuse me," a voice came out of nowhere.

I spun around and saw a Hawaiian woman clad in the traditional wrap-around dress. Embarrassed, I jumped back in the pool to hide my nudity.

"What are you doing here?" she wanted to know.

"Nothing," I said. "I just wanted to see the Muliwai."

"Well, for goodness sake," she scolded. "Put some clothes on."

When she disappeared behind a large boulder, I climbed out of the pool and slipped into my trousers and shirt, feeling like a naughty little boy. I was trying to think of what to say when I walked around the boulder and discovered the Hawaiian lady had vanished.

Strangely, I never saw her again even though I later got to know all the people who lived in that area.

But I returned many times to the Muliwai, usually with the excuse of collecting some watercress to enliven my meals. The real reason, of course, was the sheer joy of visiting such a magical place. Every time I hiked back home from the Muliwai I felt like a new person.

* * *

Everyone in Nāhiku had cats. They were considered a necessity because of the legions of rats and mice which were waiting in the bush to take over any house.

For some reason I always disliked cats and had never had one as a pet, but all of that changed one night when I was obliged to help a mother cat who was having difficulty giving birth. I couldn't help but feel like a godfather to those kittens and that marked the beginning of my love affair with the feline species.

I started with two cats and ended up with seven. Most were tame and friendly, but one was so wild she would literally climb the walls when anyone except me entered the house. They were all good pets and I never once had a rat or mouse in my place.

Having lived in Florida, where there are several types of poisonous snakes, I was very grateful that Hawai'i has no snakes of any kind.

But we had our share of other creepy-crawlies in Nāhiku. The most dreaded was the centipede, an eight-inch long insect with large fangs and powerful venom to match. I was bitten by one in my sleep and woke up in excruciating pain that felt like a blowtorch on my forehead. For a week afterward my face was swollen and discolored, and I still have a tiny scar where the bite festered.

Less common was a small scorpion which preferred to live in the bush instead of houses and had a sting no worse than a honey bee.

Although not poisonous, the bane of every household in Nāhiku was the giant cockroach, a two-inch variety which had the bad habit of flying around and landing on the nearest human body when disturbed. Cane spiders with a leg-span the size of one's fist were never killed by old-timers because they ate other insects. Farther up on the food chain were the geckos, small beige-colored lizards who hunted insects and even ate their own kind in territorial disputes.

Sometimes, when I really paid attention to what was going on in my house, it seemed like a combat zone for lower forms of life.

Outdoors, one kind of mosquito worked the day shift and another kind came out after dark. After a while I became somewhat immune to their bites as most people eventually do. I was pleased to learn that mosquitoes in Hawai'i are not known to carry human diseases, although they do transmit dog and bird diseases.

There was an ugly toad common in Nāhiku that I was prepared to hate when I heard it could kill any dog or cat that ate one. But I made peace with the Bufo toads the first time I saw one swallow a huge centipede. With a few gulps that 'pede was gone and I had a new friend in the animal kingdom.

I bought a Cuban rooster and hen from a neighbor who

raised fighting cocks. I let them run loose, fed them grain and in no time I had a flock of 17 chickens. Every morning I went looking for eggs. Usually they were under the house, but I also found some "hidden" in the middle of the front yard. Some of the hens weren't too bright.

The Cuban roosters were fierce defenders whenever a mongoose would try to grab one of the chicks. But I found out the hard way you can't have two cocks in the same flock. I got slashed on the arm one day trying to separate two roosters who were fighting. I shot the loser and ate him in a stew.

When my flock began to dwindle, I couldn't figure out what was causing it. Then I saw a stray dog running away with one of my last chickens in his mouth and I knew what I had to do.

I shot the dog and buried him. Later I found out that dog had been dropped off in my neighborhood by people who lived miles away and didn't want to feed him anymore. I felt like a damn fool for shooting the dog instead of his irresponsible owners.

* * *

About a year into my Nāhiku residency, I reached into my front pocket one day and pulled out a quarter and two dimes. It was the last cash I had left to my name. The sight made me shudder and sent little streams of panic flooding through my brain.

Looking at those three coins as if they had somehow betrayed me, I took a quick mental inventory of my situation. On the plus side the rent was paid for the next month and the vegetable garden was producing better than expected. But I was broke for the first time in my life and I had no job prospects in sight.

My taste buds protested every time I considered becoming a vegetarian. I was used to eating meat and I began thinking specifically about pork.

I decided there was only one solution to the problem:

Benzedrine Benny, arguably the best pig hunter on that side of the island. Benny and I had worked together on a ranch the previous summer and I had given him that nickname because he was always so alert and active in everything he did. Naturally he hated it, and to get even, he called me by a Hawaiian name that meant slacker. We were quite the odd couple trading barbs and stringing barbed wire through the jungle.

I telephoned Benny and asked him if he would teach me how to hunt wild pigs. To my surprise he said yes and told me where and when to meet him.

I showed up that morning with a .22 caliber rifle and a big knot of fear in my stomach. Benny had a high-powered rifle and two hunting dogs who didn't seem to like me much.

"What's that?" Benny asked, pointing to the .22 with a look of contempt.

"It's my gun," I said.

Benny laughed and shook his head. "You didn't need to bring a gun," he said.

"How can I shoot a pig without a gun?"

"You just keep the safety on," he warned. "I don't want you shooting me in the back if you get excited."

Benny sent the dogs ahead with a shout command and we started up the hill from the road. The dogs disappeared into a guava thicket. As we followed, Benny outlined his philosophy of handling hunting dogs.

"A lot of hunters won't feed their dogs before they take them hunting. They think it makes them meaner or better hunters. But I don't believe that. Dogs are no different than people. If you and I were hungry right now, we wouldn't have the energy to climb this hill so fast."

Trying to keep up with Benny's pace, I was glad I had eaten a big breakfast. He pulled a bundle out of his pocket and showed it to me.

"I always carry needle and thread and some disinfectant," he said. "In case the dogs get cut and I have to sew them up."

As that knot in my stomach grew larger, Benny recalled he once killed a wild pig but ended up carrying his badly-wounded dog down the mountain instead of the pig.

"My dogs come first," he said.

"Too bad you lost the pig," I said.

"I didn't lose anything," Benny replied. "I went back the next morning and got him."

"Wasn't the meat spoiled by then?"

"I sunk him in a stream with rocks. You know how cold that water is. And the flies can't get to the meat if it's under water."

I made a mental note of this storage technique in case I ever got more than one pig while hunting alone.

By then we were far above the highway and I was catching my second wind when Benny stopped and put his finger to his ear. At first I couldn't hear anything, but when I concentrated, I detected a faint sound in the distance.

"They got something!" Benny hollered, then bolted up the hill so fast he was out of sight before I could get my legs working. This was a particularly steep incline covered with trees and the limbs smacked me painfully in the face as I ran. Somewhere ahead I could hear dogs bellowing a deep throaty sound that scared the hell out of me.

I came over the ridge just in time to see one of the dogs go sailing through the air as a huge black monster of a pig flung his head to one side. The dog landed with a yelp, bounced to his feet, and dashed back to put a bite on the pig's ear. The other dog had a firm grip on the pig's tail. Benny stood at my left, his head bobbing as he tried to get a clear view of the battle.

With black hairs bristling on his back, the pig suddenly spun around and let out a horrendous noise, but the dogs continued to hang on.

Then Benny did something my mind could not accept.

"Here!" he shouted, thrusting his rifle at me. "Hold this!"

In a state of shock I reflexively took the rifle and saw Benny pull out his large hunting knife. What followed seemed to happen in a kind of dreamlike slow motion. Climbing the trunk of an uprooted tree, I watched in disbelief as Benny jumped on the back of the pig as if he intended to ride it. With one fluid movement he cut the pig's throat with his knife and leaped off.

I couldn't believe what I had seen. I crawled down out of the tree and watched the muscular animal quiver in its death throes. It was a 200-pound wild boar with sharp tusks protruding from its lower jaw.

I had to ask, "Why the hell didn't you shoot it?"

"My dogs are gun-shy," Benny explained. "The noise hurts their ears and spooks them. They'd still be running if I had fired the gun. I never use it unless I have to."

When the pig stopped moving, he squatted and lifted its head to show me something.

"See how the ears are almost gone? This is an old boar. Probably killed a few dogs in his time."

Silently and with a queasy stomach, I watched Benny field dress the pig. First he cut off the head and set it aside. Then he made a cut from the groin to the upper chest and carefully removed the intestines, stomach, heart and lungs. He cautioned it was very important not to puncture the bladder because a boar's urine would spoil the smell and taste of the meat. Finally he tied front legs to hind legs with rope, slipped his arms through the tied legs and hoisted the pig carcass onto his back the way other people would put on a backpack.

It would be an exaggeration to say that "we" carried the pig down to the Hāna Highway. Benny carried it the first half mile or so and then said it was my turn. Sitting on a log, I slipped into this hairy backpack and tried to stand up. Even field dressed that carcass must have weighed more than 100 pounds, and I immediately fell backward over the log.

Benny laughed and said: "You gotta do better than that."

Later I was able to manage a couple hundred feet at a time before my legs buckled, then Benny would carry it for a much longer period. Every time I had the backpack on I could feel the blood dripping down into my shorts.

"Soak your clothes in bleach water when you get home," Benny told me. "That will get rid of the bloods stains and ukus."

"The what?"

"The ukus," he said. "You know, pig lice."

Yuck!!!

By the time we reached the truck with that lousy pig carcass, I had a new respect for Benny's physical strength. Although he was slightly shorter than me and had a slender build, he was obviously much stronger than I was.

When we got the pig to Benny's family house that day, his relatives were ready and waiting. They de-boned the meat so fast I could hardly believe my eyes. It was like an assembly line from the cutters to the wrappers to the two deep freezers. The family never had to buy meat at the store because Benny kept them well supplied with wild pork.

I took part of a ham and some ribs home from that first hunt and found wild pork to be delicious if cooked properly. It was much leaner than domestic pork and had a taste more like beef.

As it turned out, the wild pigs I killed provided the only meat I had to eat during a six-month period when I had no money for store-bought.

At first I hunted without dogs and had surprisingly good luck running into wild pigs while hiking alone through the rainforest. Later I was given two of the most unlikely-looking canines who ever turned into hunting dogs.

Tote was an old spayed part-Labrador who had grown up on the docks in Honolulu. Brown Dog was a young male who looked and behaved very much like a fox. Compared to the ferocious breeds that most hunters used, these two dogs were an absolute joke as hunting dogs.

I don't know how they did it, because I never did anything to "train" them, but Tote and Brown Dog somehow knew we were looking for wild pigs the first time I took them into the bush and every time thereafter. I suppose it proves that all dogs have an instinct for hunting.

For two years I hunted wild pigs with Tote and Brown Dog. During that time, they got increasingly better at it without ever once being hurt themselves or putting me in danger. They always cornered the pig long enough to allow me to get off a good shot. Unlike most hunting dogs, they wouldn't touch raw pork and only ate some later after I had cooked it.

Since I never tied them up, after awhile they learned to go out in the bush by themselves. I would wake up at daybreak and see them limping home, exhausted and covered with mud after a long night's adventure. By noon of the same day they would be eager to follow me back into the bush if they saw me carrying the .22 rifle.

I took pride in being marksman enough to kill a pig with the first shot so he wouldn't have to suffer needlessly. One day I missed where I was aiming and hit a pig in the snout instead of the temple. Wounded, he splattered blood in my face as he ran past me to escape the pursuing dogs. I had to shoot the pig several more times before he died.

Wild pigs are not native to Hawai'i and have caused massive ecological damage to the rainforests there. Even so I decided that day I had had enough of killing them. It was the last time I ever went pig hunting.

* * *

Like pig hunting, fishing was much more than a hobby in East Maui. Besides putting food on the table, fishing was something akin to a religious experience and I caught the obsession soon after I arrived in Nāhiku.

Since very few people could afford to own a boat, the kind of fishing most of us practiced was from shore. The best shore fishing was usually in remote spots that were difficult or even dangerous to reach.

One exception was a tiny island in the mouth of Hāna

Bay where I had some of my best luck. From the pier it was a short walk to a footbridge and then a climb over the rocks to the side of the island facing the open ocean.

The channel between the mainland and the island was only a few feet wide, but I always felt as though I were boarding a sailing ship whenever I crossed that gangplank of a bridge. More than once when the sea was rough, I imagined I could feel the lava roll beneath my feet like the deck of a ship.

I usually brought a large spinning rod and reel and at least one bamboo pole cut from the forest near my house. On the spinner I used 40-pound line and floated my bait as far offshore as the wind and currents would take it. The best bait was baby akule (halalū), a kind of Hawaiian mackerel. The bamboo poles had tiny hooks and I fished directly below the lava shelf where I stood in water that dropped off from 40 feet to 200 feet in a short distance.

The unusual depth of the water so close to shore explains why I caught 'ōpakapaka (brown snapper) and hooked into kāhala (amberjack) and mahimahi (dolphin fish) when these fish are normally caught only from boats.

I landed an amazing variety of smaller fish with the bamboo poles as well. Besides the 'ōpakapaka, I caught uku (gray snapper), pāpio (baby jack cravelle), po'opa'a (rock cod), uhu (parrot fish), two kinds of humuhumu (trigger fish), manini (convict tangs), an ocean perch called 'a'awa and a delicious silver fish named Sari.

Some other fish I caught didn't suit my taste, but my cats loved them and they saved me money on cat food.

Of course the real fun was catching the big fish. On my best day at Hāna Bay it took me half an hour to land a 22-pound barracuda and a 14-pound longnose stickfish that measured 4 1/2 feet.

I also fished from the cliffs behind the Hāna airport. This was my best spot for uku. I hooked several big ones there, but I only landed two because of the near impossibility of pulling them up the tall cliff with hand-held gaff. My friend, Juanito, almost fell into the ocean helping me retrieve a 17-pounder.

The rocky bottom off the airport was literally crawling with large conger eels named pūhipaka because of their brown color. It was a tug-of-war every time I bottom-fished there, trying to pull the eel out of his hole. The biggest pūhipaka I ever hooked had a head the size of a football and broke my 40-pound line when I tried to deadlift him out of the water.

Nuʻu was my favorite place to go fishing, not because I caught the most fish there, but because it was such an alluring place to camp out. Miles beyond the last human settlement on the backside of the island, Nuʻu was a black sand beach on a large bay surrounded by old lava flows.

In the old days, Nuʻu had been the site of a cattle ranch that had an unusual way of getting the beef to market. The cattle were driven into the bay and forced to swim onto offshore barges bound for Honolulu. Some of the cows drowned and I always wondered if that accounted for the good fishing at Nuʻu.

I caught a 15-pound barracuda there once, but the time I remember the most was the shortest fishing trip I ever took.

The ocean was very rough that day and I had just put my line out when I looked toward the horizon and saw a monstrous wave building. I dropped my pole at once and tried to sprint up the rocks behind me. The wave hit me waist-high and it took all the strength I could muster to hang onto the rocks as the water surged back into the bay with all my fishing gear.

Soaking wet and still shaking, I felt like one of those cows as I walked to the car empty-handed to begin the long drive home.

As good as my luck was at shore fishing, I never caught the fish that everyone dreamed about: the ulua, or jack crevasse. Rarest and most difficult to catch was the black ulua, which grew as large as 200 pounds in Hawaiian waters.

Skippy Young was considered something of a genius when it came to catching ulua. He used to land 40-pounders from the cliffs in 'Ula'ino with a rod and reel. He once told me you had to think like an ulua to be able to catch one, but I never got the hang of thinking that way.

Ulua fishermen used one kind of bait that I would rather eat than dangle in front of any fish. Live baby lobsters were said to be the best bait. Small white eels and certain types of small live fish were also considered good bait for ulua.

The most popular shore fishing technique for the biggest ulua and other large fish involved the use of a rope line. A large guava pole is wedged in a cliff above deep water. The rope line is looped around the tip of the guava pole with the large baited hook hanging a few feet below the surface of the water. The end of the rope is tied to a larger rock or to a car tire fastened to a rock, and the excess rope is coiled on the ground.

The purpose of the guava pole is to provide enough tension to set the hook when the bait is struck. Sitting close to the coiled rope is dangerous because it could fly in any direction when the fish runs.

Two fishermen learned that lesson the hard way a short time before I moved to Nāhiku. They were fishing from a cliff near Kaupō when a fish struck and the coiled rope tangled around the neck of one fisherman, dragging him off the cliff. Trying to save his friend, the other fisherman jumped into a rough sea and drowned.

Everyone I talked to was sure the culprit had been an ulua—the fish that catches men if they aren't careful enough.

I learned to snorkel and spearfish on the placid shores of West Maui, but I soon discovered the ocean is not nearly so forgiving on the east side of the island.

Chuck Kalama took me tako (octopus) diving one day when the ocean was kicked up a bit. He forgot to tell me about a bad riptide in one place. I knew there was something wrong when I noticed I was going backwards in relation to the ocean bottom while swimming forward as energetically as I could.

I opted to get out of the rip by body-surfing the breakers over the reef. I was bleeding from multiple coral cuts and completely out of breath when I finally made it back to the beach.

Another time I allowed myself to be talked into going spearfishing when I knew the ocean was too rough. As soon as we hit the water, we started going up and down like we were in some kind of liquid elevator that was out of control. Even the fish seemed to be hanging onto the rocks on the bottom.

I immediately surfed a wave into a rock beach where the outgoing wave sucked the diving fins off my feet while I held onto a rock for dear life. The other diver also barely made it to shore alive.

Tom was an 'opihi fisherman who came close to death more than once. 'Opihis (Hawaiian periwinkle) are single-shelled sea creatures that attach themselves to the rocks and cliffs where waves break. A gallon of shelled 'opihis could fetch as much as $200 and were used as traditional food at Hawaiian lū'aus, eaten raw or briefly cooked in a dish called Hawaiian stew.

Tom made his living one year harvesting 'opihis around East Maui. He told me he "died" once. He got hit by a wave, swallowed so much water and was unconscious for such a long time he dreamed he was dead. He said he never felt like the same person after he woke up.

* * *

To this day I still don't completely understand why I did it.

I decided to bulldoze the land below the house so I could plant an acre of banana and papaya trees. I can only offer the most feeble of excuses: it seemed like a good idea at the time.

It was easy enough to get permission from the landlord to have the bulldozing done at my expense. And the price was right when I checked with the owner of the ranch next door. Bully told me the small job would just about cover the cost of servicing the D-9 bulldozer.

"Only easy, brah," Bully said as he walked the dozer

across the stream bed and ripped into the land with that mammoth front blade.

As always, Bully did his work quickly and efficiently. It was all over in less than an hour.

The sight of what I had done plunged me instantly into a state of depression. There was nothing left. The pig pens, rabbit hutches and trellis posts were gone and so were the trees, bushes and vines that had held this jungle homestead together in one big tangle. The only thing that remained was a big ugly wound in the earth. I could almost see it bleeding.

Don't ask me what I expected. I had seen plenty of bulldozing on other people's land, but for some reason that didn't prepare me for the grim aftermath I witnessed.

Overwhelmed by a terrible sense of guilt, I worked like a peasant for the next couple months planting banana and papaya trees and also putting in some ornamentals around the perimeter. I was obsessed with the idea I had to make the place come back to life.

The effort resulted in much less than I wanted. For one thing, my neighbor's cows ate all of my papaya saplings in a single night. The banana trees did well, but the price at the local store was so low I wound up giving away most of the fruit to my friends. In the end, I didn't even recover the original cost of bulldozing.

I really didn't care about the money. What haunted me was that the place never felt the same afterward. Something magical had been lost and I knew it was my own damnable fault.

* * *

Eventually I left Nāhiku and moved to another island where I bought a piece of rural land and started over again. I went to college and majored in anthropology for three years before I realized I had already studied the subject first-hand in a way that no college course could ever equal.

Ten years later I returned to Nāhiku for a visit. The travel agent grossly misspelled the name of the owner of the house I was to rent for a few days, and he turned out to be someone I knew from the old days. Bill was older and fatter like me, but still the same likeable guy I remembered.

It took me an entire day to gather my courage to return to my former homestead. I assumed the old house would be replaced by a new one, as the owner said he intended to do when he retired.

But there it was—the same old house still looking like a bunch of termites holding hands! It looked smaller than I remembered and slightly more pathetic. I'm sure houses don't really shrink with age, but they do seem to grow a coat of melancholy.

I wanted to go knock on the door and introduce myself, but there was a mean-looking dog in the driveway, so I walked to the ranch and looked across the stream to the back of the land. I literally jumped in the air when I saw a healthy stand of banana trees so overgrown with jungle you couldn't tell a bulldozer had ever touched the place.

Mother Nature is the great healer of mistakes that men make.

* * *

I remember everything that happened to me in Nāhiku as a learning experience that was almost larger than life. Thoreau put it this way: "If one advances confidently in the direction of his dreams, and endeavors to live the life he has imagined, he will meet with a success unexpected in common hours. He will put some things behind, will pass an invisible boundary; new, universal, and more liberal laws will begin to establish themselves around and within him . . . and he will live with the license of a higher order of beings."

I sometimes dream of wandering through the Nāhiku wilderness as I used to. In the dream I always pause beside a waterfall to take a drink. The water is cold and sweet-tasting. Mangoes and bananas lay ripe on the ground. A wild pig runs past me and disappears into the thick underbrush. I look up and see the endless dark canopy of the jungle where I am lost but feel somehow just on the verge of finding myself.

Dreams like that can haunt your waking hours.

KIYOSHI YOUNG NAJITA

I WOULD LIKE TO DANCE THE HULA
WITH YOU

Please forgive me for what I'm writing. It's been long years since we've seen each other, and so much has changed. We both married and had sons; my sister died from all the drugs and alcohol she devoured; your parents fled from each other, shouting and cursing. When I try to picture you, it's either Thanksgiving, Christmas or New Year's Eve.

Please forgive me, but I must recreate the death of your husband. I know it is not right to do this. I know that I do this only for myself. I beg you to forgive this indulgence. I admit to having little knowledge of what actually happened or how you really felt. It is my lack of accurate information that allows me to do this at all.

Even the actual time we spent together will be distorted by the lens of my recollection. I will alter facts to suit my needs, or entirely fabricate certain details and situations. I do not do this out of any consideration for you, and for this I apologize and plead for your forgiveness.

It is not my wish to hurt you, but I must write this. I hope you will never read this, but if you do, can you find it in your heart to forgive me?

* * *

We began our fifth game of backgammon as the aroma of roasting turkey gradually filled your house. I'd won every game, and at moments you were on the verge of tears; you could never stand to lose. We agreed to switch to cards or Mad Libs after the game, and ventured down to the kitchen for some hors d'oeuvres.

Your father was taking his lemon meringue pie out of the refrigerator. Since he was the only one in your family who liked lemon meringue, he baked one for himself every year. Your mother always seemed humiliated by the pie, and tried to hide it behind other desserts. There were many guests that night; it was traditional for your father and mine to invite their graduate students for Thanksgiving—they were poor singles and couples who eagerly accepted an offer to be fed and cared for. These familiar faces became like older cousins for us during the years they studied with our fathers; they often seemed more at ease with their professors' children than with their professors themselves.

Wine and beer always flowed freely, and you dazzled me with your taste for burgundy, my capacity to enjoy a room-temperature beverage as yet undeveloped. We moved through the crowd, piling our paper plates with carrot sticks, cubes of cheese and stuffed mushroom caps. The legs of the adults around us were like a forest, their conversation as unreachable and distant as the highest branch—until some friendly students briefly engaged us in chummy small talk:

—*So what grade are you two in now?*
—*Boy, you sure have gotten taller since last year.*
—*Seen any good movies lately?*

We made secret plans to hide a tape recorder under the dining room table to document examples of adult drunkenness and scurried back to your room to finish our game.

I rolled another double six and you twirled your ponytail in frustration. On these long nights together we often became bored. There were only so many games to play, so many schemes to annoy our older sisters, chatting in the next bedroom about their lives in high school; in many ways they were further from our grasp than the adult world downstairs. We would plow through Clue, Sorry! and Monopoly. We had outgrown the imaginative games of our younger childhood—science fiction scenarios that were largely my domain and with which you grudgingly went along. The idea of acting out dramas in hastily improvised costumes cobbled together from your mother's wardrobe had become embarrassing to us; we couldn't even admit to each other that only a few years before it had been our favorite pastime on those prolonged holiday nights.

Instead of Mad Libs, we opted for talk—something we found ourselves doing more often, and with less awkwardness. Our conversations at that time were increasingly dominated by talk of the opposite sex, an area where, unlike backgammon, the advantage was yours. You had already held hands with boys at rollerskating parties while I tried to muster the courage to try skates on. I would see you in the halls of our school, your back pressed against your locker as three or four boys would agree with every word you said. You would laugh at them and touch them on the shoulder, or yank their baseball caps down over their eyes, and I marveled at your ease with them; I marveled, because you were the only girl I'd had a real conversation with.

That night, you became especially curious about which girls at school I admired. I wanted to say you, of course, but that wasn't possible. It was enough for me that you'd always wave as we passed in the halls, causing tailspins of jealousy in your many suitors. Even though you always told them I was "an old friend," it was enough for me to spend holidays with you, and to grow up with you. So when I finally revealed some of my most hidden crushes to you that night, and you leaned back on your pillows with a smile of satisfaction on your lips, I learned that being a good backgammon player was, at best, a secondary talent.

* * *

It's been months since your husband's last operation, and it went so well that you've finally stopped lying awake at night and listening to his breathing. You've put away the pocket mirror for under his nostrils; you've watched the red in his face pale into a pleasant pink; you've started sleeping again.

So when you feel your nightgown sleeve being tugged, you're slow to wake up at first. And when you see that it is your son, you assume he's had a frightening dream and needs his mother's comforts.

But when you see the tears brimming over his eyelids and when you see his tiny, beautiful finger pointing over your shoulder, pointing urgently to look behind you, that's when you suddenly feel the bed shaking.

That's when you grab the phone and hit the speed dial that you'd prayed never to use. That's when you order your son back to his room, telling him not to be afraid, even though fear has already swallowed your legs. That's when you hold your son's face in your hands and tell him everything's going to be fine, while you curse yourself for a liar and your husband's fists yank the sheets off of you.

* * *

I first met your husband on Christmas Eve, at your parents' new highrise apartment. I had brought my fiancee; it was the first Christmas our families had spent together since we'd been out of college. Your husband was stout, bearded and red-faced with wine. His eyes flashed like warning flares when he laughed. You had just married, and it seemed like you were still becoming acquainted; it was odd to meet a stranger who had become such a major component in your life. You still hadn't taken your honeymoon because he couldn't get away from work. You joked that he worked too hard for someone with a weak heart, then scratched the short-cropped hair on his neck to soothe his look of irritation.

At your wedding, your parents had fought about whether or not your father would walk you down the aisle; it was the last in an extended series of arguments concerning virtually every aspect of the ceremony. You wearily commented that it had been years since there had been any simple agreements between them. Your father's strident Armenian temper still seemed resistant to you marrying an Irishman, even as he fussed in the kitchen with his trademark Yorkshire pudding and your sister brushed melted butter on the braided rolls she was baking.

My fiancee whispered that she thought you wore too much make-up, while your parents actually hollered at each other in the kitchen about the gravy. There were no intervals in their tone with each other; there was silence or shrieking. I noticed you and your husband exchanging a brief, telepathic caveat—*we will not become them*— then your mother shouted for someone to set the table. Always our job as children, it fell on us once again.

As I passed you a stack of salad plates, we smiled at each other through the strain of this reunion. Even wine hadn't helped us to remember being children, being friends. Suddenly there were husbands and fiancees and jobs and apartments; suddenly you were putting your plans "on hold" to stay at home, take care of your new house and prepare for a family. I looked at the back of your neck and couldn't imagine your being a mother.

You complimented me on my fiancee, approving of her and prognosticating a good marriage. Your expertise in the field of love had reached a culmination, and it fortified you against the harsh storm raging in the kitchen. Even so, I was annoyed that you still had advice for me—I had always consulted with you about how best to approach a girl I was interested in; how to get out of trouble with my parents; what kind of Christmas gifts to choose—and here you were, still teasing me about putting the silverware on the wrong sides. You said my fiancee would have to handle these matters, and I privately regretted the remark she had made about your make-up.

Your sister was just starting to complain about her flute recital at the midnight mass we always attended. Married, with a daughter and a second child pending, it was a chore she had thought she'd outgrown. Your mother insisted, despite the loud disagreement from your father. I looked forward to the mass despite this subplot—loaded with Christmas roast and wine, it was one of the few occasions when I enjoyed public singing. My fiancee, although Jewish, liked the musical program enough to agree to join us. That year, however, my sister was not there. My mother and father felt the weight of your parents' collapse like an anchor chained to their hips; their daughter's absence only added to their agitation, fueling their drive to behave as though nothing was wrong. It was the first of many holidays that she missed as her life became increasingly hidden from us, until at last she was nowhere to be found.

From the kitchen came the sound of your mother bellowing at your father to make sure his pudding was ready on schedule. Your father, in turn, shouted for someone to remove your huge, aged sheepdog from her favorite napping spot in front of the oven. You quickly attended to this; she was your dog, and one of your biggest childhood indulgences. When you moved to New Jersey with your husband, the dog stayed at home, getting older and smellier, the burden of her presence growing as your parents became more of a burden to each other. You hustled her into the living room with fierce affection, desperate to remove even the smallest bit of kindling from the fires that were scorching your mother and father's feet.

Your husband walked up to me and asked what I did for a living. As always, I had trouble answering that question; I still do not know how to say that what I do is to make things up. Your husband worked for a major New York bank. His throat swelled beneath his necktie, and it looked as though he might burst his top collar button and propel it into my eye. He poured himself more wine and perspired. He spoke loudly and brightly, complimented everyone and totally ignored the gloomy fog floating through the house. He told me and my fiancee that you were the best thing that had ever happened to him, an empty cliché which he filled with meaning as easily as he filled his glass. He was unaware that you had overheard him speaking, that you were sneaking up behind him to ease your arms around his waist, a comfortable pillow amidst a tangle of briars. He spilled a few drops of wine, but you held on tightly, and he spilled some more.

* * *

Your husband is dying next to you in your bed and you're

helpless to stop it. You try to unclench his fists, to engage his eyes with yours, but most of him is no longer there. You knew this might happen, but your hope had caused you to forget, and you became comfortable in your forgetfulness.

Now that his breathing is shutting off like a closing valve, you want all the years that you'd hoped were ahead. You want to raise children and send them off into the world; you want to grow old together, to sleep less and eat quiet meals; you want to see his beard, so thick and red, shade with silver strands as though woven through with fishing line.

You tell him the ambulance is coming, the paramedics are on their way and you ask him not to leave you and your son, you beg for him not to go.

* * *

Our families sat in my dining room, listening to Ahmad Jamal playing "Poinciana" on the stereo. Their forks clinked occasionally against their plates, scraping and shoveling the last remnants of salmon and asparagus. They drank toast after toast to the New Year, the "Year of Orwell", as they called it. Your father's gravelly guffaw harmonized pleasantly with my father's metered chuckle; your mother whistled out of tune with the music while mine asked if anyone wanted more pilaf. Our sisters no longer had a room of their own to retreat to in my house, so they remained at the table. Your sister chatted amiably about her new job and fiancee; mine looked stranded and drank furiously.

We excused ourselves and smuggled a bottle of champagne up to my room, waiting for a surge in the music downstairs to mask the pop of the cork. We flopped on my bed and shared sips from the bottle, the fizz running down our chins. We'd flopped on this bed throughout our childhood—to play Mille Bornes and crazy eights—but never to drink champagne. Now, as high school was crawling to a close for both of us, we'd lie on this bed and compare our weekends— who "partied hardiest" and who got into more trouble. It always seemed you were less in your parents' favor as the years went by. You were always sneaking out, wearing a little too much lipstick. In some ways, I aspired to your level of trouble-making, but in the wake of my sister's, what little turbulence I caused was relatively tame.

That night, we talked about the colleges we had applied to and what we hoped our first autumns away from home would be like. We passed the champagne rhythmically, the dark green bottle chiming against the string of pearls you were wearing. I laughed at our ritual of dressing up for each other on holidays, and loosened my tie. You kicked off your shoes as the music from downstairs grew louder. My parents had put on one of their old Hawaiian records, and soon they would all begin dancing.

I reached for the champagne, touched the rings on your fingers and decided to leave my hand there, on yours. We both laughed, softly, breathing and laughing into each other's mouth as our mouths drew closer. We laughed at what was happening, even though we always knew it would happen, we'd been feeling it would happen for so many years. The swell of your breasts against my chest and the moisture of your tongue on mine was like a fabulous joke. Your fingers in my hair and my palm on the coarse nylon covering your thigh was hilarious. Our bodies were no longer those of children, but we clung to each other as though we were playing, as though we were acting out a scene from a childhood skit. We rolled on my bed and felt the cards of a thousand games of war crumpling beneath our backs; we reached inside each other's clothes and heard dice rattling inside the felt-lined cups of endless backgammon games. We held on and pressed closer, crushing our childhood between us.

Then, your hands were on my chest, pushing me away—and we laughed a little more. We went downstairs in silence, each of us smiling, but probably for different reasons. The hula dancing was well underway, so we found an open bottle of champagne. We watched our parents and sisters cavorting, drunk and dedicated to each other, and laughed yet again. Soon, we joined in the dancing and I watched your hips and feet move, remembering, as though years had passed, how they had felt under my hands. We all counted the final seconds to the New Year and shared embraces, oblivious to any portents of the unbearable days to come, blissfully unaware that we were marking the end of so many happy times for all of us.

Suddenly, you and your family were putting on your coats and our front door was open, letting in the wind and snow. We hugged as you left, and both of us knew we would never again speak of that night.

* * *

I wish I could walk down the suburban New Jersey street that leads to your home, up the driveway and through your front door. I would walk through your living room, down the carpeted hallway and past your son's bedroom.

I would like to silently enter your room to find you draped across your husband's chest, your tears soaking his pajamas. I would close his eyes for you, then gently lift you off of him.

I would prepare a meal for you and your son, and set the table properly. I would serve roast beef and Yorkshire pudding, braided bread and asparagus, with plenty of wine.

I would like to play backgammon with you; after you won every game, I would tell you all of my most secret crushes.

I would like to dance the hula with you.

I wish I could do all of this for you—but there is one thing that I cannot do:

I cannot save your husband's life in this story.

CARRIE O'CONNOR

THE MAD PEOPLE IN THE ATTIC

I have lived in the white, frail house at the edge of Kuli'ou'ou for more than six summers. The house's sun-worn wood body remains cracked and dry like the tops of the taro plants we pulled from the front yard two weeks ago.

I live here with Tutu, my daughter Julie, and a cat named Jasper. People say that I came here as a single mother for convenience. Really, I came here to learn what degree my genes carry the coded message of madness.

One December morning, a long time ago, in my East Village apartment in New York, I swallowed a vial of my roommate's blue, oval valiums. I had just turned in a paper on the lotus sutra in contemporary design for my graduate art history class. Dressed in fire engine red long johns that I hadn't washed all semester, I crawled into bed for my long winter's nap. Only the glaring ER lights and clear tubing that prodded my passages disturbed my slumber.

The psychiatrists play with words from the DMS III. Post-Traumatic Stress Disorder. Depression. Panic disorder. Believe me, the possibilities are endless.

Sometimes I look in the mirror at my round face and dark eyes, wondering if I am the mad woman that everyone shuns. Medusa. Emily D and her attic. Sylvia Plath and her fatal gas oven. The slut. The old, eccentric biddy with 13 cats crowding her studio apartment. The welfare queen. The housewife having her 19th nervous breakdown.

I imagine them all as cotton stuffed dolls in a coin-operated dryer, spinning around, their cries muted by the thick glass. The professionals will quiet them with drugs, restraints, cognitive therapy.

I have lived in this house for six years. The neighbors still watch me carefully for signs of lōlō mentality—excessive weeping, harried response, a wart on my nose. When I call my father he says, "Where are you?" Mrs. Manu, an old family friend, brought over liliko'i and asked me if I took my medicine and saw the doctor. I can't tell her that she is nīele and would probably get lost in Chinatown, let alone Manhattan. But they watch and wait. Will I crack again?

I patched the roof this year. I replaced the 20-year-old, white ceramic sink in the kitchen. The one in the bathroom that we share looks like a dentist's white ceramic spit bowl with rust oozing from its openings. I have no money to fix it so I just keep scrubbing the Comet hopelessly into the red brown spittle marks.

Every creak in this house sounds out the pulse of memory, buried alive in the grey matter of our minds.

My daughter sits next to Tutu at the black lacquer table in the dining room. She has her father's straight, pious nose. She never knew him and I'm not cruel enough to show her the pictures of us, in love at the wrong time and in the wrong place. How do you tell a six-year-old that her daddy has a wife and children in another part of the country?

Julie can add double figures in her mind. Her chestnut brows squeeze together in a Super Fly pose when she asks me how much it will cost to reconstruct Kalaniana'ole Highway. The other day she was shining the flashlight in my eyes to check for healthy pupils and any "sleepies" that might be stuck in the corners.

She knows too much, this child of mine. I watch her, amazed, as she eats from her Mickey Mouse dishwasherproof plate.

Silver-haired Tutu stands slowly from her aqua blue padded chair, surrounded by pieces of spaghetti noodles, lettuce dabbed with Thousand Island dressing and chocolate pudding cake. She grabs her cane and sets forth to watch white-spangled Vanna White turn the letter boxes on Wheel of Fortune. As she moves, a stream of flatulence follows her like a long stream of fire crackers, as she walks the length of the table.

Julie, clamping her spoon like a three-year-old, starts to writhe with laughter. Her cheeks turn pink like the strawberry ice cream that she is eating.

"Really, Jules, everyone farts," I say. But I smile because my daughter can laugh like a six-year-old, thank God.

I take Tutu her ice water. She sits dignified in her floral print house coat with embroidered blue trim. She stares me down with ice blue eyes sunken in tiny flaps of skin.

"I don't approve of using four-letter words like 'F-A-R-T.' I like to use words like 'kūkae' and 'shishi.' And I would like less water and more ice in that glass please," she says.

I go up to the kitchen that my friends and I painted sunflower yellow and follow her orders. For the remainder of her life, I claim the posture of the indentured servant. I live in her home, bathe her, wash her night commode, serve her meals. I exchange this role for rooms in the old white house where I raise my daughter.

The house subdues me with its memories. Sometimes I walk around this house awed with the thought of the memories.

My great-grandfather, a Portuguese pig farmer, killed himself in the attic where I sometimes go to sleep to avoid the summer termites that swarm and drop their paper wings. He used a hunting rifle. Tutu's sister used a razor to cut out the bloody squares of blue carpet.

Some men in the family called him courageous to perform such an act because he was tired of living. "It's very Hemingway," my cousin explained to me once. But a woman wouldn't be called courageous if she did that. They would call her crazy, selfish, a quitter.

But the family still tries to forget it. Each generation washes the awful stain away. But then I halted progress when the ambulance pulled into NYU medical center and the EMT handed the admissions clerk my identification. Admitted as a psychiatric patient, the curse began again.

I have dreamt of the old one. He poses tan with white hair in front of an old-fashioned telescope. He smiles at me. I tell him that I spent a week in the hospital long ago and I now understand madness. I has to do with nerve synapses, tricyclic anti-depressants and vitamin B. He laughs and tells me not to be afraid. His laugh has volume and fills the room. His eyes cut through me like brown porcelain balls.

My neighbor, Jane, believes in spirits. When her Okinawan grandmother died, she lit incense and suddenly the other end of the black stick began to curl with smoke as well. That night as she crawled beneath her blue stitched comforter, the light switched back on. Grandma crossed over.

Jane babysat Julie last year and slept on the hikieʻe. She woke up at 2 a.m. and saw a white-haired man, lithe and tan, cross the living room and disappear. Jane swears that just before daybreak she felt a strong arm hold her down and grab her left tit. She shrieked, but no one woke up.

A Catholic priest blessed this house when the old man died. But his angry spirit finds no rest. During *Bon* season I set up an ancestral altar. I burned red candles from the Maunakea Street gift store, and incense I got at Longs. I put two *anpan* and half a glass of Cuervo Gold on the attic table.

Then I told him to leave me alone. I have a child and a nagging old woman to take care of and I'm tired. "I don't have the luxury of checking out, old man," I say. "Go bother the cousins."

* * *

The wheel of the year grinds slowly to summer. We fish the ripe mangos from the trees with long catchers. I peel them at the sink and Julie grabs one, sucking the juicy orange flesh that stains her mouth and cheeks.

Lately, I fold origami. Every day, I take squares of the gold foil, creasing, folding and turning until the cranes emerge. The birds, so delicate, so beautiful, join a flock on the koa coffee table in the living room. I might just fold 1,000. Not to get married, as is the custom. I'll matte and frame them in flight from the darkness, the winter and my great-grandfather's eyes.

JOAN PERKINS

CONVERSATION WITH MY EIGHT-YEAR-OLD SON

It is true, what you say: I have never understood you.

It takes more imagination than I have
to understand someone as different from me as you are:
an eight-year-old who wants a soldering iron for Christmas.

It is true, what you say: I have always understood your
 brother better
than I understand you.

Your brother's mind is a familiar room: even in the dark, I
 know where everything is.

But your mind is not familiar. To me it's like an enchanted
 forest, full of goblins and talking trees.

Your mind is a kaleidescope of the unexpected, and I'm
 always afraid I may not leave it in one piece.

We had our first fight soon after you were born.

Each day I would try to give you vitamin drops; each day you
 would fight me off.

Your pediatrician said you had to have the iron. I cried.

After a month you were so angry that you began to aspirate
 the liquid and choke on it.

I was afraid you would be the first baby ever to drown in his
    own Tri-Vi-Flor.

At two, you refused haircuts. You grew shoulder-length gold
    ringlets, and the other boys called you a girl.

I was afraid you would become confused about your sexual
    identity, and you did.

At two and a half you could shinny up street signs. You
    climbed the drapes, the drain pipe, the neighbor's
    fences, and the door jambs.

I was afraid you would break your bones—and you did.

At three you insisted that all strangers were good, and that if
    one asked you, you would go away with him.

At four you ate a bottle of children's aspirin. When I found the
    empty container you said you had only taken two.

In the emergency room, we watched twenty-five little pink
    tablets crawl out your nose and down the plastic tube.

You explained that the only reason it looked like there were
    more than two was because they had broken into little
    pieces in your stomach.

Later, when I tried to make you promise you would never do
    it again, you said that you never know what you might
    do when you get excited.

That was the year you decided to wear a rhamphoryncus
    costume for Halloween.

You refused to believe that Longs didn't sell them. Proven
    wrong, you decided I could make you one.

And after I spent a week constructing bat-like wings from
    wire and black vinyl,
you refused to wear them because they weren't anatomically
    correct.

Instead you wore a brown paper Safeway bag you colored
    yourself with a green crayon.
At seven, you invented your own language. You refused to
    speak to me except in Hoghs.
You wouldn't let me hold you, even for a hug.
But yesterday when your guinea pig had her baby, you
    climbed into my arms as if you had never been away.
    We sat there for almost an hour, watching the baby
    nurse, and neither of us said a word.

And you are not adopted. The day you were born

    I walked for seven hours to make you come.
    The nurse in obstetrics begged me to lie down,
    but I was mad to have you, could not wait
    for the moment I could hold you in my arms.

And you were not switched in the hospital. Only you, your
    father, and possibly rhamphoryncuses have teeth like
    that.

And you're right—I don't understand you. You're the one-
    eyed jack, the wild man, and I don't like taking chances.

But I am not afraid any more.

All I can do is love you.

And I do.

RAN YING PORTER

Excerpt from BLACK DRAGON RIVER

It was always a gloomy afternoon. I followed a group of enthusiastic boys and girls to a newly constructed classroom building. I always went right up to the double doors and pressed my nose and forehead against the glass to see what was inside. It was a huge empty room with a small red flashing light twirling on the floor in the middle of the room. I could not see the source of the light. It went around and around in a steady pace. I felt the heat on my nose and forehead. I could not stop staring at it. All of a sudden, it grew dark around me. The children broke into a run, and somehow I knew the building was about to blow up. I tried to run but my legs felt like jelly. Choked with fear, I gave up on escaping. Kneeling, I pressed my hands on my ears and waited for the explosion. The explosion never came, and I always woke up wondering, "Haven't I dreamed of this before?"

* * *

I was the youngest old timer in the preschool run by the Foreign Ministry. I knew all the teachers in the school because they took turns staying with me on weekends when others went home, children and adults alike. Loneliness did not become my company, for weekends allowed me to play with all the toys I could not get my hands on otherwise. Those toys were usually monopolized by older and stronger children. I could sit on any of the seats on the merry-go-round for as long as I wanted. There were also tricycles of all colors, red, green, blue, yellow, purple, and they were for me alone. I could pick any one of them and change to ride another color without it being taken away by someone before I was ready to give it up. When I was tired of playing with the toys and riding tricycles, I sat and rested on the back of one of the two small stone lion statues by each side of the double doors that led to the front yard. Again, I did not have to fight anyone over which one I preferred.

My tree stood in the corner of the school yard. It was an ancient willow tree. The trunk of the tree was enormous with the twigs swaying a cheerful welcome every time I came to it. From there, I could see all that was going on in the playground. Sometimes, I liked to see what was going on outside the school. There were chickens, pigs, goats, and horses out there. But I liked this tree mostly because I came to talk to an old lady. She was my friend.

The old lady dressed differently from everyone else I had ever seen. She always wore a long black dress which was tight around her waist and spread out down to her feet. It was made of some thick material. Around the neckline and the wrists was white lace. It was simple and pleasing. She had a brown triangular shawl over her shoulders. It was knitted in a pattern that reminded me of a chess board. Her snow white hair was pulled back into a tidy bun just above her neck. It made her look kind. She had deep set small eyes. Her cheeks were smooth and shiny. Her toothless mouth gave the impression that her chin thrust forward like a forever smiling puppet.

I came to talk to her whenever I felt sad because of a scolding I got from a teacher or a toy taken away from me by an older child. I came to talk to her when I became lonely on weekends. I also came to talk to her when I just felt like seeing her.

"Where is your home? Do you live in the little log cabin in the middle of a dark forest?" I thought her home must be in a forest because she appeared from inside the willow tree every time I saw her. I could see inside the old willow tree a road, as ancient and twisted as the tree itself, stretching into a magnificent forest. "Will you take me to your cabin? Will you take me home with you?"

"Dear child, your mother and father will come for you soon." She said tenderly.

I looked toward the playground, I envied how happy and cheerful the children were. I heard the teacher calling. It was lunchtime. I turned to ask the old lady to hurry and take me away, but she was gone.

Impulsively, I ran up to the teacher and said, "My mother and father are coming for me soon." She patted my head and smiled.

"Where are they?" I asked the teacher.

"Far away. In a foreign country, Poland."

"Why are they there?"

"They work in the Chinese embassy."

"Why don't they come back?"

"The Party and the government sent them there to work. They followed the instructions of the Party as everyone should." She pushed me gently into the room. "They will come for you when their work is done."

"Like when I listen to teachers and do what you tell me to?"

"Smart girl!" The teacher was pleased.

* * *

One cold and rainy afternoon, my mother came to the preschool to pick me up. For some reason, I became upset. Being a creature of habit, I knew I was not supposed to go home on a weekday. It was against the usual pattern of the life I had known for four years. I wanted to sleep in my bed in preschool, I insisted. My mother finally promised to bring me back at bedtime. I ran quickly to my tree to tell the old lady goodbye. But she was not there.

On the way home, I watched the rain fall slowly in the streets. The street light reflected in the wet street making me feel slightly off balance. Something was not right, but I did not know what. My mother was talkative. She was pointing at something, but I could not concentrate on what she was saying.

When I got home, my father was sitting at his desk writing. I ran to him. He asked why it took so long for us to get home. My mother explained my reluctance. I felt a little uncomfortable but was relieved that my father did not scold me. Instead, he showed me a ceramic gourd with some money in it. It was a piggy bank. He told me to put the money people gave me in it. "This is your Treasure Gourd." He said. "When it's full, you will be the richest little girl in China."

At bedtime, I asked to go back to the preschool. My mother said it was too late and I had to stay. I started crying and for the first time, my father looked at me sternly and told me to do as my mother said. I went to sleep wondering why my mother had promised me something she had no intention of honoring.

I was awakened early the next morning. My father accompanied my mother and me to a train station. Holding the Treasure Gourd in one hand and cuddling my dolly close with the other, I boarded a train with my mother. Wherever we were going, my father was not coming with us.

* * *

Four days later, on an afternoon, the train arrived in the city of Wuhu in Anhui Province. Some aunties, uncles and cousins were waiting for us at the train station. They pointed and waved when they spotted my mother, happy to see her. When we stepped off the train, they rushed over and spoke to my mother at the top of their lungs in a language I did not understand. Pulling my mother to my level, I asked her in a whisper, "How come these people are already mad at you?"

"No," She said, laughing. "This is how they are when they are happy."

The crowded city was located on the bank of the Yangzi River. We made our way to my great-grandfather's house. It was a big two-story house with lots of rooms. An auntie took me to meet Great-grandfather. He was a tall man with a big stomach. He wore a snow white mustache and a long beard, but on the top of his head, he had very little hair. He sat there and ran his hand down his beard slowly. In his other hand, he held a miniature teapot. It looked worn and as ancient as Great-Grandfather himself. The look on his face made me think of a picture of an angry god I once saw, red and twisted with untold irritation. He nodded without a word when my auntie introduced me. I wanted to hide behind my mother, but she was not there. For the rest of the day, whenever I saw Great-Grandfather, I ran and hid behind furniture.

The next morning, I followed my mother to a place that looked like a tiny mom-and-pop store. A dark, narrow walkway led through the store to the back. The store faced the busy street with a long L-shaped counter on the right side. A short, skinny old man with a face like a dried up twig stood behind the counter. The few teeth he had left in his mouth were black. He mumbled something under his breath to my mother. My mother said something to him in a respectful manner. Just then, an energetic middle-aged woman charged out from the dark walkway with a bald-headed skinny little boy of about three following close behind. She pushed the little boy forward and pointed to my mother. She urged him in a loud squeaky voice. It made me think of the time my father and I were taking a walk when we heard a loud annoying noise, a donkey had become annoyed with its driver.

My mother brought out some candies and gave them to the boy. After some exchange of words, my mother told me to call the woman Grandma. The old man behind the counter was addressed as Grandpa. And the little boy turned out to be my brother, Little Tiger. All this was making me uncomfortable. The strangeness of the people irritated me. The dark walkway bothered me. Slowly, I situated myself behind my mother. When the introduction was over, Grandma motioned toward the dark walkway. I grabbed my mother's shirttail and said I wanted to go back to Beijing. My mother ignored my request and told me to follow her. When I retreated toward the street, Grandma came up to help my mother drag me in. Determined not to set foot in that creepy place, I started screaming. I struggled and kicked. Little Tiger watched us and ate his candies with the utmost indifference.

I won the battle. My mother took me back to Great-grandfather's big house. I clung to my mother that day for fear of losing her. I missed my father, my preschool, my tree, and the kind, old lady terribly. At bedtime, I did not stop crying until my mother lay down beside me and promised that we were going home the very next day.

I woke up next morning with a light heart, the thought of going home made me happy. Turning my head to look for my mother, I saw only my golden-haired dolly lying next to me. An auntie came into the room and said in broken Mandarin that I should brush my teeth so that I could eat breakfast with her. Sitting on the edge of the bed and holding my dolly, I asked her where my mother was.

"Oh, she's left." Auntie said in a carefree manner.

"Where did she go?" I did not catch the hint.

"Beijing. She had to go back to her job," Auntie said kindly, but matter-of-factly.

I was stunned.

"But she said . . . " My words were drowned by the flood of tears rushing down my face.

Auntie came over and wiped my face with a warm towel. "Now, now. Stop crying. Dolly's hair is getting wet." She gently brushed away the wetness from dolly's hair. After breakfast I went with Auntie to Grandma's house, this time without a struggle.

Grandma turned out to be a pleasant and knowing woman. She left me alone in my grief. Lunch was simple: rice with a dish of vegetable that I have never seen before and some salted fish. I had little appetite for the strange food. Grandpa, on the other hand, seemed to really like his lunch. With those few rotten teeth, he quickly cleaned his bowl of rice. He lay down the chopsticks. Holding the rice bowl with both hands, he started licking the bowl like a dog attacking some juicy table food. With each stroke of his ancient tongue the bowl turned in his hand. In a few seconds, his bowl was so clean I was sure he could see the reflection of his own miserable tongue in it. He set the bowl down, satisfied.

After lunch, Grandma put a bowl in front of my brother. Little Tiger proceeded to urinate into it, acting as if he had done this many times. I looked with horror while Grandma drank the urine like it was a nice soothing bowl of tea. Between the homesickness and shock, I measured the possibility of ever getting used to the strange people living in this house.

That first night lying in bed in Grandma's home, I heard strange music floating in the quiet darkness. The tune was melancholy yet soothing. It felt like soft, invisible hands caressing me. Grandma said in her heavily accented Mandarin that it was the old tailor next door playing an *erhu*, a two-stringed bowed instrument. Next day, I stood outside the tailor shop and saw a tiny hunchbacked old man with a rope ruler hanging from his neck. He busied himself with measuring, cutting and ironing and paid no attention to anything around him. Looking at those bony and deformed fingers, I could not imagine that the painfully ugly fingers could create such beautifully magical music. Every night the spellbinding melody seeped into my subconscious and led me into the darkness. It gradually erased the details of my memory, the memory of my mother and father and the kind old lady under the big willow tree.

I got used to my new life. Without knowing when and how, I began speaking the local dialect. The strangeness wore off. Bowl-licking and urine-drinking turned into normal routines. Even the creepy walkway lost its black magic. Behind it was a three-room apartment. One room was used as a combination of kitchen, dining room and living room. Grandpa slept in one room and Grandma, my brother and I slept in the other. The rooms were dark, sparsely furnished with a hard, dirt floor. It was not nearly as comfortable as Great-grandfather's big house. I went to Great-grandfather's big house often. Even

Great-grandfather lost his severity. For the next four years, I called the place behind the creepy, dark walkway, home.

I also learned Grandma was not my real grandmother. She was my real grandfather's younger sister and Grandpa was her husband. Both of my real grandparents died as refugees during the World War II far away from home when my mother was two years old. Great-grandfather provided for my mother. The woman I now called Grandma had always had a tender spot for the orphan girl and now for my brother and me.

* * *

The morning of my preschool graduation, I took out the one and only dress I had brought from Beijing two years earlier. The dress was green with white peonies printed all over it. In the center of each peony was a pinch of yellow. It was sleeveless with big ruffles over the shoulders. I was excited, for the teacher had told the class that the best dressed boys and girls were going to be seated in the front row for the picture taking. Standing in front of the big mirror, I carefully pulled the dress over my head. Grandma came over to button the back for me when my brother walked in the room. One look at my new dress, and he proclaimed that the dress was his. When told otherwise, the whine turned into a full-blown tantrum. He screamed and rolled on the floor, refusing to get up unless I took off the dress.

I went out to wait for Great-grandfather and hoped that his arrival could put an end to my brother's ridiculous demand. Although Grandma often gave in to my brother, this time I just knew she would not allow him to walk out of the house wearing a dress. Usually when things got out of hand with Little Tiger, Grandma would give me a sign and I would run to the big house and bring Great-grandfather. This morning, knowing he was coming to take us to school soon, I waited anxiously outside the store. I wanted to get to school early to show off my dress.

It had rained the night before and the street was full of

puddles. I took care to stay away from them. My cousin came and commented on how nice I looked. She told me that Great-grandfather was not feeling well so she came to take us to school instead. My heart sank. I went back in the house with my cousin. My brother's scream went up a notch when he saw me. Grandma said the only thing to do was let him have the dress.

"No! What is a boy doing with a dress on?" I refused.

Little Tiger was rolling and screaming on the floor.

"You are older and know better. Let him put it on for now. You know he has a heart condition and ought not to be over-stressed."

"But it's *my* dress." I twisted my body in disbelief.

She whispered. "When he gets to school and kids laugh at him, he will know to take it off. Then you can put it on."

"What if he doesn't?" I asked. I hated myself for always giving in to the two of them.

"He will. Come on. Take it off." She was getting impatient with me. Although incensed with the plan, I was not in the habit of disputing Grandma, and she knew it.

It was amazing how quickly Little Tiger calmed down when he got his way. We set out. The dress was too big for him. It fell right above his feet and if the opening on the neck had been an inch larger, it would not have stayed on his shoulders. Every now and then, I looked at Little Tiger from the corner of my eyes hoping he had changed his mind and worried that he might trip. There was no sign of his changing his mind. Worse, he seemed to be enjoying his look of absurdity. My spirits were so low I did not even want to attend my graduation. I stopped and stared into the department store window, then, I heard my cousin's voice, "Aiya . . ." I turned and saw my dear little brother on his stomach in the middle of a big puddle of dirty water.

* * *

After I became a school girl, I assumed some easy domestic

duties, like washing dishes and sweeping the floor. I was also directed to take a thermos full of hot soybean milk to Great-grandfather every morning. The thermos was big and heavy, but I was glad for the opportunity to spend some time with Great-grandfather, who had not been feeling well since my graduation. He seldom went out of the house now.

As much as I did for Great-grandfather, I had a feeling that I did not please him that much. But for some reason, I did not mind. Something about him was like a magnet that attracted me regardless of how he treated me. When he was in a good mood, he let me sit on his lap and touch his long silver beard. Other times, he let me hold and look inside his miniature teapot. It was an old teapot, the inside stained into dark brown by the tea leaves. I imagined Great-grandfather's stomach the same color as the teapot's insides for the amount of the tea he drank. He kept the teapot filled with steaming hot water and tea leaves. When he felt like a shot of tea, he held the bottom of the teapot in his palm with one finger guarding the lid down. He simply stuck the spout in his mouth, tipped the teapot a little, and took a slow sip. There was always a sense of serenity about Great-grandfather's every movement, slow, deliberate and soundless. Occasionally he would tell me that I was not anything like my mother, but at least I probably would not be a rascal like her. He seemed to find consolation in the thought. When I asked what a rascal was, he slowly shook his head and never gave me an answer.

* * *

Great-grandfather was born a poor man in the city of Nanjing. He was a devoted Chinese Muslim, a minority group not often found in the South. For many generations, the male members of the family worked on the Yangzi River as river rats. Great-grandfather followed the family tradition. However, he did not allow the weight of tough burlap bags filled with rice, grain and raw coal to break his zeal for life. He taught himself how to read and write by studying the characters on the bags of rice, the street signs and the names of shops. He carefully observed the businessmen who came to the river piers to conduct their transactions. He quit his job on the river and started working for a rice merchant when he was in his late twenties. The merchant was impressed with Great-grandfather's instinct as a businessman and promoted him to be his assistant.

Great-grandfather worked diligently and saved enough money to open his own restaurant. He called the restaurant Mu Lixin, New Creation, which was selected by a fortune teller for good luck. It was a Muslim style restaurant which meant pork was forbidden. However, Mu Lixin's Muslim style spicy beef noodle soup, along with its Southern style white salted duck, roasted cow tongue, and its vegetarian dishes such as stir-fried sticky rice cake with assorted vegetables and sticky rice shumai, quickly became the local favorites. Great-grandfather became one of the most successful businessmen in the city. He bought a big house and provided the best education for all his grandchildren.

My grandfather was the younger of Great-grandfather's two sons. There was only a handful of Muslim families in this city, so to secure a wife from a Muslim family for my grandfather, Great-grandfather bought a 10-year-old girl from one of the poor Muslim families across town. This child bride was my maternal grandmother. Following the tradition in those days, the child bride served the family as a maid until she was old enough to be married to her future husband.

My mother was the fourth child. The first child was born with a white foam all over her body. A fortuneteller was brought to the house to determine the significance of the omen. With one look at the newborn, the man reported that the baby was wearing funeral clothes for her parents, a sign of bad luck. Great-grandfather immediately arranged to have a peasant woman adopt the baby. The peasant woman was overjoyed for her own newborn had just died. My grandmother had two more babies, both boys, but neither survived their infancy. By the time my mother was born, my grandmother was terrified of losing her. She did everything she knew to take care of the baby. Still, my mother was a sickly baby. Doctors were consulted and medications administered. Nothing seemed to work, but my mother demonstrated an unusual will for life. In desperation, she wrapped the baby up one cold winter morning and went to see a blind fortuneteller stationed just down the street. After feeling the baby's tiny hands and reviewing her birthdate and time, the blind man read his stack of cards slowly and carefully with his fingers. He must have turned all his cards over at least five times, mumbling all the time under his breath.

Squatting beside the blind man with the baby cuddled close, my grandmother waited impatiently. Her eyes shifted from his fingers to his empty eye sockets.

"What do you see?"

Not getting any response, she leaned over and nudged the man with her elbow.

"What do the cards say. What do they say?"

The blind man was methodical in his reading. He refused to be distracted or hurried.

Finally, stacking up his cards, he carefully put them away. With a heavy unfamiliar accent, the fortuneteller announced this baby girl had only four of the five essential elements needed to make a healthy being. Instead of having metal, wood, water, fire, and earth, she had only metal, water, fire, and earth.

"Please, master. Explain that to me," my grandmother begged.

Clearing his throat, the fortuneteller explained, "Your baby is an exceptionally smart girl for she possesses unusual amounts of metal. She will be an energetic creature for she is full of fire. Earth is not abundant, but no matter. A little lack of practicality does no harm to anyone. Water, she has enough to allow flexibility. But without wood, she has no physical wellness. So, all else she has is wasted."

"What should I do?" She panicked.

"What's the baby's name?" The blind man asked after a little consideration.

"Oh, a beautiful one, Mu Hongxia, Rosy Cloud," she replied proudly.

"You've got to change it. Forest would be much better."

"Forest it is," my grandmother agreed. My grandmother trusted the stranger completely. Within days, my mother's steadily improving health surprised everyone.

My mother was Great-grandfather's favorite grandchild. She was a pretty little girl, feisty but very smart. She had her prose and poetry published in the local newspaper and magazines when she was an elementary school student. Great-grandfather was very proud of her. He made plans for my mother to enter religious service at the local mosque and took it upon himself to teach my mother Muslim prayers and the Koran. My mother was quick at grasping the prayers and language which pleased Great-grandfather. He placed his hopes for the future of the family on her.

Great-grandfather set strict house rules for the whole family. Girls were not allowed to linger after school. Once home, they were not allowed to step out of the front door without permission from him. But my mother, born with a restless spirit, defied the rules of Great-grandfather and often sneaked out with the help of her cousins and aunties. One early spring day, my mother was sent to accompany an auntie and a cousin to the opera. The cousin had not been allowed out of the big house since her graduation from high school the year before, because Great-grandfather believed that young ladies should not go out in public until they were properly married. The three enjoyed the opera thoroughly. The next day, the cousin found out why she had been allowed to attend the opera: a matchmaker was arranging for her marriage. But the groom had refused to give his consent without seeing his future bride. The would-be groom had arrived early and positioned himself to observe the Mu ladies. Once satisfied with her looks, he gave his consent.

My mother was mortified by the trickery. Fearing a similar destiny, she decided to leave this feudal house. She packed a few belongings in a suitcase and left town with a girlfriend. They took the train to Nanjing with only a couple of names and addresses given to them by their friends.

Great-grandfather was furious when he found out that my mother had run away from home. A girl running away from home brought shame to his prominent status. She owed him everything. How could she do this to him? He dispatched Grandma to find her.

"My job was to bring your mother home." Grandma remembered. "I had to find her, or else I could not go back home. This was your great-grandfather's order."

"But Nanjing was a big city. How were you supposed to find her? What if she was not even in Nanjing?" I was skeptical.

"I had a hunch I would find her. Every day I went and walked around the streets and back allies. On the third day, I saw your mother, walking aimlessly on the street with her friend. I grabbed her, just like this," she grabbed her left wrist with her right hand and chuckled. My mother and her friend could not find anyone at the addresses they had. They stayed in a hotel and their money was running out. So she had no choice but to come home. Great-grandfather locked her up in Grandma's apartment behind the dark walkway and allowed her out only when the school started that Fall.

My mother's chance to leave home came when the Korean War broke out in 1950. When the new Communist government called for volunteers to serve the country, my mother was literally the first one in the city to become a volunteer. Her name was all over the newspapers and she was invited to give speeches to recruit others to join her. This time, Great-grandfather could do nothing to stop her. In early 1951, my mother was assigned to study English in the Beijing Foreign Language School. This was to prepare her to interrogate American prisoners.

Though he still adored her, Great-grandfather accepted the fact that he had lost my mother forever. He kept in touch with my mother and my mother returned home for visits during holidays. However, the final straw was three years later when my mother and father were married without permission from Great-grandfather. Great-grandfather could not find it in his heart to forgive her because my father was not a Muslim. Great-grandfather instructed Grandma to write to say that he no longer recognized her as his granddaughter. For the first time in her life, Grandma told Great-grandfather that she would not do what he ordered. The matter was dropped. Grandma said Great-grandfather was a smart man, and he knew the times had changed. There was no use fighting it. He never spoke to my mother again.

I remembered now that I did not see my mother speaking to Great-grandfather, although they were in the same house at the same time. My mother must have been just like Great-grandfather, the way they struggled to establish themselves. I understood, because of it, the hurt was deeper and more unforgiving. To Great-grandfather I was the product of my mother's disobedience. Kind and gentle as he was, I never could please him.

* * *

Great-grandfather passed away in his sleep when I was seven years old. In the center of the spacious front room in the big house, Great-grandfather's body lay in a shallow wooden box brought in from the mosque. A piece of red cloth was thrown over the body. Grandma was so busy with the funeral that an older cousin took care of Little Tiger and me. The cousin explained that having lived for over eighty years, Great-grandfather had a full life. Therefore, the color red represented a happy funeral. When a younger person passed away the funeral was a sad one because the young person did not get to live a full life. The cloth that covered the body would be white. A large white cloth screen separated the box that Great-grandfather was lying in from the view of the visitors. A *baxianzhuo*, an old-fashioned square table for eight people, was placed in front of the screen. Smoke coiled up from the burning incense on the table.

A stream of people came to show their last respects for two days. The adult women in the family took turns sitting on the left side of the *baxianzhuo*. Their job was to cry with women friends or relatives who came to show their last respects. It confused me because I thought my cousin said that this was a happy funeral. I wished the adults would get their feelings straight. However, seeing the women crying like grief-stricken kids, I wondered what Great-grandfather would have said. He used to always tell my brother to wipe his eyes and stop crying. I did not cry because I was sure Great-grandfather would not have liked it. Besides, I did not feel sad, although I thought I should because Grandma said they were going to bury him. That meant I would never see him again. But I just did not feel any sadness inside me. So I sat and watched others feeling sad. When they were off-duty from crying, the women in the family worked day and night sewing shirts, pants, caps and sashes with mostly white and some bright red cotton cloth for family members to wear at the funeral.

Many men came, too. Most of them were old and wore the same mustache and beard like Great-grandfather's. Some stood rigidly in front of the table and bowed toward the direction of the body. Others kneeled and kowtowed. An adult male family member always accompanied the visitor and did the same. My cousin said that the ones standing were friends and relatives of the same generation as Great-grandfather. The ones who kowtowed were friends and relatives of the younger generation.

The night before the funeral, I watched while Great-grandfather's body was washed. The box in which the body lay had a small opening. The washing took a long time, the water streamed out draining away the last bit of humanness of Great-grandfather. I worried that Great-grandfather's body was melting in the water. I breathed a secret sigh of relief when the water was finally turned off. The coffin was then carefully dressed in white clothes made of a type of rough material.

On the third day after the death of the Great-grandfather, Grandma helped my brother and me put on our white shirts and pants before the funeral. We wore white caps that had a bright red dot in the front. Grandma said because we were great-grandchildren, we only got a little bit of red. The garments were big and baggy on us. Grandma tied white sashes around our waists. I noticed that my aunties and uncles wore baggy white garments and red caps while Grandma, her husband, her brother and his wife wore garments made of undyed rough hemp. In the big house, a tall cover was placed over the box where Great-grandfather's body lay. A large red cloth with elaborate gold flowery design embroidery was thrown over the cover. The cover was so big I thought it looked like a small fancy house. The family members knelt in front of the box, their friends behind us. There must have been hundreds of people, all kneeling quietly. Grandma stood next to the box waiting for all the visitors to find their place. The room was quiet, except for the constant prayers of several Imams. I could hear an occasional sob. Grandma announced in her loud scratchy voice that the time had come for us to pay our final respects. With an even louder voice, she commanded, "Kowtow, once!" All the people lowered their heads to touch the floor. I did the same. As I was lifting my head up, I heard the second order. "Kowtow, twice!" In a hurry to comply, I bumped my head on the floor. Then, "Kowtow, three times!" Following the ceremony of Kowtow, the box with its bright and cheerful cover was carried out of the big house. A procession of white and red followed.

The only family members missing from the funeral were my mother and father.

ALBERT SAIJO

NIGHT LIFE
WAKING STATE ZOMBIE

SMOG OVER ARCTIC SO WSZ CAN ALTER NATURE'S
PLAN TO HAVE DIURNALS ASLEEP SHORTLY AFTER
DARK—WE DON'T HAVE THE ROUND EYES OR
ECHOLOCATION OR ELECTROFEEL TO DO IT BUT WE
WANT TO CONTINUE DAYLIGHT CONSCIOUSNESS INTO
NIGHT WHEN PROPER DIURNAL MAMMALS ARE IN
THE RADIANT BLACK OF DEEP SLEEP OR IN THE PRE-
TERNATURAL DREAMSTATE—BOTH WHICH STATES WE
CONTINUE TO BELIEVE IRRELEVANT TO WHAT IS CON-
SIDERED THE REAL ONE & ONLY LIFE ZONE FOR
HUMAN—THE WAKING STATE—VISIBLE & INVISIBLE
SMOKY RADIATIONS POISONOUS TO LIFE SPREAD OUT
FROM SPOILED 4 CORNERS OF SW SO VEGAS & LA CAN
MAINTAIN THEIR WAKING STATE ZOMBOID MODE
THROUGH THE NIGHT—WE WON'T CLOSE DOWN THE
WORLD WHEN IT GETS DARK—WE WANT TO GO INTO
THE NIGHT WITH OUR DAYTIME WAKING STATE CON-
SCIOUSNESS—WE WANT OUR NIGHT LIFE & WE'LL
TURN EARTH TO CINDER FOR IT—WE'RE GOING TO
MAINTAIN ZOMBOID WAKING STATE OVER EARTH 24
HOURS A DAY EVERY DAY INCLUDING HOLIDAYS—BUT
NOW EARTH GETTING STRUNG OUT FROM LACK OF
DEEP SLEEP—TOO MUCH LIGHT—TOO MUCH NOISE—
EARTH EYES FEEL GRAINY—EARTH FEELING JANGLY
GETTING IRRITABLE EVEN HAVE TANTRUM & THROW
BACK GROSS MEDICAL GARBAGE ONTO BEACH—
EARTH LOSING TREES LIKE MAN LOSING HAIR—EARTH
BEGINNING TO HAVE BAD MORNINGS—EARTH COUGH
HAWK UP SHIT—EARTH HAVING DRY HEAVES SO US

CAN STAY UP—STAY UP PAST DARK WITH OUR MEANINGLESS DISPLAYS OF WAKING STATE RATIONAL BULLSHIT—TURN OFF THOSE FUCKING LIGHTS AND COME TURN IN

ALBERT SAIJO

KARMA LOLLIPOP

WHITEMAN CENTRAL BREAK DOWN—THINGS START
TO WOBBLE & FALL APART—GLASS SHATTERS METAL
CORRODES FERROCONCRETE WEATHERS &
CRUMBLES—WHITEMAN CENTRAL BECOMES POOR—
DIRT POOR—MORE POOR THAN A 3RD WORLD
COUNTRY—SO POOR IT CAN'T EVEN SUPPORT A
WEALTHY CLASS— WHITEMAN RETURNS TO HUNTER
FORAGER MODE—WHITEMAN'S LAND BECOMES TERRA
INCOGNITA—THEN ONE DAY INTO THIS NOT NECES-
SARILY UNHAPPY SITUATION IN WHICH HARDLY
ANYTHING IS HAPPENING BUT LIFE THERE COMES
NOVELTY—1ST IT'S THEIR MISSIONARIES—THEY ARE
NOT WHITE—THEY ARE ELFIN & YELLOW— THEY HAVE
HIGH CHEEKBONES SLANT EYES & BLACK HAIR—THEY
SAY THEY ARE FROM AN ADVANCED HYPERTECH
CIVILIZATION ACROSS THE GREAT WATER TO THE
WEST IN THE DIRECTION OF THE SETTING SUN & THEY
POINT IN THAT DIRECTION SO WHITEMAN UNDER-
STAND—THEY TALK LOUD—THEY SAY WHITEMAN OUR
BURDEN—THEY SAY BUDDHA LOVE WHITEMAN EVEN
IF WHITEMAN BACKWARD DIRTY & HEATHENISH—
THEY WANT WHITEMAN TO CLEAN UP & PUT ON
CLOTHES—THEIR TRIP SEEMS TO BE BUDDHA LOVES
YOU SANITATION & DON'T LET NUTHIN HANG OUT—
SO BIG DEAL IF THAT'S ALL THEY WANT—BUT THEY
BROUGHT THE KONG HONG FLU—LESS SAID ABOUT IT
THE BETTER—THEN COME THE SOCIAL SCIENTISTS—
THEY ARE FROM ANOTHER ADVANCED
TECHNOCIVILIZATION OF SMALL BROWN PEOPLE
WHERE ALTERED NEURONAL TISSUE CULTURED ON

SEWER SLUDGE GROW INTO GIANT BRAINS THAT RUN EVERYTHING—ORGANIC BIOTECH TO THE MAX OR NOTHING—A MARVEL OF THE NEW GOOK SCIENTIFIC IMAGINATION—THEY SAY HEY WHITEMAN YOU DON'T MIND IF WE SET UP OUR CAMP IN YOUR YARD DO YOU—WE WANT TO STUDY YOU—YOU'RE VERY INTERESTING TO US—HEY WHAT'S THAT TOOL YOU GOT IN YOUR HAND—LOOK FELLAS IT'S AN ARCHAIC VICE GRIP—WE WANT THAT—THEY GIVE WHITEMAN A MESS OF CHEAP BEADS & A TIN MIRROR & THEY TAKE HIS VICE GRIP—AND THEY LEAVE THE YELLOW YAW YAWS—ALMOST 100% MORTALITY FOR WHITEMAN ON THAT ONE—CLOSE—THE YELLOW YAW YAWS ARE LIKE THE HEARTBREAK OF PSORIASIS ONLY MUCH MUCH WORSE—AGAIN LESS SAID ABOUT IT THE BETTER— THEN COME THE POWER & BUCKS PEOPLE—THEY ARE SHORT WITH BROAD FLAT FACES & PERFECT ALMOND EYES YOU'D DIE FOR—THEY DON'T GIVE A SHIT FOR NUTHIN BUT POWER & BUCKS—DERE DA GUYS WHO GOT THE VAPORIZOR GUNS—YOU GET IN THEIR WAY THEY POINT THE VAPORIZOR AT YOU & PULL THE TRIGGER—WHEN THE FORCE HITS IT TURNS YOU INTO A PUFF OF INNOCUOUS VAPOR—NO GORY CORPSE— MAYHEM MADE SANITARY—A GIANT STEP FORWARD FOR CIVILIZATION—A MARVEL OF THE MONGOL SCIENTIFIC IMAGINATION WITH ITS SURREAL MATHEMATIC TURNS FLESH TO VAPOR—NOW BEFORE THE VERY EYES OF WHITEMAN THESE ADVANCED NONWHITE NATIONS ARE DIVIDING UP WHITEMAN'S LAND INTO WHAT THEY CALL SPHERES OF INFLUENCE—THEY ARE GOING TO PUT A GRID ON WHITEMAN'S LAND & SELL IT OFF DIRT CHEAP FOR KIWI PLANTATIONS WITH WHITEMAN DOING THE GRUNTWORK—THEN ONCE THE PLANTATIONS ARE IN THEY AUTOMATE PLANTATIONS—NOW WHITEMAN ON THE DOLE & REALLY BEGINNING TO GET IN THE

WAY OF PROGRESS—SO THESE SUPERTECH NATIONS
ROUND UP WHITEMAN THAT IS THE REMNANT POPU-
LATIONS OF WHITEMAN STILL SCATTERED HERE &
THERE & THEY PUT THEM INTO WHAT THEY CALL
RELOCATION CENTERS THAT CAN MEAN ANYTHING
OR NOTHING LIKE RESERVATIONS—NOW THESE NON-
WHITE ADVANCED MEGATECH NATIONS BEGIN
FIGHTING AMONG THEMSELVES—INEVITABLY—ALL
POLITICS IS BULLSHIT—THEY MAKE WHITEMAN'S
LAND INTO A BATTLEGROUND FOR THEIR WARS—
THESE WARS HAVE NOTHING TO DO WITH WHITEMAN
BUT THEY ARE TRASHING HIS LAND—MEANTIME
AMIDST ALL THE CHAOS OF THIS MOTHER OF ALL
WARS ONLY THE MENEHUNES OF THE WORLD REMAIN
CLEAR CENTERED ON TIME NEUTRAL EACH A VERI-
TABLE SWITZERLAND OF THE UNIVERSAL POETIC
GENIUS

MARJORIE SINCLAIR

SENSEI

Under eyebrows like the crests
of bulbuls he looked
where I couldn't see—
an old man of infinite gentle power

sitting on the lanai shaded
by a mango tree hiding
the sea and the houses below.
In afternoon sun the leaves

shone dusty green or new yellow,
motionless, silent
and heavy in September air.
The old man looked into the foliage

as if he were the tree
and not the tree—that's
the only way I can say it.
He was among the leaves and outside them.

He spoke softly, "The bitter fruit
and the sweet" then looked at me
until I knew I was there with
him while he was there—

back from wherever he had been.
He smiled to reassure me,
"A beautiful great tree."
Uncertainly I said, "Past the time of fruit."

* * *

We climbed the wooden stairs among
the reaching arms of pine trees and rocks
here and there, as if they were naturally
there instead of artfully placed.

At the doorway we removed our shoes,
walking across the mats
to a room overlooking a garden.
Suddenly rain fell from the eaves.

"This is the Teahouse of the Spring Rain,"
they said. The rain suddenly stopped
then started again. Sensei
laughing, clapped his hands.

"Just as good as any rain.
It sounds and smells sweet."
I thought of the pine laid
along the eaves to make certain

the guest saw the garden through
a silver fall, and Sensei
like a child clapping his hands
in simple approval.

Could this be what I tried
so hard to understand—
that the rain in actuality
is not rain; yet it is rain.

It can't be put in words,
Sensei always said, his eyes
bringing me to the edge
of the immediate moment.

LIA SMITH

SAFE

On the last morning of their three-day retreat at Tassajara, a Zen monastery in the hills east of Carmel, Christine and Sam discussed separating for the day, he to join the rest of the guests for a hike in the back hills and she to stay behind and relax.

"Aren't you curious to know what delights they've packed us for lunch?" a woman who was sharing their breakfast table asked. "The food here is absolutely divine."

"I don't like trips without definite destinations," Christine began to explain but Sam cut in to defend her.

"We did come here to rest," he said.

"Go ahead," Christine urged. In their everyday routines, she happily depended on Sam to get her from one place to another so now she felt herself having almost to force him to leave her on her own.

Christine returned to their cabin and read for a while, wanting to make sure the hikers were gone before she ventured out herself. She didn't want to hear the sounds of their voices disappearing into the trees or run into someone who'd come back to shed a sweater or grab a forgotten pair of binoculars, but before ten minutes had passed, Christine began to feel uneasy. She rose from her chair and shivered when the cool air of the cabin touched the backs of her arms. From the cabin, she hurried to the main grounds of the monastery where tree-lined paths wound through miniature groves and branched off in all directions within a small garden park. She didn't want to be observed nor did she want to encounter anyone, so she chose what she felt were the most unused routes. Being in the garden gave her a strange sensation. She wanted to feel the garden had no edges, but also felt a need to patrol its boundaries, to make sure no one was there with her. She came upon several benches in the garden and sat for a time on each one, trying to relax and enjoy her surroundings. But she soon tired of this and, finding a path that looked particularly unruly and untraveled, hurried down it. To her surprise, it led directly back to the buildings of the main grounds, the first one of which was the monastery's huge baking kitchen. It was a large, open room with wooden tables and mixing bowls. All the wood surfaces were unfinished and, except for the permanent wall which housed huge, clay-white ovens, the kitchen had the appearance of a covered stall. The northern wall, a lightweight bamboo structure, was hung from the roof on hinges and had been swung open and propped up like the doorflap of a huge tent.

It wasn't until an acolyte spoke to her that Christine realized she was rudely staring at the bakers.

"Would you like a tour?"

"But I should be away on the hike. I'm not supposed to be here."

"You are our guest. No one is required to do anything here." The man approached her. "We keep this wall up through most of the year to keep the area cool enough for us to work in comfort," he said.

Christine stepped into the room and noticed how bright and vast it seemed. It was as if the sunlight were reflecting itself off the suspended particles of flour in the air. Christine felt as if she had been removed from the outside world and into infinity. Abruptly, she grabbed at the man's arm.

"Is something the matter?"

"Sam!"

"Excuse me?"

Christine feigned a cough and shook her head. How could she explain that for a moment she'd lost track of Sam, had panicked, as if she'd inadvertently left one of her children in a dangerous place.

"I need to get away from the flour dust, I think," she said.

Once they were outside, she was able to calm down.

"It's like being lost, being in that room," she said.

The acolyte nodded. "When I'm not baking, I often feel a sense of complete chaos," he said to show they were in agreement.

Christine nodded. She didn't know how to tell the man she had meant *forsaken*.

At the evening meal, Christine forgot all about her day as she listened to Sam describe the beauty and peace he had experienced in the woods. She listened eagerly to him explain how the day had reminded him of forgotten things that were really important.

"And you, Christine, what was your day like?"

She wanted to tell him she was falling in love with him all over again. "My day? I saw quite a few residents engaged in their daily meditations," she said. "They spend hours and hours reflecting on their contact with God. And, Sam, I saw the kitchen where they bake the bread." She felt as if she were about to bring him into the kitchen with her, into the infinity, but his attentiveness startled her. It was as if he were willing to follow her and she faltered. What if she told him how lost she had felt? How she had wanted him? Her eyes lighted on the torn loaf of bread between them on the table. "It's just flour and water," she said.

Sam's look made her shift in her chair, as if she'd said some grossly absurd thing.

"Yes, it is very good bread," he finally murmured.

She saw his hand reach across the table to touch her but busied herself with her cloth napkin, folding it carefully and then placing it neatly on the table.

Sam had already packed their bags into the car so they could linger a while in the dining room before leaving Tassajara but as soon as their plates were taken away, Christine excused herself from the table to use the restroom and told Sam she'd meet him in the parking lot.

"I was thinking, Christine," Sam said, as he steered them down off the high mountain passes through the twilight and into the deeply shadowed valley, "That maybe it would be an idea for us to take a day or two to ourselves. I mean, each of us, on our own. I don't mean to be insulting but wasn't it refreshing to have so much to talk about at dinner tonight?"

"But we share our days every evening, Sam, don't we?" Christine asked. She no longer rested her hand on his thigh while they were driving and instead kept her arms at her sides, often unconsciously holding onto the edges of her seat. "We talk about things. Books, movies, our jobs," Christine's voice trailed off as she tried to think. "We used to talk about our plans for our house."

"We've finished with that. The dream house is complete." He laughed. "We got our picture in *Sunset Living*, after all."

"Our dream house," Christine said.

"That's just it," he said. "What are your new dreams, Christine?"

She looked out the window.

"So," he said. Christine wondered whether she should love Sam as much as she did. "With both of us working again, we can afford it. The kids don't need us and we have the money. It's something I want us to think about," he said.

Sam had plans to go up to Tahoe for the weekend again. Dutifully, Christine thought, he invited her each time to join him on his cross-country ski trips, but she declined, saying she feared a broken leg.

"What would the children do then? With a crippled mother?"

Sam's invitations seemed genuinely sincere, but Christine hadn't been able to trust him since the weekend at Tassajara. In her mind, a man who could tire of vacations with her could also tire of her. Sam was always the one with the ideas, the dreams, the need for new things. Christine was unlike him. Her editorial position at the magazine more than fulfilled her. She had worked hard and achieved her goals, to have her own office with windows looking out at the Bay. She was content with her private secretary and both of them shared the feeling that they would work together until Christine's retirement which Christine looked eagerly towards as a time to spend her days knitting, reading and pickling vegetables. It bothered her, too, that Sam had made his suggestion as if she would know where to go for a weekend on her own.

"I can't understand why you won't come with me." He seemed to have forgotten the conversation they'd had six months ago. "The snow hasn't been this good in years. I'm hoping you'll change your mind."

What would convince me, she thought as she heard him working in the basement oiling and waxing both their pairs of skiis, *is if you'd forget the trip altogether and stay home.*

As soon as Sam left, Christine felt relieved, released from a vague feeling that she ought to find some way to tell him that although she was angry at him for going off without her, she was also secretly enjoying her weekends alone with the children. She had forgotten how much she'd been in love with them after their births, through the years she'd breast-fed them, Brenda until she was three and Sammy until he was two-and-a-half. When Sam was at home, her behavior and actions could be judged: as over-indulgent or overly harsh, undermining their shared parenting or not allowing him to be her equal, too much a mother and not enough a wife. With Sam gone, she could freely give herself over to them without the complications of Sam's presence.

After dinner, Brenda complained that she felt hot. She was running a temperature and when she got up later that night to vomit, Christine rushed to help and lovingly held back her daughter's hair as she knelt in front of the toilet bowl. But the next time, inexplicably, Christine pretended she couldn't hear Brenda's calls. Lying in her bed stiffly, Christine made snoring sounds to prove that she slept, surprised at how easy it was to ignore her daughter's distress. Staring up at the ceiling in the darkness, Christine was unable to close her eyes, and she tried to imagine a safe place. When she heard her daughter flush the toilet and return to her own bed, she realized that

Brenda would never consider the possibility that her mother hadn't been asleep, unaware.

The next morning, Christine checked on Brenda and found her in a deep sleep.

"Aren't we going to the park?" her son asked.

"We have to stay home and let Brenda rest, Sammy." Christine found herself smiling at him as she'd smiled to herself whenever she'd sneaked into her children's rooms to watch them sleeping.

"It *used* to be fun around here. Can't you play with me?"

"Not right now."

"Then you should have let me go with Sam. On the skiing trip."

Christine disliked it when Sammy called his father by his first name. She scowled at her son, hoping he would leave her alone, but he came and joined her at the kitchen table.

"Can't you tell me a story?"

She had begun flipping through the issue of *Sunset Living* their house had been featured in and pushed it towards him so they could look together.

"Once upon a time there was a young woman and a young man and they spent a lot of time talking about what would make them happy. The woman wanted to fill her house with fresh flowers she had picked from her own garden. The man wanted a see-through kitchen so he could see everything and never run out of things like coffee beans and whipped butter and elbow macaroni which he liked to make into soup with chicken-flavored bouillon cubes." Christine pointed to things in the photograph as she talked. Most of the things she pointed to were props the people from *Sunset Living* had brought with them for the shoot. She was against the idea of cut flowers.

"Did they have children?"

Christine looked at the picture. She could easily see that the house in the magazine hadn't been made to live in. It had been made to have its photograph taken.

Sammy wanted her to finish the story.

"That's all," she said. Her voice boomed up among the high rafters overhead and she felt a surge of well-being at how level her tone was, how reasonable and mature.

"It has to have an end."

"No. There's no ending."

"I don't believe you. You're just being mean by not telling me the rest," he accused.

Christine looked at her son and was filled with a rush of love for him, something she hadn't felt in some time; the feeling was powerful and re-awakened the pride she felt for being able to love her children no matter what.

The next morning, Christine made pancakes for herself and Sammy and vegetable broth for Brenda and she carried both her children one by one into her and Sam's bedroom, settling them all in the king-size bed to eat breakfast together.

"Aren't we lucky to have a super mom like Christine?" Brenda said and Sammy agreed.

On his return, Christine told her husband she wanted to go away by herself. "I feel a bit like a cooped up housewife," she said. This wasn't true and Christine watched his face, thinking he suspected the truth about her, that he knew she was contemplating dangerous things. "I thought I'd go to Tassajara. You can give me exact instructions for how to get there."

Her weekend came and Christine took Sam's orange Ferrari. It was hot in the Carmel valley and she drove with the windows open. To keep from getting lost, she kept exiting off the freeway to check the map and Sam's directions. After making the final turn-off, Christine didn't recognize anything. The landscape was unfamiliar and the road, winding. She stayed below the speed limit and pulled onto the shoulder as soon as possible whenever a car appeared in her rear view mirror. She wished for road signs and wanted a hitchhiker to appear so she could ask for reassurance about being headed in the right direction. It was late afternoon when she arrived at Tassajara. The inside of her face seemed caked with dust and she wanted very much to speak with someone.

"I thought I would never get here," she told the monk who opened the large wooden entrance gate for her car to pass. "The road was so long and I was frightened of falling into a precipice." The man nodded. He had a strange smile on his face and she wished she knew whether she hadn't mispronounced *precipice*. Wanting to appear as if she knew her way around, she had asked for the same cabin she and Sam had shared, but when she moved up the gentle slope above the main grounds, she became confused. The trees seemed to be conspiring against her, casting moving shadows onto the bare ground and preventing her from making out any path. She tried to make sense of the numbering sequence, to find some footprints or a narrow lane leading from one cabin to the next but found herself circling boarded-up cabins that were apparently out of use. When she did find her cabin, the sky was dark and without going inside, she set her bags down just inside the door, relieved it was dinnertime and she had somewhere to go.

In the dining room, Christine told the waiter she would happily share her table. The waiter nodded and she tried to decide whether he was the same man who had opened the gate for her. Christine began eating but the food seemed cold and bland, a hodgepodge of colorless and over-cooked vegetables. Each dish seemed to have the same cloying cinnamony-sweet aftertaste and she motioned several times for a waiter, wanting to ask for some bread which, for some reason, hadn't been placed at her table. No one came to share her table and when a waiter did approach her, to ask if everything was all right, she replied too quickly that everything was excellent.

Later that night, Christine lay uncomfortably on her bed, her stomach burning with indigestion. She wished Sam were beside her to cuddle against. He always rubbed her back when she had trouble getting to sleep.

The next day came abruptly and Christine awoke slowly, her feelings seemingly unattached to her body. Her vision felt blurred, but looking in the mirror, her features reflected clear and sharp, her eyes bright. Christine finished brushing her long hair and went to sit on her bed. It wasn't quite time for the dining room to open and she didn't want to be the first to arrive, as if she had nowhere to go, nothing else to do with her life but eat breakfast.

One of the windows looked out into some trees and Christine pulled a chair close, wanting to make the window's mosquito screening unobtrusive. She thought of how slow life seemed, and, thinking of her children, realized she missed the kind of love she'd felt for them as infants. She loved them much more now, but a complex of feelings for them had replaced the baser, instinctual attachments that had kept her unable to say she loved them, in the sense that she had always understood that word before their births, until they were both well over a year old. The love she'd felt for them at their births had been, almost eerily, dispassionate in a way because it had been so unfixed, so unbidden and unconnected to anything she perceived in them. They had been living beings to care for. Now her love for them was deep and complex, inextricably bound up in her responses to the love they had for her, a love she was convinced they had begun feeling for her only with their first utterances of "I love you" which had come with speech, in their third years. As her thoughts tumbled through her head, Christine wanted to laugh out loud. Was this perhaps how people who went from one affair to the next felt, wanting to be in love again, she wondered. *The children don't need us.* Those had been Sam's exact words. Remembering them made her wish for Sam, to be able to console him for his innocence. How could he have known his words would strike at her heart? Brenda and Sammy didn't need *her*. The trees before her began to take on an odd texture, as if she were seeing them through a haze. She laughed self-consciously, reminding herself that she was, after all, looking through window screening, but she was unable to shake her uneasy feelings. When exactly had Brenda and Sammy stopped needing her? Abruptly, she realized that she was asking herself the wrong question. When, more to the point, had she stopped loving them (because now she knew what she meant when she called those feelings "love") in that overwhelming and absolute way? It was a gradual thing, she thought, like weaning, quite natural. And then another answer came swiftly, tersely. The *day* she went back to work, *the day*. Horror filled her as she truthfully remembered the reasons she had gone back to work when Brenda had turned five months and then again when Sammy had turned eight months. She had done it to compete with Sam, to lessen her responsibilities for their children, make them more equal to his. She stood up and pressed her nose against the metal screening. Why had she seen herself as vulnerable for having had a larger hunger, a bigger appetite for their babies than Sam had seemed to have? Why had she feared exploring what it would have meant to stay at home with them? Acutely, she could remember leaving her babies behind with the caregivers. How easy it been to swiftly rationalize away the aching and the tears on those two separate but identical mornings of her life. She could remember how the ease had confused and disturbed her.

Her thoughts stilled and she stood at the window silently, holding herself quietly. It wasn't until she heard the conversations of a group of people coming towards the cabins that she realized the breakfast hour had ended.

The appearance of the other guests jarred her, and Christine hurried out of her cabin, pausing only long enough to grab her bathing suit, feeling she would end up remaining in her cabin until lunch if she did not begin moving at once. When she reached the bathhouses she was out of breath since she had forced herself to get there quickly, not wanting to give herself any time to change her mind. The bathhouses were built alongside a small river and Christine fell in step beside a monk on the short bamboo bridge leading across the river. The monk had to tug at her arm to get her attention.

"The women's bath is to the right," he repeated, pointing.

Christine looked into the man's face. Again, he looked

like the man at the gate and the man in the dining room. *Why are you bald?* she felt like asking him though she knew everyone at Tassajara had their heads shaven when they joined the monastery, both men and women.

The dressing room was a large room with wooden benches and pegs for clothing along four walls. Several pegs had bathrobes hanging from them. Christine got out her clothes and put on her bathing suit, a bikini patterned with a blue and red checkerboard-like design. The shiny synthetic material clashed with the bare concrete walls and floor. Christine turned the corner into the baths and saw no colors. The bathers were all naked. At the stair descending into the bath, she dipped her foot in to test the water.

"It's warm like a bathtub, honey," an older woman with sagging skin told her. "You ought to be careful about coming in here with your suit. This is a sulphur bath. Might discolor your pretty suit. I don't know how sulphur acts on bathing suits. Turns silver and gold dull." The woman held up her hands to show she wore no jewelry. Christine slid her right hand behind her back, wanting to conceal her wedding ring from them. Wordlessly, she sat down at a far edge of the bath. She had to scoot her thighs over the sill so her feet would reach the water and she remained there for a while, dangling her legs, wanting to join them.

"Come in," one of the women beckoned. Christine shook her head slowly and then, thinking the other women were laughing at her, quickly shook her head again. The women gave her a few more friendly smiles but soon drew their attentions back to themselves and Christine felt herself flushing with embarrassment, as if she were a shy teenager again, unsure of how to be herself. She watched them for a while, their large bodies floating calmly in the waters, their eyes closed, and she envied the relaxation they seemed to be enjoying.

At the bath's edge, she quickly became cold and decided to leave the bathhouse. In a sink in the dressing room, she wetted her suit completely and then balled it tightly into her fist to hide it from anyone who might notice she had brought one to the baths. It was time for lunch and she dropped her suit off in her cabin, dropping it into a plastic bag and stuffing it down into the bottom of her overnight bag. It angered her that Sam had never explained the baths to her.

The dining room was almost empty since most of the visiting guests had chosen to take a bag lunch at breakfast. A woman and a small child sat together at a table near the windows and Christine chose a table as far away from them as possible. She wanted to eat quickly and leave. She didn't want to hear the sound of the child's voice. After lunch, Christine returned to her room and stayed there until dusk, until it was time for her to return to San Francisco.

"I was worried about you," Sam said when she arrived back at home. "I was afraid you might have run into problems."

"Oh, no. Nothing. I'm sorry. I was so busy I forgot to call like I promised. You should have seen me racing around the curves in the dark with the high beams. Just like a pro. I guess I stayed later than I should have."

Sam hugged her tightly and she waited until his grip loosened and then stepped away. "It's good to be back, though. Tassajara wasn't much without you."

"No?"

"I probably should have left this morning. The beds were hard," she explained. "And the religious aspect. I guess you're supposed to feel humbled by their devotions, but I felt more that they're simply foolish people." Christine shook her hair down out of her scarf and caught Sam watching her. He loved to see her dark hair tumbling down. She touched herself nervously. "Everyone there is bald," she said. "I guess if I joined I'd have to shave my head too." She laughed, waiting for Sam to join her. "I'm joking, honey."

"I'm sorry to hear you didn't have a good time." He seemed disappointed for her and gave her what she felt was a conciliatory hug. "We had such a nice time there together."

"I'm not saying we didn't, Sam," Christine said. "Really, it was all right. I'm just not the meditating type." She let herself out of her embrace. "I should go in and kiss the children goodnight. I'm pretty tired and I want to be well-rested at work tomorrow. Deadlines for our annual report."

Two days later, Christine left work early and went for a drive by herself. She took the Golden Gate Bridge to Marin county, to the highway that ran along the ocean. With the windows of the station wagon wide open and her hair loose, she sped down and around the winding, curvy, narrow road. Air, cooled by the water down below, fanned gently into her windows, making the warmth from the sun pleasant. On the straightaways, she daringly passed other motorists, waving a hand when they deferred to her, when they eased into the shoulder to let her by. She wished for a way to take Sam's Ferrari on her secret drive. The next day, Christine left across the bridge again. This time, though, the traffic was backed up on the coast. The cars surrounding her were filled with surf-boards and teenagers in bathing suits and sunglasses. Radio music changed the quiet countryside into a noisy thoroughfare. She wanted to be separate from these beach-goers; they were going somewhere, she had come to drive. Christine noticed the car behind her was following too closely. She tried to keep him at a distance, fearing he might hit her. How would she explain being here to Sam? Distracted, Christine let the car ahead of her advance without moving herself. It had just disappeared around a bend when she heard a loud honking and realized the tailgater was passing. He dodged in front of her and she slammed on her brakes.

"Hey, lady!" Voices yelled and horns blasted from every direction. In a panic, Christine pulled out into the opposite lane, wanting to get away. It took her half a dozen moves to get turned around. The drivers in the cars around her beeped their horns and one driver stood up out of his side window and watched her with disbelief. "Someone could be coming," he was saying. "It's a blind curve, lady. She could get knocked off," he told the stopped traffic. "Whammo. Right off the cliff." Christine drove wildly back up the highway. Her crying was heavy and blinding, but she kept on until she had left the slow-moving line of traffic far behind her. The noise of the wind helped to calm her and she laughed out loud to release the tension she felt.

Because she had some time left before she had to pick up her children from their after-school activities, she decided to stop and look at the ocean. She pulled off the road and got out. The air felt bracing and Christine shrugged against the firm breeze, closing her eyes for a moment. When she opened them, she was looking out into a vast field of blue and she cried out loud in fright. She was falling and groped blindly for a glimpse of the road snaking out beside her, an edge to transform the blue infinity back into the sea. Christine fell to her knees and when they struck the ground she lifted herself up and ran from the cliff's edge back to her car. It hurt her eyes to look at the ocean and back inside her car, she thought of bathing naked in the shallow sulphur baths at Tassajara.

That evening when she and Sam were getting ready for bed, she told him she would be returning to Tassajara.

"Tassajara? I thought you didn't like it there."

"No." She shook her head. She watched a change come over his face and as she looked at him, she knew their faces held the same expression. Surely, if he could go skiing on his own, without her, he could look after his own children.

"You're leaving me," he said.

She frowned slightly, thinking he was making it sound like something that could happen just like that but then realized he was right.

"Yes. But I didn't know it, until right now, right this very moment. You must believe that." She stood away from him, beyond his reach. "I went driving today, down Highway 1. I drove with the windows open so I could feel the wind rushing against me. Sam, when I drove to Tassajara last week I was scared to death. The mountains frightened me horribly." She was trying to explain how what she was doing was merely the next logical step in some larger plan she had yet to understand. She didn't know it, but she would go back to Tassajara for another weeknd and then several weekends, one after another, and then a week; she would return many times and each time she would stay longer, each time her children would wail at her betrayal, crying like wounded animals, and she would become a Buddhist. "I can drive, fast and free. I'm a good driver," she said for something to say but she stopped. She would never tell him how she felt. She could feel defiance rising up in her. She would not help anyone understand her, not her husband, not her children, not the neighbors, not anyone. She had already given up a self that she had once longed to be, a self which had she been able to accept, might have blissfully stayed with her babies until they had started school. She would never get that time or those babies or that self back. And now, she would be damned before she would give up this trade off, this reckless, rationalizing self. She could not remember a time when she had felt so strong. She was filled with something she now knew she had never felt before and she knew it was desire; she would take risks no one had ever dreamed her capable of taking and be able to rationalize each and every one of them. She would take risks without her family's encouragements and approvals. She would explore exactly how far she could free herself of them.

INDIGO SOM

MISSING

At dinner w/ deep-fried
crab & red bean soup
for dessert, the imitation
sparkling apple cider
circling lazy around,
Uncle Yuen tells this story:

Sojourners sailing
back to China wd
gamble away their
life savings on board
the ship, & then
jump. There were always
men missing when
the ships docked. Even
when gambling on board
was banned, they wd
pay off the captain &
gamble down in the
hold. how many sojourners
swallowed the sea?

if it's all gone,
why go back?
if it's all gone,
no reason to go back.

because it wasn't enough
what you had. you were
supposed to get rich here

growing from fifteen to forty.
Return home to build a proud,
lasting house. But the shirts
you pressed w/ starch, & all
those washed white dishes,
your wrinkled fingertips,
were never enough.
It was never enough & so
you tried to double it, last
chance as you moved
closer to those waiting
eyes, open mouths asking
how much? how rich?
double or nothing,
nothing & you jumped, your
empty pockets heavy now
with waterlogged lint.

INDIGO SOM

CORVINA

everyone was scared of Corvina. except me. it's not what you think. it wasn't that i was as big & bad as she was, it was the opposite. sort of. i mean, she picked on the people who picked on me. i just knew she wd never hurt me, that she might even protect me. it was because we were both Chinese, although i never thought about it at the time. i just knew, that's all. she said she'd been to juvy, & nobody knew for sure, but i figured i might as well believe her.

well, i guess it wasn't just cause we were both Chinese. it was how we both hurt from it. i know, cause Corvina used to always pick on darlene. darlene was the goodygoody, perfect Chinese daughter type. she spoke the language. she wasn't hurting from it. after i grew up some, i realized she probably lived in the richmond w/ lots of Chinese friends, & i was jealous. but when we were kids she irritated the hell outta me. Corvina must've felt the same way. i don't think she ever actually beat her up, though, probably just liked to scare her.

heather levenson was always pickin on me. nothing serious, just spoiled brat kind of stuff like pulling my scarf off my head, or stealing gum from my bag when i wasn't looking. i put up with it, mostly because i was a scared kid who didn't know how to fight back, but partly because i knew that Corvina terrorized heather a lot worse than heather wd ever bother me.

years later, all grown up & everything, after heather levenson had changed to heather fenton so she cd be michael j. fox's girlfriend in back to the future, i ran into Corvina on the unthanksgiving ferry to alcatraz. she said her mom's family liked to go every few years. i was surprised cause i never knew her mom was indian. i just figured she was all Chinese. things were simple when everybody else was white. you were either Chinese or japanese or black. nothing else seemed to exist.

she said she saw mike ziegler around now & then, & he wd ask, are you gonna beat me up, Corvina? he doesn't understand, i'm not that kinda person anymore. i don't beat people up anymore. i'm different now. i wanted to tell her thanks, or something. i wanted to tell her so many things about how she made it okay for me to be Chinese back then, how i might not have made it if she hadn't been there. but there wasn't any way to say it. i mean, it's not like we were ever really friends or anything.

JOSEPH STANTON

SPRING TRAINING IN 'AIEA

On this raised ground, this April playing field
high on the heights above the ships and subs
of Pearl Harbor my nine-year-old and I
play pitch and catch, hurrying against
the coming dusk. We would have all the field
to ourselves if not for the gathering
of plovers preening the wide wings that will
carry them through three-thousand miles of flight
unbroken across the unforgiving
blue expanse of Pacific sea—a trip
they will take any day now. Today
perhaps we will see them leave. We are
ready for our season and they for theirs.
But our suburban world and this vast
plover place do not touch. Even when we
switch to batting practice and my son's hits
send the birds scattering this way and that.
We are no more to them than wind or grass.

It is so lovely high and breezy here;
the clouds steep against the Ko'olaus;
the Wai'anaes in the distance heave stark
silhouettes against the sun that plunges
down to the Leeward sea. The ball
floats so cleanly and true through the high blue
and orange of the day-ending sky that all
this could almost be song. The stitchings
of the high pitch go round and round, flickering
red against the smudged white as the aria
tumbles its aerial trajectory.

The plovers, too, sing a note now and then
as they fly from one spot to the next.
Every bird or ball must come down somewhere
and always ground or sea is waiting, but
the sky is capable of holding so much—
turning it all carelessly in its hands.

EILEEN TABIOS

NEGROS

"Daaaaaa - deeeeeeeee! Daddy, daddy, Daaaaaa-deeeeeeeee!"

My mother did not look dignified yelling down the mountain. Her hands flapped like the wings of chickens we chased for dinner, her blouse escaped from the waistband of her skirt, her hair streamed in all directions from her loosened bun and her mouth thinned around a circle of prominent teeth. She screeched from the balcony of our house which stood on top of Mount Asawa. She, most assuredly, would have been dismayed if she realized that her voice topped that of Auntie Feling's whose water broke when she was visiting the previous month. Clutching her belly, Auntie Feling's exhortations to call the doctor had been audible even to the traffic on the road circling the bottom of the mountain.

Mount Asawa is actually a hill, but everyone was accustomed to calling it a mountain because of its name. The other thing about its name was that "Asawa" can mean "wife" in Tagalog. Thus, my father's friends always enjoyed a rollicking good time discussing the many ways to "Mount Wife" when they first heard of it.

Anyway, there was my father's *asawa* ordering me and my father as we were half-way up the mountain to hurry in a voice loud enough to carry to Manila. We broke into a run, wondering what disaster had befallen the household. My father had gained weight over the years but he easily ran ahead of me—his quivering backside, encased tightly in brown polyester, looked like the rump of a fat water buffalo.

As we burst into the house, the servants were running through the living room, much like the time Mama stood barefoot on the sofa and screamed with regard to the unexpected visit of a neighbor's pet monkey who slipped in through an open window, "Ayyyyyyyy-susssss! Everyone get that lice-ridden creature before he tracks his diseases through the house!"

This time, my mother was instructing all the servants, "Black, black, as much black as you can find!" before dashing off towards the servants' quarters.

"What's going on here?" my father demanded as we followed my mother. We entered Manang* Inday's bedroom where we found the maid lying on her bed, clutching her knees to her chest, mumbling and shivering despite the heat.

"Ayyyyy-susssss!" we finally deciphered some of Manang Inday's mutterings. "I am freezing!"

My mother started layering the clothes bundled in her arms over Manang Inday as my father and I watched, open-mouthed with amazement. I reached for my father's hand which returned my clasp firmly.

"Her body has been taken over by a *mamau*," Mama explained, her perspiring face looking back at us and inviting us to share in the horror of the matter.

"*Mamau*—a ghost?" I repeated, concerned and moving behind my father. My father closed the cavern of his mouth and snorted.

"Another ghost? Why did we move to this place," my father complained, releasing my hand as he disgustedly flung both of his up in the air. "Ever since we arrived in this city, I've been haunted by floods, neighbors who eat the evidence of their depletion of my chickens, a roof that won't stop leaking and a different ghost showing its pathetic presence every month! Are these *mamaus* breeding behind the chicken coop?"

Then my father laughed at the ceiling, apparently thinking he inadvertently displayed some wit. I smirked, too, as his lack of fear made me unafraid.

"Well, and what does this ghost want this time," my father asked after he stopped barking to himself at the sight of Mama's frown.

"Have you no respect? The body of Inday, who could

never hurt a soul and, undoubtedly, was just minding her own business, has just been invaded by an unwelcome visitor from the other realm!" my mother, her hands on her hips, chastised my father.

"The other realm?" my father mocked in a high-pitched tone. As the warning look became murderous on Mama's face, he calmed himself, smoothing back the sparse strands over his glistening scalp. He sat in the lone chair of the room which, next to the servant's bed, allowed for a direct look into Manang Inday's grimacing face. He pulled me to his side and whispered, "We're in this together, buddy. Let's discover the surprise *du jour!*"

Du jour is French and means "of the day." My father loved to teach pieces of trivia that he thought I would not learn otherwise from the nuns at my elementary school.

"All right, let's hear it," my father said, sinking his chin into his chest with the demeanor of preparing for a long, tedious story. His profile was that of a multi-bellied Buddha in a yellow, short-sleeved golf shirt. "But first, why did you cover Inday with your slips? Isn't it better to cover her with a blanket than your underwear?"

My mother dropped her eyes and blushed before she responded, "My slips are black. Nana Sitang said that if ever a ghost takes over the body of someone in our household, we should cover the body with black material because black feels more comfortable to a *mamau*."

I remembered Nana Sitang's visit to our home and the conversation turning to the nature of ghosts. But Nana Sitang could not explain, however, why black was more comfortable to *mamaus* or why the comfort of ghosts was significant, only that she had managed to pick up these gems of wisdom from her village's witch doctor when she was a teenager. Of course, she cackled through tobacco-stained teeth, this was before Nana Sitang's parents discovered and put a stop to her visits to the witch doctor who also dabbled as the bookie at local cockfights. Before my father could remind Mama of these points, we heard a slight scuffling noise behind us.

"Oh, good, Neta, you found more black," my mother said to one of the servants who stood just beyond the doorway, her head tilted away from looking into the room as if there was a disease she could catch by just looking. Manang Neta blindly held out a bundle of clothes. Sighing, Mama allowed Manang Neta to avoid entering the room and went over to take the pile from her hands.

"Hey, that's my jacket," I piped up as I noticed one of the articles of clothing my mother was layering over Manang Inday from the results of Manang Neta's forage through the closets.

"Shussssh, boy," my father ordered. "Why do you need a jacket when you live in a tropical country?"

"But it's American and from Uncle Cosmo," I mumbled to myself, ignoring his lesson that I lived in a "tropical country" and wishing only to retrieve the jacket my favorite uncle had sent me for my tenth birthday. My jacket was black with a picture of Captain Kirk, Mr. Spock and Dr. McCoy on the back.

"Okay, Gloria, what does *this* ghost want?" I could tell my father was losing patience by the way he emphasized his words. Since we moved from Manila to Baguio City three months ago, we had been visited by three ghosts, including the one who inhabited Manang Inday's body.

The first was a dark shadow that hovered outside my parents' bedroom window and pleaded for any old clothes that they could spare. The ghost made its request in what my father called "a whining, toadying tone that no self-respecting ghost would ever use because real ghosts should have no reason to behave towards humans in a servile manner!" In disgust, my father threw out his old bathrobe but refused to let my frightened mother empty the drawers for more clothes to dispense out the window.

"It's only a *loko-loko* from the neighborhood trying to stiff us," he said, waving at her to return to bed and slamming the shutters closed. However, since my parents' bedroom overlooked the air over a steep-sided valley created by one side of Mount Asawa, we have never determined how a person could have managed to throw a shadow from right beyond my parents' bedroom window.

The second ghost appeared a month later and took the shape of my father's old bathrobe floating beyond the bathroom window when my mother had to exercise an act of nature in the middle of the night. With one frayed sleeve pointing at my mother, the *mamau* chastised my parents for their selfishness. The tunnel-like darkness of the empty sleeve reminded her, my mother later said, of the throat of a shark who had opened its jaws at her when she was a little girl swimming in the seashore by the fishing village where she was born. My mother decided to make a generous donation to the local orphanage the following day, much to my father's dismay.

"You weren't there!" Mama replied heatedly over breakfast after my father berated her for confusing dreams with reality. I sneaked a forgotten mango slice from my mother's plate as I waited for my father's response.

"Of course I wasn't there! Since when have I ever accompanied you to do your Number 2? It does not smell sweet, madam!" my father roared back, stabbing his fork in the air and breaching one of my mother's rules of never pointing an eating utensil towards the direction of another. But my father's anger did not accomplish anything as my mother proceeded later that day with her gift to the orphanage.

"*Susmaryosep*! Don't use that tone of voice with me," Mama snapped back at my father as they discussed the third ghost. "You can listen, too, with your elephant-sized ears as I question the spirit."

By expressing "Susmaryosep" instead of the shortcut, "Ayyyyy-sussss," I could tell my mother was really agitated. "Susmaryosep" is short for "Jesus, Mary, Joseph" whose names my relatives frequently invoked in moments of stress.

My mother bent over Manang Inday's quivering face. Poor Manang Inday, I thought as I always did whenever I happened to pay attention to her. Her face bore a distinct resemblance to Uncle Fillmore's bulldog: the same mournful brown eyes surrounded by drooping lids; the slack, multi-layered folds below the chin; and a bulbuous forehead. Uncle Fillmore also had noticed the resemblance upon acquiring the bulldog, and so named it after Manang Inday, much to the distress of his wife, my Auntie Feling, who surely must have busted one of Uncle Fillmore's eardrums with her views on the matter.

"Now, now. You should be warmer now," Mama crooned, her face about an inch away from the bump protruding from the tip of Manang Inday's nose. "Who are you and why are you visiting us through poor Inday's body?"

Manang Inday started to act like a fish, disconcerting my mother and causing her to move closer to us. The servant's lips kept shifting as she breathed through her mouth. Finally, the ghost discovered that one can breathe more easily through a nose and, after a few times of becoming accustomed to this notion, used Manang Inday's mouth for speaking.

"Is that you, my little garbage can?" Manang Inday, or rather, the *mamau*, asked. It had to be the ghost because the voice did not sound like Manang Inday's voice. The voice was melodious instead of Manang Inday's that has reminded many listeners of the braying of a discontented goat.

"Is that you, my little garbage can?" the ghost repeated lovingly.

"Yes," Mama could manage only one word through the surprise, then the prolonged wince contorting her features.

"Mama, why is she calling you a garbage can?" I asked the question, as well on behalf of my father as, both wide-eyed, we looked at her.

The *mamau* laughed with Manang Inday's face: soft rolling peals that sounded like the hymn being outlined on air whenever the bells tolled from the church another hilltop away.

"My little garbage can, this must be your son, Matthew," the ghost said. "Well, I'll tell you why, my sweet boy."

I scowled at being called "sweet" but leaned closer with my parents toward Manang Inday's body. The *mamau's* voice was full of mischief, courting us with the manner of sharing confidences.

"When your mother was a little baby, I helped take care of her. We would spend many afternoons in the shade of the biggest star apple tree in your grandmother's yard. There we would sit, I rocking her back and forth while I feasted on my little bags of sweets.

"Oooohhhh, I had such a sweet tooth," the ghost said with an air of self-congratulation. "I always carried around bags of *churros, susporos de casuys, palitaos, polvarons, maja blancas, maruyas* and *bibingka*. My favorite was *puto maya*; I loved to watch my mother make it with sweet rice, coconut milk, brown sugar and grated coconut meat. My, my, they were so delicious!"

Here, the *mamau* interrupted herself with a few choice smacks with Manang Inday's lips. My mouth also started to water.

"One day, your mother started crying and crying. I kept rocking her and patting her on the back but she wouldn't stop bawling. Then I noticed her small chubby hands reaching into my bag of sweets. Your Mama wanted some, too.

"Well, she was just a baby and couldn't have eaten the snacks with her soft, little gums. So, after much thought, I chewed and chewed a tiny piece of my favorite *puto maya* and then fed the result to her. She loved that so much. And that's how she became my garbage can. Because I would chew sweets and feed them to her, directly from my mouth with a kiss."

"Eeeeeeuuuuuuuwwwwwwhhhhhh," my father cried out before we both burst into laughter and pointed our fingers at my mother who was standing still with a pained look on her face. Mama tried to hide her embarassment by starting to straighten her blouse and smooth her hair back into her bun.

"That's why you're a garbage can, because you ate her leftovers when you were a baby?" I wheezed between my laughter.

"Aaahhh, but Matthew, she was *my* little garbage can and

I so loved my honey honey bun bun," the ghost noted, screwing up Manang Inday's lips into a grin wide enough to display the blackened fillings in all of Manang Inday's cavities.

My father elbowed me to look at him. Cross-eyed, he started whispering in a sing-song, "honey honey bun bun." Choking on my laughter, I bent over and crossed my legs as I felt my bladder begin to expand.

My mother cleared her throat and asked in as business-like a demeanor as she could manage, "Auntie Lina, why are you here? What can we do for you?"

"I'll tell you, my darling, but before I do could, you please bring me something hot to drink? I am so co-o-o-o-ld," the ghost replied and made Manang Inday's body shiver exaggeratedly.

Mama quickly called for Manang Neta. Manang Neta showed the back of her uncombed head again as she still refused to look into the room. "Yes, Ma'am?" she squeaked.

"Heat up some Campbell's," Mama instructed.

"Yes, Ma'am," Manang Neta squeaked again and ran away to the kitchen.

"Campbell's soup? How kind of you to share such luxuries as American food," the ghost said gratefully.

"But now, let me tell you why I'm here. Do you remember, my little garbage can, your distant cousin, Eliel?"

"Only vaguely, Auntie Lina. Doesn't he now live in Negros?" Mama asked, referring to Negros Occidental, the country's primary sugar-growing province.

"Yes, yes. Things are bad in Negros for your cousin's family. My heart breaks to see Eliel so skinny. He refuses to eat because his children do not receive full sustenance from the little that he can offer them. Yet he's the one who must remain strong to be able to harvest the sugar cane and do any other work required to feed his family," the ghost nodded Manang Inday's face up and down as she sighed.

"That is sad," Mama said. Solemnly, my father and I nodded our heads in agreement.

"Well, you and Andrew are doing so well here in Baguio City, two well-educated professionals that you are," the ghost continued. "Congratulations, Andrew, on your recent promotion to Senior Vice President at Banco Baguio! My goodness—you've become such a big-shot banker! And, Gloria, to be principal of Baguio High School—what a coup!"

"You don't have to explain, Auntie Lina. We will be more than happy to help," my mother quickly interrupted. Mama later told me that hearing the *mamau* recite our family's good fortunes made her uneasy. "Never take blessings for granted, Matthew," my mother warned.

Unlike the other two ghosts, my father did not utter a single word of complaint over my mother's offer to provide assistance. He only pulled me closer and looked sadly at my mother.

After my mother agreed to assist Uncle Eliel, the *mamau* did not speak again, despite my mother's questions and other attempts to engage her in conversation. She only indicated her presence by intermittently making Manang Inday's body relapse into a fit of shivers until Manang Neta brought the soup. The ghost still uttered no words as she finished a bowl of Campbell's noodles in chicken broth. After she emptied the bowl and emitted a loud burp, Manang Inday's body sat up on the bed with a startled look on her face, the layered clothes flung off in a disarray around her. When Manang Inday brayed at us familiarly like a goat, then we knew the ghost had departed.

* * *

Before we emigrated to the United States three years later, Uncle Fillmore and Auntie Feling agreed to my father's request that they provide assistance to Uncle Eliel and his family. But until we left, Mama dispatched a servant with packages of food and money every six months to travel the hundreds of miles to Negros which was located on the southern part of the Philippine archipelago.

As I helped my mother the day after the incident to pack

the first set of provisions to Negros, Mama mentioned that she doubted that the *mamau* was actually Auntie Lina because she inhaled and drank the soup so loudly.

"Your Auntie Lina never would have slurped. She was a lady," my mother emphasized, her hands patting at the bun on her head to ensure that it had trapped all the stray strands of her hair.

"Yes, Mama," I agreed dutifully, and then asked, "But Mama, why did you consent to helping Uncle Eliel if you didn't believe that the ghost was Auntie Lina?"

"Because Negros is Negros, my son. And I had no doubt Eliel's family needed help. The ghost was just reminding me, that's all," Mama replied before turning aside and bending down to look at something in the rug.

She would have been upset if she knew I saw the teardrop sliding down her nose, I thought as I allowed her to pretend to rub away at an invisible stain on the rug.

Later, as we were packing to leave the country, my mother stumbled across a shoebox of correspondence from Uncle Eliel. She read from some of them and gave me the first letter Uncle Eliel wrote to her. Mama said I should bring the letter with me to the United States so that I will remember those who are left behind. My letter said . . .

> "We are so grateful for your help. We ate meat that day, the first that we have had for over a year. We usually eat only rice and vegetables, sometimes with fruit and, of course, we have our water and salt.
>
> The last time that we ate meat, we found some frogs in the fields. We put on pieces of old clothes—of course, all of our clothes are old, heh-heh—and kerosene in a bottle to make a light. Then we went frog-hunting at night. But, more often than not, we are too tired to hunt at night. When we get back to our barracks, it is late and we are so tired that all we can do is sleep."

My Uncle Eliel's letter mentioned other things but I usually thought about how his family did not have much to eat. Many years later, I conducted some research as an aide to a United States Senator who was being lobbied by Amnesty International regarding certain labor incidents in Negros.

I learned that about 70% of the province's sugar-growing land was located in *haciendas*, a remnant from Spanish colonial days which has been compared to American Southern plantations before the United States' Civil War. The workers' houses were typically rough-hewn wooden shacks, with no more than twenty-five square yards of floor space. Most families possessed only sparse furnishings such as thin straw sleeping mats and a few utensils. Many *haciendas* also contained barracks that were partitioned by cardboard walls to house *sacadas*, seasonal farm workers, from the poor of neighboring provinces. The *sacadas* were treated the worst among all workers, usually assigned the most menial and harshest jobs such as cutting the cane. I remembered my mother telling me that Uncle Eliel originally moved to Negros as a *sacada* and never managed to earn sufficient money to leave what he thought would be a one-year posting.

I learned that most *hacenderos* belonged to a tight-knit political oligarchy. Some were absentee landlords, enjoying the fruits of their wealth in Manila, Hong Kong, London, New York and elsewhere outside of Negros. Some paternalistically defended the *hacienda* life as the best way of life for the people of Negros who, some *hacenderos* said, were unable to become self-proficient. At this notion, the representatives from Amnesty International scoffed before adding that, in any event, truly benign dictators would have been less inclined to ignore the widespread hunger and illiteracy surrounding them.

I learned that the landless comprised as much as 98% of Negros' population and that the province's poverty rate exceeded 80%.

I learned that the land reform promised by Corazon Aquino when she overthrew Ferdinand Marcos never materialized and that the landless and impoverished continued to provide fertile ground for labor and political agitation, driven not only by communists but also local priests and nuns responding to the grinding poverty afflicting their flock.

I learned that Negros Occidental was a microcosm of the extreme economic and political inequities that affected the entire Republic of the Philippines. I grew to picture it vividly in my mind as a place where darkly-windowed luxury cars drove around malnourished children too hungry and deprived of energy to do anything but mimic puddles on the dirt.

Finally, to finish my research, I tried to live on water and salted rice for as long as I could. I did not last long—a failed experiment that also made me recall the aftermath of the ghost's visit to my home in Baguio City. I remembered once more my consternation over how Uncle Eliel and his family would have hovered on the brink of starvation without my parents' aid. My childhood sense of security had been uninterrupted until my exposure to Uncle Eliel's dilemma as he worked the sugar cane fields of Negros. It was the first time in my life that I felt the ground shake beneath my feet. Uncle Eliel was not a stranger to my family; he *was* family. I never met him but for a long time after the *mamau* took over Manang Inday's body, I felt Uncle Eliel's presence everytime I sat down at our dining table.

Ahhhhhh. Delicious, isn't it, my little garbage can, my honey honey bun bun? I would hear his voice behind me as I ate. When I turned around, there would be no one there or only one of the servants looking quizzically at my frightened expression. I came to imagine Uncle Eliel as a diaphonous, floating face with an elongated chin exagerrating the size of his mouth, an open chasm trickling saliva from one corner as he coveted my food. I lost weight that year. It was also the year when, with hunger as my teacher, I first learned how to faint.

---

* "Manang" is a title courteously used by a younger person when referring to or addressing an older person.

KOBAI SCOTT WHITNEY

KONA GLITTER, 1964: A GHOST STORY

I wonder what that dumb, gum-chewing high school girl behind the counter at Dave's thinks of me: The fat, old maid white lady who comes in (all too often, I might add) and swoons through her one scoop of lychee sherbet—eyes crossed under closed, fluttering eyelids, lost in her mid-life fantasies?

How could I ever explain to her what the taste of lychee sherbet does to me, how immediately it brings me back to the Kona of 1964 when I had my first taste of Calvin Ah Siu.

This is the year of our thirtieth high school reunion; that's why all this has come so vividly back to mind.

For the life of me I can't remember what word we used for "hunk" in 1964. It seems to me that hunk did not appear until the 70s or 80s and that the girls of Kona Waena High in 1964 must have said things like: "he's a dream," or just plain "wow."

Whatever word we might have used in those days, it would certainly be connected to my prom date that year, Calvin. He was taller than most of the other country boys in our class, more muscular, more poised. The dream of not just yours truly.

I was one of four haole girls in that senior class. Even today, my habit is to think of the word "haole" as being a routine descriptive designation. Often we didn't know each other's last names so, for instance, Dexter Ito was "you know, the Japanese boy with the eyes" (poor Dexter's eyes crossed or stalled unpredictably in their tracking), or Ellison, "you know, the rascal Japanese one who hangs around with the jocks."

I was known as: "you know, Lisa, the haole girl with the Buick." It wasn't my Buick, of course; it was Daddy's—a sleek baby blue showboat with the innovative transmission called "Dyna-Flow." In later years, when the Buick started showing signs of age, Daddy used to refer to the transmission spitefully as "Dyna Flush." But that Buick, plus my haole-ness, was simply the way I got identified.

Although our family never thought of ourselves as rich, I know that my classmates did put me into that category. This social class distinction started in elementary school, where wearing slippers to school was a sign of affluence. The ordinary kids—I don't think anyone thought of themselves as "poor" in those days—the ordinary kids just came to school barefoot. Because of this classification system, and much to the frustration of my mother, I was continually managing to lose my slippers between home and school.

If you didn't know Calvin's last name, he was "you know, Calvin, the pākē boy with the Mother." Calvin's mother was famous, and feared, by the rest of us. It was because of her, and despite a dramatic personal appeal and home visit by Coach Ikeda, that Calvin was not on our football team. He was more coordinated and more confident than the other boys on the team, and the coach wanted him badly. Yet Mrs. Ah Siu would not budge in her conviction that football was a barbarian American invention—something too risky to allow her son to play.

She didn't like surfing either, but occasionally Calvin snuck away to ride the waves with his friends. Yet he would never complain about her strictness, nor would he ever dream of defying her in any direct way. Stealth-surfing was the only minor rebellion he ever allowed himself. So, with the exception of surfing, he was totally loyal to Chow Fun Lady—as I used to call her in the peevish privacy of my adolescent mind. (In Elementary, Calvin always had chow fun in his bento box, instead of rice, but since he was universally loved by his peers, he rarely got teased about it.)

The coup of my senior year was landing Calvin as my date to the prom. What he never knew—even to this day, thirty years later—is that I had also slated him to become my husband.

I had watched Calvin with the cunning of a huntress since eighth grade. I knew his every movement, stance, posture, habit of speech. Fortunately, first love—a love which is that intense and tragic and idiotic—only comes once. My love for Calvin was the kind of love that breaks your heart on a daily, or even an hourly, basis.

I would see some other slut flirting with Calvin and my heart would break. ("Excuse my French," as we used to say so urbanely in 1964, but I'm a mature, single professional woman who has no need for euphemisms anymore.)

Such glimpses of the competition would launch me off into dark fantasies of abandonment and solo jumps from the sides of steaming, desolate volcanoes. Suffice it to say that for nearly five years Calvin was the pivot, the center, the axis of my swirling schemes and feelings.

* * *

Here is prom politics in a nutshell: Get yourself on the Dance Committee. The Dance Committee gets to choose the "team." (It was not until I was in my first English Composition class at U.H. that I realized that there was an English word spelled THEME.) Our "team" was to be MOONLIGHT FOR LOVERS, but Mr. Clark, the principal, finally made us change it to "Moon River." Does anyone remember Andy Williams anymore? I think they trotted him out on a stage last Christmas for a television special, like some mainland Don Ho, crooning his long-ago memorized medley.

So I got myself on the Dance Committee, and I got the love-of-my-life to agree to take me to the prom. I was at the pinnacle of senior year politics.

There was one committee battle I lost, though. I didn't like glitter, even in those days, but for the rest of the committee it was just too irresistible: all that silver glitter on the cardboard moon, with a blue-green glitter river (down which we'd all float, I supposed, with our dates, into an ocean of spangled bliss).

I went along with the rest of the decorating scheme for the gym—no hotel ballrooms in those days. The main thing was to hide the two basketball backboards and to create enough of an illusion of glitz that only the sense of smell would reveal the true identity of our dreamy, sophisticated ballroom.

We accomplished the hiding of the backboards with a false bamboo ceiling—which turned out to be a bit too low for some of the taller boys, including Calvin. Several thousand yards of colored paper streamers and several hundred acres of freshly picked Kleenex tissue flowers completed the gym's disguise.

When I talk with school friends now about these details, it all seems so tacky—and we do nothing but laugh at ourselves. But it was so serious then, so huge and romantic and other-worldly. For most of us that shoddy prom was as important as our graduation, for some of us, probably more. And though we can't remember what we did the day before or two days later, our collective memories can fill in every detail of that bewitching night on Moon River.

As the sons and daughters of my classmates prepare for their five-hundred-to-thousand dollar proms in 1994, we remember our own preparations for that big, but much cheaper, night. No limos. We were lucky if the boys washed down the coffee jeeps before they picked us up. No dinner out. Where, for instance, would one go? Teshima Restaurant?

If the sixties were supposed to be a time of sexual license, you wouldn't have known it by Kona. Ignorant farm boys and naive would-be Annette Funicellos, that's what we were. Maybe others were getting some in the cane roads at night, and I heard rumors of some clumsy groping in the back rows of the Kona theater, but certainly the Kona coast was not exactly the free love capital of the world. In my own home, sex was never mentioned, except for some brief and evasive medical mumbo jumbo when I first started my periods.

Our house was filled with the Christian haole women of my mother and grandmother's generations. They were women who referred to themselves as kama'aina, as if it were a designation of royalty—as if they were baronesses with right of succession. It had nothing to do with being "children of the land." It had to do with entitlement and imagined grandeur and a place in society that would never have been possible in the New England of their (much humbler) origins. In this lily-white world, sex was never on the agenda—except as some vague and euphemized danger to young ladies.

But I did, once, have a taste of Calvin. And I mean that quite literally. We kissed one evening about a month before the prom—where else but in Daddy's Buick. I had picked him up one late afternoon at the school and we parked off the road between the Greenwell House and the main road. For what seemed like hours we talked and watched the sky go dark. I escalated things by reaching for his hand and holding it while I dreamed up more things to say.

Finally at a loss, I pulled him toward me and we kissed. For him, it must have been the first time he had kissed anyone but his mother or his aunties. I taught him as best I could, and in that teaching I got my first, elusive taste of him. The closest I can come to describing the taste of Calvin's body is the flavor I have since discovered at Dave's Ice Cream: Lychee Sherbet. It has that same vanishing sweetness that I tasted on his body that night so many years ago.

For a long time I thought of it the Man Flavor, but with more experience I began to realize that it was a uniquely Calvin flavor. Since discovering its replica at Dave's, I've been extremely careful only to have one scoop on the premises. (Much like the dangers of off-premise liquor sales, I fear total loss of control should I ever have an unlimited supply in my own condo. I can't risk it.)

* * *

Before our thirty-year reunion, I had last seen Calvin at Ellison's funeral in 1986. That memorial became an unofficial class reunion too, since every one of us had watched our televisions and seen (over and relentlessly over again) that lonely rocket split in horrid, smoke-trailed pieces... and we each must have thought to ourselves: "There goes Ellison—you know, the rascal one."

For the people of the Kona coast, especially the older ones, the Challenger disaster became a kind of cautionary tale, Kona's own version of Icarus as local boy. For many of our elders, Ellison's daring demise was proof, once again, of the dangers of life on the Mainland, or, alternately, a parable about the perils of haole-made hardware.

It seems a frivolous thought, but all of us who were his classmates knew that no one of us would ever die in such a dramatic, showy, or unimaginable way. Like speeding off a road at 100 miles an hour, it was an adolescent way to die.

But if he was Icarus to the older people, he was James Dean as local boy to us. Because of that, our own late childhoods also went up in smoke 21,000 feet above Florida, with brave, rascal Ellison.

* * *

Here is what happened in 1964 to my perfect prom politics: let's call it, Revenge of Chow Fun Lady. About a week before the prom, when Calvin had finally gotten the nerve to tell his mother who he was taking to the prom, the pork hash hit the fan. Mrs. Ah Siu apparently interpreted the prom as a serious precursor to marriage, and Calvin was ordered to go to the prom alone.

I must admit too that my own mother was not overjoyed at the thought of my going to the prom with a Chinese boy. The miscegenation fear of her age and class were never stated verbally, but that brief tightening of the right side of her mouth told the story all too clearly. (I had actually rehearsed for a direct prohibition from her. It culminated with the line, "There aren't any haole boys to go with!" But I realized that this would have been too much of a temptation for her—and I was sure she would have taken up the challenge, unearthing some pale-faced cousin, descended perhaps from the Maui planter aristocracy she so admired.)

Now it must be said that going to the prom alone was no big disgrace in those days. A lot a people, especially the fat girls, went to the prom alone. Well, actually, the fat girls usually got one of their māhū boyfriends to go with them. This worked out perfectly since the māhū were the only boys who loved to dress up. They were also flashy dancers—and they were the only ones who could give their dates tips on makeup and hairstyles. (Secretly, I think the parents were also relieved, since they knew their daughters' virginity would go unchallenged during their gay night out.)

But I was NOT a fat girl—not then, at least—and the idea of showing up at Moon River without a date sent me back into my tragic-maiden, volcano-jumping fantasies.

I tried to convince Calvin to meet me outside the gym that night so we could walk down the concrete stairs together into the ballroom and be announced as a couple. Quite sensibly pointing out the smallness of the Kona community, he refused, convinced that his mother would find out.

So I went alone, driving Daddy's Buick into the parking lot like some rich, spoiled mainland girl, in hooped crinoline and a ratted-beehive-hairspray-helmet that pushed up against the inside lining of the Buick ceiling. (This left an indelible chemical stain that neither I nor my father ever spoke of.)

Holding back the tears which would have told of my tragic aloneness, I entered early through a side door and threw myself into last minute decorating details with the other girls on the Dance Committee.

Calvin showed up an hour or so later, also entering through the stag side door. I pretended not to see him. I pretended to be absorbed in the business of the glitter. One boy, poor Dexter Ito ("you know, the one with the eyes"), had already guided me out on the dance floor. His breath was sweet with what I now know was Sloe Gin and his fickle eyes were bloodshot. "You are so beautiful," he whispered carefully into my left ear as he lurched his crotch into my crinolined left hip, quite impressively demonstrating his arousal.

"Poor Dexter," the old ladies of Kona used to say, "such a nice Japanese boy—too bad, yeah, about his eyes." Dexter's cousin, Lily, a fellow Dance Committee member, saw my plight on the dance floor and redirected her cousin outside the gym—where he later upchucked streams of purple projectiles. (I know now I should have given myself over to Dexter's advances. After high school he was able to get corrective lenses for his eye problem and he has now become one of the richest men on the Big Island.)

Calvin did, though, come over to the sidelines and ask me to dance about midway through our Special Night. That seemed brave enough to me at the time. It was a slow dance too. (How weighted that term was in those days: "Slow Dance!" We pronounced those two words with the same caution and awe that surrounded phrases like "Heavy Petting" or "French Kiss.")

So for just a few minutes my prom dreams came true. I closed my eyes and leaned my head against Calvin's neck as we swirled down Moon River. It was then I decided on one more taste. As I opened my eyes—fully intending to lick his earlobe or taste his dreamy cheekbones—my line of sight panned the side entrance where the chaperones were huddled.

Like the little square in the center of the viewfinder (that video game target-finder we got so used to during the Gulf-Oil/CNN War) my vision zeroed in on Mrs. Ah Siu standing in the doorway—her own serious range-finders fixed right on me.

I immediately shut my pre-moistened lips and guided the two of us toward some glitter camouflage. "Calvin," I whispered, "your mother is here." I could feel his muscles tense, and we broke off our duet, parting from each other, fading into the sidelines as far from her iron stare as possible.

I guess I have greatly romanticized Calvin's bravery in my convenient recollections of that evening. The visuals of Calvin and me dancing under the bamboo sky are still filed in my memory as a scene from *Romeo and Juliet*—brave Romeo defying his family, and hers, to woo the girl he loves.

But, let's face it, I was no Juliet, and Calvin didn't exactly defy Chow Fun Lady.

The evening was wrecked, of course, and I don't remember much more after that, except that I stayed to help with clean-up and ended up getting drunk with the fat girls and the māhū under some coffee trees. Someone drove me home in the blue Buick as the dawn light diffused above the waters of Kona. I'm sure I got in trouble with mother, but all I remember is a tragic hangover.

* * *

Calvin has since married a Chinese girl, just like his mother wanted, and is a big-time lawyer in L.A.—with all that implies: poofy silk shirts, pants with pleats for days, gold chains, and a cellular phone. He's become a very 90s kind of guy.

Mrs. Ah Siu died in 1981. Calvin and his brothers and their one sister all appeared in Kona for the funeral. I know; I watched them carefully from a distance.

Now, thirty years later, our reunion was to be held at the Kamehameha IV Hotel, not in the gym. There was no glitter, thank God. It was an elegant and expensive evening and I hoped, at least, that the interior lighting would be dim enough to hide our aging faces.

I went alone of course, as the only Old Maid that class produced—except, of course, for Sister Mary Cordeira who still teaches at a Catholic school on Maui.

I had enough gumption to sit next to Calvin and his wife. She was actually quite nice to me, and fun to talk to. At least I didn't have to arouse her suspicion by saying that Calvin and I had gone to the prom together.

As my second white wine began to kick in, however, it was all I could do to keep from leaning toward her nearest ear and asking, in a whisper, how Calvin tasted after all these years.

I danced with him only once that night, after asking my new friend, his wife, for permission. As we talked on the dance floor, it became clear to me that he did not remember his mother's prohibition—or her prom-night appearance at all. He seemed to recall that we had both gone to the prom alone and he didn't acknowledge that there had ever been any other plans. Somehow I was deeply shocked at this discrepancy in our separate memories.

In a fit of boldness, I closed my eyes briefly and licked my lips—and I was about to have myself a taste of Calvin when he whirled me around in sync with the music.

As my vision grazed the side entrance to the ballroom, there she stood, floating phantom-like next to the white-coated busboy: Chow Fun lady with her eyes fixed on me—no legs visible below the knees, just like the Hawaiians say. Just those burning eyes.

I gasped and separated myself from the puzzled L.A. lawyer. I mumbled something about too much wine and fled outside to the hotel parking lot.

Standing in the night air, afraid to glance over my shoulder for fear that Ellison too might appear, I thought: *Where are they tonight—the fat girls and the māhū—when I need them again?*

* * *

The next morning, I took the plane back to O'ahu. While airborne I wouldn't let myself think about anything that had happened the night before. For a while, I closed my eyes and took refuge in my habitual fantasy about the perfect brown legs of Honolulu's UPS drivers.

I took the bus home from the airport, and as I walked along the last block between the bus stop and my condo, I noticed a new abandoned car—now almost totally stripped and trashed—where nothing had been before. There was also some new graffiti on the wall of the warehouse across from my building.

LONELY GIRL LOVES KENNY, it read, and I was overwhelmed with the impulse to wish her well.

LOIS-ANN YAMANAKA

THE CROSSING

Emerald-green feathers Father and me pluck off of the peacock from Pu'uwa'awa'a Ranch off the old Kona Road. The body cold but defrosting, smelling a little bad already. We pluck and sort so there's no double work, sort them into rows and rows of fishing-hook trays. So many bird feathers in plastic trays like feather apartments, one on top of the other.

It's Father's new moneymaking idea, and though we've worked hard—taking those long drives to the countryside to get the dead birds or shooting them ourself, it's been good money.

And Daddy talks to me all the time, sometimes like I'm not even there. Just going on and on. And he drives real slow even when the speed limit is 60, Daddy goes the minimum, which is 35.

If we come home Volcano way, he gets a good start, puts the Land Rover in neutral, and rolls all the way down from Glenwood to Pana'ewa. My mother gets mad if she's in the car, so he does this only if I'm there. It takes us double the time to get places. Daddy and me.

We're going to Wai'ōhinu. The sky gray, rain slanting sideways. Daddy soaking wet after fixing a flat outside of Kurtistown, he finishes, stops, and stares at the sky, the rain pouring on his glassy face.

When he gets in and we drive for a while, he says, "I tell you one story, Lovey. About the three of us—Tora, Uri, and me. This been bugging me for all these years. But Daddy like you know the one thing I rememba about my small kid time. This is it."

It's like this all the way to Wai'ōhinu to pick up the three

Chinese ring-necked pheasants. Daddy telling me things that he may never say again. Sometimes like I'm not even there.

"Tora, he nine years older than me. He was one good-looking bugga, dark his skin, and one good leader. My brudda, he was brash. And cocky. But everybody was scared him in Rice Camp 'cause he like for fight. You know, he used to lick this Filipino guy once a week for nothing. I think his name was Pablo. No, the guy's name was Pundo. He was Tora's classmate and was smarter than my bradda. The teachers, they all thought my bradda was dumb—but he wasn't. Just playful.

"Uri, he one year older than me. Ho, I tell you, Uri was the fastest runner in the camp and the best tree climber. And him, he follow Tora whereva he went. Every time, just the two of them going hea and there. Had other kids in our family and other kids in the camp but they was my big braddas right above me, Tora and Uri, but always only them two—and then there was me.

"I going tell you some things right now and what I tell you, you betta rememba, 'cause there was nothing to say about this before and now there is."

He pauses and looks at me. The landscape changes fast out on the drives to South Point side. Rain, then 'ōhi'a forest, then lava field, Ka'ū Desert, cane field, fog, hail, cow pasture, within yards of each other, they change. And Mauna Loa to the right of us.

My father says, "I had one shirt. Was one blue one with white flowas. You know that shirt belong to four braddas before me. Had fifteen kids in our family and we no could have new stuffs. You know, by the time I got that shirt, couldn't tell if was blue before. I only knew was blue 'cause my braddas rememba it that way. But me, I neva really care back then. I was only six, what the heck. You know what I mean? Small-kid time, you dunno the difference, right?

"My fav'rite thing for do was hang around with Tora and Uri when they let me small kine be with them. I tell you, I use to wait on the roadside sometimes one hour if I hear Tora and Uri talking about going fishing at breakfast time. I no like them leave me, eh? So I make sure I there, waiting. How many days like that I listen to them buggas talk, then try be where I can follow, so I can go with them all their secret places, you know what I mean? But had one time, I swear, I neva going forget.

"You know what I rememba about that morning? I rememba kicking some small stones in the open ditch. The water in that ditch, all greasy and dirty from the kitchens and furos in the camp. I rememba how dirty that water was—Rice Camp, us neva have sewer system.

"That morning I remember thinking how your grandma make our camp house look so nice. She plant the African daisies, carnations, and Easter lilies all in the front. And on the side of the house, she wen' grow won bok, spinach, beans, peas, and turnips.

"I seen Tora and Uri with their bamboo fishing poles and other fishing stuffs with them, but I neva say nothing when they wen' walk pass me. I go pretend like I looking something way down the pasture side. Then I follow few steps behind. Uri, the bugga, go whisper something to Tora. All of a sudden, Tora, he turn around and whip the pole upside down on the ground.

"He draw one line deep in the dirt. 'See that line?' he tell me. 'You see um, Hubert? You try cross um. I going lick you with this bamboo pole. You cannot come with us. You too slow, not like Uri. Try cross um," he threaten me.

"I know that Tora and Uri was going up Turning Pond or Scharsh Pond, maybe even up the O'va. If the buggas went up Hulē'ia River, they was going for mullet or pāpio. In the upper river, had 'o'opu. You dunno how I wish I could see the fish they was going catch while the bugga thrashing on the line, not all dead and ready for the frying pan like I always seen um when my braddas come home.

"I just stand there behind that line on the road. I watch my brothers until they small specks up the road. Then I push my foot through the line. I erase um. No mo' line now and I run forward fast as I can. Ho, in my mind I can see all the mountain apple, the guava and liliko'i. So I run faster, maybe I get to heaven before them. I can already see my braddas ahead of me. Then Tora turn around. 'Go home, Inky,' he yell. He draw another line. 'You try cross this line, Inky. You going get lickens when I get home, I tell you. Stay home.' My braddas, they call me Inky Dinky Bali Boo. Sometimes they sing um.

"Me, I stop behind the new line and pull my faded shirt. I look at the long line Tora wen' draw across the whole road. The bamboo grove on the side of the road creak and brush in the wind. I sit behind that line and draw in the dirt.

"Then I yell loud as I can, 'T-o-r-a. U-r-i.' I know they cannot hear me. But I wait behind the line, all day that day, that's what I rememba. Had plenty days after that I wen' wait behind one line in the dirt. I always waiting behind the line my bradda draw for me.

"And I was small boy that time waiting, waiting. Some days I feel so scared all by myself waiting till dark, I sing some songs the haole lady teach me at school. Then I whistle little bit but I call the obake lady from the trees 'cause I whistling and I one small boy all by myself. She laughing 'cause look like I no mo' madda and fadda. I feel so shame, one obake laughing at me like that, and I all by myself.

"Some days I waiting, I think I missing out on heaven, the way Tora and Uri make um, the places they seen while I was behind that goddamn line he drawn in the dirt. And I so damn sad I cannot see heaven with them with *my own eyes*. Gotta wait at home with all my sistas for the guava, liliko'i, mango, and 'o'opu.

"Not the same, probably no even taste as good as when you got um straight from God."

* * *

By the time we get to the Mark Twain monkeypod tree, by the Nishimoto Motel in Wai'ōhinu to meet the man with the birds, my father's story is over. He wraps the frozen birds in newspaper and puts them in the Igloo in the back of the Land Rover.

Daddy and me on our way home, we stop by Wood Valley up the hills behind Pāhala. Wait in the cane and see, Chinese ring-necked pheasant, red face and orange eyes watching the sky. And Daddy lets me shoot first, aim away from the white neck so blood won't stain the most pure feathers on this bird.

* * *

Jimmy Lee, who runs the chicken hatchery, says that his friend at the Ali'i Feather Company on Mamo Street, next to AnToinette's Beauty Shoppe and Hilo Camera and Comic, wants golden pheasant.

What a lei that would make. Like strings of gold, the feathers that fall in shiny strands. And the red breast feathers, fine like the 'ōhi'a lehua blossoms. Daddy knows a breeder all the way up in Hāwī and makes a deal for dead birds. Not a real good deal, but he says, "The return going be three times when I sell the feathers, you watch, Lovey. And you see a real businessman in action."

We leave the next morning way before sunrise so we can make it home early in the afternoon to pluck the feathers. All the way to the halfway mark, Tex Drive-in, my father tells me about ghosts 'cause Daddy got the ghost-eye.

"I can still smell the smell of that pillow, you know, stuff with pigeon peas, rice parchment, and beans, if I think real hard."

I learn that if I let him go, the stories get real good. Never stop and ask questions—he gets grouchy and stops talking for miles.

He says, "Uri's snoring next to me, and next to him, Tora tossing and turning. Five of us younger boys in that room.

"I turn my face to the wall. The rice-bag pillowcase always feel rough, even when dirty. I pull the futon my madda made from leftover rags close to my chin. Ho, I had to piss but I thought the outhouse was haunted.

"My madda use to tell me for wake her up or one of my braddas if I gotta go bathroom nighttime. So I turn to Uri. But I neva wake him up. I was mo' scared for make him mad than go outside face the obake.

"I look at Tora. Everybody in Rice Camp call him Captain. He use to wear army hats. He had plenny army hats but nobody know where he got um from. Ho, the night wind shake the mango tree. And when the moonlight come inside the room, I seen Tora's hats all stuff under the corner of his pillow.

"I look outside by the outhouse. Had one spooky bamboo grove around um and the whole grove whistle and brush when the wind blow. Sound like squeaking and whistling, like one old Japanee song on one flute. And the worse part was wheneva one of us kids went out there for use the bathroom nighttime, the next morning the person tell the whole family about the ghost that he seen.

"I wen' stand up and already the wind crawl up my pants leg. Uri wake up, he tell, 'Where you going, Inky?'

"'Come with me, please, Uri,' I tell, and he come with me. Nighttime get plenny light, you know, if get full moon. And the sounds real loud, every sound, even your feet walking in the gravel.

"And right by the bamboo grove, right when the flute music from the bamboo reeds wen' start for play, I seen her. The obake lady with long white hair, no mo' legs, with one red mouth. Me and Uri, right by the outhouse. And you know what, I wen' piss right in my pants and by the time I was pau, she was gone."

Then he pauses for a long time. I see Tex Drive-in ahead of us. Still dark but I smell the malasadas from miles away. And Daddy says, "Remember I said I going take you up Kīpū Plantation? First get that long road with pine trees. Get plenny obake in those trees at night.

"Rememba the pictures of the pile of stones I shown you?

That use to be my house when I was small. And all the rusty totan roofs, all corroded in the middle of the stones—that was our roof.

"Hā'upu Mountain. You going see um. Thass where Tora and Uri use to go. That get my goat, man. How come I neva went there? Even when I got mo' big, I neva went there, 'cause I wanted for see um with them.

"Get one statue of Mr. Rice that says, 'Erected in his memory by his Japanese friends.' My fadda built the foundation part of that statue, you believe that?

"And I show you in the pictures, over there was the outhouse. Over there was the garden. Over here was the kitchen. But I get hard time even see um in my head sometimes.

"One day, you and me going climb Hā'upu Mountain and look around, 'cause I imagine get plenny for see. What you think? You eva thought you might see heaven when your heart was still going and your lungs was still breathing, or what? You be my company when we go visit God."

* * *

Something tells me I don't want what comes next. I don't want the dead barn owls this haole man from Volcano Village says he has. He tells my father on the phone that field poison the sugar company uses to kill cane rats make the owls brain dead, dizzy, and dazed by the time they die.

He tells Daddy he has *four* of them. Four white speckled birds, rare feathers for a lei that I would *never* wear around *my* lauhala hat. And the haole man tells my father he has a pueo he'll throw in for the right price. Daddy doesn't even want to consider this bird. He's mad that the haole even said he had it. Even if it died naturally.

The morning slides cold through the car windows. Pink light behind the African tulips in the back as we leave the house for Volcano Village before my mother defrosts the lup cheong for breakfast.

And Daddy begins, "Mornings are always the same. The

men from Rice Camp, few Filipino, plenny Japanee, and one Portagee left for work at five in the morning. They end at five in the afternoon. All of them had for wear straw hats. Hot, you know, working twelve hours a day. And had to wear linen shirts bumbye the cane leaf cut your arm. Cane leaf get fine hair on top, and when you sweat, the bugga cling on you and you get one mean rash.

"Some workers make better pay—they get leather gloves. The poor ones get cloth. Everybody get arm protectors. All us get tabi 'cause was cheap and had socks kine leggings so the centipedes no bite your feet.

"My madda them had for work too. All the ladies had big hats with scarf around their neck and face. The wahines had linen 'āhina pants so the cane no scratch. When they had babies, they put um in cloth slings and hang um by their hips when they work the fields. All day.

"This plantation was fifteen hundred acres but was small compared to some others back then in the 1930s. We earn one dolla a day. One dolla, and we bus' our ass, laying train tracks—that's heavy steel we carrying all day till our back feel broken, and cutting cane, hoeing, dig and plant and cut, bend ova all day long—we work mo' hard than you eva will in your whole life, and dirty work, pilau, break your ass. Yeah, we had free house and water and free medical but big deal.

"That goddamn doctor—he okay, but the bugga had one bad habit of taking out your appendix for one stomachache, I tell you."

My father shows me a scar across his stomach. Shakes his head, and soon after this, past the field of white ginger near Mountain View, I'm not in the car, as fas as Daddy is concerned. And I'm glad, because he tells about my grandpa that no one talks about.

"My fadda was born 1890. Came Hawai'i 1907 for be one laborer in the sugar fields. He the only one came from his family. My fadda, and this what get me even now—he neva seen Japan again.

"He work that plantation all his life. Set the train tracks in the just-harvest fields. That's hard labor, I tell you. Broke your heart, then your body. When the old man was forty-something, he bus' his hips in one industrial accident. Afta that, he was kinda cripple, no can walk good no mo'.

"My fadda, he love for go fish for koi nighttime. But koi, gotta fish nighttime, eh, so kinda spooky. But my fadda, he no let nobody go with him even if we ask plenny times. On his way home from fishing, he stop up the graveyard for pay respect to all his dead friends. This usually around midnight. Ho, I tell you, my fadda seen mo' ghosts than anybody in the camp. Thass where I get my ghost-eye from. And now Calhoon get um, that ghost-eye. Not everybody get um, you know. You no mo' the eye. See what I mean?

"You know, my fadda, he neva say nothing about going back Japan. Was pau, everything he had with Japan. Except for one small package he had. He brought um with him from Japan when he was seventeen years old.

"He neva tell nobody what was inside. But he told all fifteen of us and my madda that we could open um when he die. In 1952, you wasn't even in my dream yet—I was seventeen, my fadda, he die of one heart attack. He was dead right there off the plantation truck. And where I was? I was in Milwaukee with my big sista working in one brewery. I neva had nuff money for come home say goodbye to my old man. But Uri tell me what happen.

"When my madda open the package, was soil—from Japan. My old man, he wanna be buried in Japanee soil. He carry that package in his one bag in 1907 all the way from Japan and keep um under his bed all those years. That was his way of going home."

* * *

On our way home, my father makes me hold the barn owls on my lap. I feel them pulsing. I don't want to pluck the feathers with him. I don't. But I know I will, one by one of the floor of the garage, feel the cold come up the legs of my pants, see blood drip out of each owl pore.

The white owl feathers worth plenty of money. And my father imitates their cry, goes "Kuri-kuri-kuri-ko" over and over again, and tells me he learned this from a pair who flew past the porch of his plantation house on Kaua'i every night near six. Learned it enough to sing it.

* * *

At the Ali'i Feather Company, a smell like the taxidermist's shop comes out the door. The chemical they use to preserve the pelts all hanging on the far wall. Rows and rows of plastic hook trays and bags of feathers sealed airtight.

Daddy and me park in the unpaved lot next to Mamo Theatre. Walk slow with our Ziploc bags full of barn owl feathers. The golden pheasant feathers, brilliant reds and golden strands.

The money we make, thick in an envelope. Daddy feels rich, goes to the '76 station and says, "Fill 'er up." He calls my mother from a pay phone and says we're driving to Pāhala. "The Japanese Blue," he says, "we go get um up Wood Valley. You know I kept nuff feathers from every bird we had for one lei for me and one for you? You be far away from home one day, you see the golden pheasant in China, you going think about the time you and me went up Hāwī. Put your lei on your hat in the streets of Shanghai and you be on Mamo Street with me again."

We get to Hirano Store and my father buys us two boiled eggs each, gravy burgers, One Ton chips, and two Japan apples for dinner. We each have our own chocolate milk and sit outside the store. He tells me, "Hamamoto Store in our camp had wooden floors all cover with oil. Old lady Mrs. Hamamoto use to tell me, 'Keep the dus' off mo' betta. Too much dus' planting time.' When I look up from the doorway, I could see Mr. Hamamoto in the office on the second floor.

"I rememba had one soda machine right by the door and

the soda bottles all full of cool moisture beads, make my mouth wata, but I neva have the five cents I need for buy one. Only had nuff money for buy bread." Father looks around the store we're in as if seeing his store.

"I dunno why my madda send me. I one small kid, youngest boy, eh, and I get seven sistas too, but me, I always the one gotta go. That day, Mr. Sadanaga, one of the reg-la workers, he come up to me with the pencil he wear on his ear every day and he tell me, 'So what, Hubert, Mama forget orda the bread? You know where stay. Go get um.'

"I rush past him, I look inside the chill box where get all the meats for little while, then grab one loaf bread. Mr. Sadanaga, he helping somebody else, so that day, I wen' look long time at the glass case with all the pocketknife and watch. I neva know my face was so close until I seen all the steam in front of my face.

"'Your papa buy you one wen' you mo' big, Hubert.' Was Mr. Sadanaga talking to me. The bugga knew us had fifteen kids and I could neva have my own knife but the way he said um, I knew he wasn't being mean. He lead me to the front of the store. 'Hea, you one good boy,' he tell me, 'I give you one Hershey's.' My mouth like take the candy. My head tell me no take um—we poor but I no need take um.

"I put my eyes down, slide my hand across the counter, say thank you small kine, and run out real fast bumbye he see my eyes, eh, and how much I wanted um."

I don't look at him and he don't look at me. I climb into the Land Rover and make my body small. Don't want him to remember how I ask for lots of things bigger than a knife sometimes that I throw around or break. Sleep all the way to Pāhala.

* * *

Our feather business ended after our last drive to Laupāhoehoe together. It was a long drive because of the sugar cane harvest mud sludge on the roads, the rains, and the slow-moving cane trucks full of muddy arms of cane hanging from their chain belly.

When we get to the Portagee man's house, he takes us in the back of his garage, lifts the foggy mouth of the freezer full of icicles, and what I see, worse than anything I've ever seen before: frozen bodies, a freezer full of animals.

Some aren't even wrapped and their eyes frozen open, mouths wtih tongues hanging out—goats, sheep, pheasants, quail, all those animals. The Portagee takes out six bundles in newspaper and unwraps them. "Four pueo, and check this out, brah, check this out, I get two 'io."

"Sorry, man," my father says, "Thass native birds—and if I was you, brah, I defrost them and go put um back where you got um before they come get you. I ain't talking the feds, brah, I talking those birds."

Walking down the man's muddy driveway, my father mutters, "Stupid goddamn Portagee. Look what we all stooping to for a few fricken feathers. I pau, Lovey," my father says. "Game birds, thass one thing. But pueo and 'io—that Portagee's ass is rats and the pueo and 'io going hunt his stupid ass down. Let's get outta here."

Once in the car, I get Daddy to finish the story he started on the road. I ask questions about Uncle Tora and Uncle Uri, and when he starts to answer, I make myself not there fast. He's talking about home again.

"Let me tell you about Hā'upu Mountain," he starts slowly, "so that when we go there, you going know you died and went heaven with me. Thass what you call one pristine forest. They always talk about the pristine forest on TV. I know my mountain pristine. Nice word, eh?

"Get 'ōhi'a trees all over. Mokihana ready for pick. And staghorn growing all over. Get tall eucalyptus and plum trees with plenny liliko'i vines. That's how you going know we there. On the day we get there." Daddy stops for a long while and looks ahead, leans on the steering wheel.

"Last summa when Uri and Tora came home, us three,

and only us three, no other braddas or sistas, no wifes or kids, went up that old road line with pine trees.

"I watch them two old buggas walk slow up the road. You know, I look at them and 1930 seem so far back. I dunno why, but I wen' pick up one long stick for tap on the road as I walk.

"Tora tell me, 'Hey, Hubert, not so fast. We've got all day.' The bugga talk kinda haole, he been away from home so long. Then my bradda, he lean on one old 'ōhi'a log that somebody made into barb-wire-fence post long time ago. He look into the mountains like one old hermit man. Study the fog little bit. 'Hey, Hubert,' he tell me, 'you gotta remember, I'm older now. Slow down.'

"Then I wen' tell him, no ask me why, if he rememba this, and I wen' draw one line in the dirt road. This where you use to draw the line for me, rememba, I tell him. I couldn't cross the line for go fishing with you two guys.

"My bradda, he frown little while. Then he look at Uri. But Uri, he turn his face away, he rememba too how he use to whisper to Tora.

"'Yeah,' he tell. 'I remember.' He no look at me afta that and all day. He no smile in the pictures I wen' take by that pile of stones that we use to call home. He act funny kine all day and I regret I wen' bring um up. I neva mean no harm."

From his wallet, Daddy pulls out a neatly folded piece of paper and makes me read the letter.

Dear Hubert,
 When we last saw each other, you asked me if I remembered something from our childhood. Yes, I did, but I wasn't aware of its importance until I was about fifty years old.
 William and I were always together—fishing at the lakes for Charley fish, for 'o'opu at Hulē'ia Valley, picking guavas and mountain apples up in the mountains by Hulē'ia School.

Whenever I felt the trip wasn't too hard, Hubert, I would let you come along. Being the oldest of the younger boys, I decided who could come and who should stay. If I didn't want to take you, yes, I would draw a line in the road and tell you not to cross it.

You were only six or so and I was fifteen, so you stayed back. I didn't realize what I was doing to you. I only knew this when you told me last summer how you felt.

It was a cruel thing to do. You were six. I'm sure you just wanted to show William and me that you could do whatever we did.

I've spent many nights wondering how I could undo what I did to you some forty years ago. I should have never denied you the right to go anywhere with us. I promise you, if not in this life then in the next, I will take you past the lines I drew for you as a boy to the mountains where we played, even if I have to carry you.

Tora

Nobody says nothing. No questions so Daddy can go home. He's muttering again about all those animals in the Portugee's freezer, those birds, the pueo and the 'io, so mnay of them, mouths plugged with bloody toilet paper—they were shot and wrapped in newspaper for somebody to pluck and sell to the Ali'i Feather Company for an envelopeful of money. Daddy continues his story.

"Mountain apple bigger than my fist and so juicy the red drops going plop off your lips all red.

"And gingers, I no think you seen all the kind gingers one place like this—yellow, torch, kāhili, white.

"And mokihana—sheez, this place get nuff for make ten strands easy.

"And maile—I told you about the maile? The leafs so

sweet and big, and when you pull the vine off the stalk, the bark smell stay unda your fingas for one week, the smell of the maile.

"Staghorn over the whole floor and the 'ōhi'a lehua, the rain hang from her red flowa.

"I imagine the plum trees and liliko'i all sweet, what you think? I neva did taste the one from Hā'upu till this day.

"And the guava, we pick um and Daddy make jelly, so much, gotta give all my braddas and sistas at the next reunion.

"See, me and you, next trip we go over there, we starting from that statue of Mr. Rice, and this time, I swear I holding my head high and we walking up past the old house and up Hā'upu Mountain and eat our lunch up there and look around the pristine forest.

"Maybe I grab me some soil off Hā'upu Mountain and put um in one package under my bed, 'cause when you and me see this place, that's the only time I wanna go there. And maybe you rememba, when I die, you know what for do with that package. Just pour um on me and I be home."

CONTRIBUTORS

Margo Berdeshevsky, born in New York City, lives in Huelo on Maui, published in *Hawai'i Review, Excursus, Soviet Woman, Bamboo Ridge, Calyx, Caprice, Cicada*, and *Visions International*, concerning global and island perspectives.

Arlene Biala, born and raised in San Francisco Bay Area, currently working on her M.F.A. in Poetics and Writing at New College of California, into performance poetry with her brothers Jimmy Biala on percussion and Billy Biala on saxophone.

Louie Bliemeister: When I was twelve, my parents took my sister and me out of school and we spent a year and a half sailing the South Pacific. I learned more that year than any since, and long ocean passages started me writing.

Meredith Carson has been a resident of Hawai'i since 1970. Her poems have appeared in *Bamboo Ridge, Chaminade Literary Review, Hawai'i Review, Poetry East/West, Sister Stew, La'ila'i*, and *Kaimana*.

Sue Cowing's poems and short fiction have appeared in a number of Hawai'i and mainland journals and in the Bamboo Ridge anthology *Sister Stew*. She is editor of *Fire in the Sea*, an anthology of poetry and art published by the University of Hawai'i Press in June 1996.

Brian Cronwall teaches English at Kaua'i Community College. His poems have appeared in *Makali'i, Chaminade Literary Review, Art Centering, Storyboard*, and numerous other periodicals and anthologies.

Diana J. Eicher is a visual artist who received her M.F.A. from the University of Hawai'i. Her secret desire to become a poet unfolded in a workshop taught by Cathy Song.

M.Evelina Galang teaches creative writing at Old Dominion University. Born in Pennsylvania, Galang grew up in Illinois and Wisconsin. Presently, she lives in Norfolk, Virginia.

Mavis Hara never believed Wing Tek Lum's claim that a child could give someone a "knowing look" until she received one.

Steve Heller's literary relationship with Hawai'i began with editorial work on *Hawai'i Review* in 1972-73, continued with his fiction in *The Man Who Drank A Thousand Beers*, and a new novel-in-progress about Lāna'i. He directs the creative writing program at Kansas State University in Manhattan.

Laura Iwasaki was born in Hawai'i in 1950. Her short fiction has appeared in *Rafu Shimpo* and *Bamboo Ridge*. She lives in Bellevue, Washington.

Milton Kimura is a public school teacher in Honolulu. He received notice of this, his first appearance in *Bamboo Ridge*, while on sabbatical leave in the midst of record-setting snowfall in New England. It made the news doubly welcome.

Jeanne Kawelolani Kinney lives in Honolulu and is working on her first novel. A collection of poems, *Redrawing the Big Island*, is forthcoming. On the third Sunday of each month, she reads tarot cards in Maunakea Marketplace, Chinatown. She invites you to stop by.

Peter C.T. Li is a two time winner of the Myrle Clark Creative Contest at the UH-Mānoa and a runner up in the Honolulu Magazine/Borders Bookstore Fiction Contest. When not planting words on paper, he spends his time hacking codes as a Windows Programmer, WAN Administrator and Webmaster at ICE Systems, Inc.

Shirley Geok-lin Lim's first book of poetry, *Crossing the Peninsula* (Heinemann, 1980) received the Commonwealth Poetry Prize. She has four books of poetry published, two collections of short stories, and two critical studies; and has also edited/co-edited four anthologies, including *Reading the Literatures of Asian America* and *The Forbidden Stitch*, which won the 1990 Before Columbus American Book Award. She is currently Professor of English and Women's Studies at the University of California, Santa Barbara. Her memoir *Among the White Moon Faces* is out with Feminist Press in 1996.

Mary Lombard lives with her husband Herman Mulder in Kailua, Hawai'i. Her stories have appeared most often in *Bamboo Ridge*, but also in *Honolulu, Chaminade Review, Sister Stew*, and *Mānoa*.

Wing Tek Lum's first collection of poetry, *Expounding the Doubtful Points*, was published by Bamboo Ridge Press in 1987. His poems in this issue were modeled after Wang Wei's *Deer Enclosure, Written on Returning to Wang River*, and *Farewell*.

Noel Abubo Mateo was born in Baguio in the northern mountains of the Philippines. He was educated at the University of California and at Yale. He lives with his family in Encinitas, California. He remains a Baguio Boy at heart.

Michael McPherson lives in Waimea on the Big Island and practices law. Recent poems appear in *Kaimana, Mānoa, Hawai'i Review*, and *Chaminade Literary Review*.

Wendy Miyake is a graduate student at the University of Hawai'i. She lives in Mililani and still dreams of one day becoming Wonder Woman.

Kiyoshi Young Najita lives in Waimea on the Big Island with his wife and son. He teaches middle school, writes stories and songs, body boards and mountain bikes. His stories have appeared in *Other Voices* and *Into the Fire, Asian American Prose*.

Carrie O'Connor is a journalist, free-lance writer and novice prose writer. She co-edited *Sharing Secrets*, an anthology about domestic violence. She is currently working with a team of writers and artists to produce *FACED*, an anthology by Hawaii's teens.

Joan Perkins has received degrees in creative writing from Vassar College and UH-Mānoa, where she is currently enrolled in the Ph.D. program in English. A recipient of the American Academy of Poets prize for UH in 1995 and two Myrle Clark Awards, she teaches in the Poets-in-the-Schools program on O'ahu.

Ran Ying Porter was born in Copenhagen, Denmark and raised in the People's Republic of China. She has recently completed her first novel *Black Dragon River*. She lives in Hawai'i with her husband Ed and their triplet sons Michael, Patrick, and Ron.

Marjorie Sinclair has published fiction, poetry and biography. She lives and works in Honolulu.

Lia Smith's stories have appeared in *Ms., Other Voices, Fiction, Painted Hills, Sequoia,* and *Seventeen*. She writes novels as well, lives in San Francisco with her husband and her three-year-old daughter, and teaches English as a Second Language at City College of San Francisco part-time.

Indigo Som's "Corvina" is featured in her artists' book, *no one to call home/girl*, available from bitchy buddha press, PO Box 5053, Berkeley CA 94705. She is also published in *Asian Pacific American Journal, The Very Inside: An Anthology of Writing by Asian and Pacific Islander Lesbian and Bisexual Woman*, and *My Lover is a Woman: Contemporary Lesbian Love Poems*.

Joseph Stanton has lived in 'Aiea since 1972. His poems have appeared in *Poetry, Poetry East, Harvard Review, New York Quarterly*, and many other journals.

Eileen Tabios is the co-editor of *The Asian Pacific American Journal*. She recently released a chapbook, *After the Egyptians Determined the Shape of the World Is A Circle* (Pometaphysics Publishing, 1996). Also in *Poet, ELF: Eclectic Literary Forum, River Oak Review, WordWrights!, Green Hills Literary Lantern*, and the anthology *Writers of the Information Age*.

Kobai Scott Whitney is a hermit with a writing problem who lives in Kalihi. He also serves as contributing editor for *Honolulu* magazine.

Lois-Ann Yamanaka is the author of *Wild Meat and the Bully Burgers*, (Farrar, Straus and Giroux, 1996) and *Saturday Night at the Pahala Theatre*, (Bamboo Ridge Press, 1993). Her novel *Blu's Hanging* is forthcoming from Farrar, Straus and Giroux in 1997.

Got those dishwashing blues again mister?

OKINAWAN SWEET PURPLETATO

WON BOK!
don't buy much nowadays

Brighten up your KP duties with these Cane Haul Road dishtowels!

THE UNCOMMON MANGO